KEY GOVERNMENT REPORTS

VOLUME 33

BUSINESS AND FINANCE – JUNE 2019

Key Government Reports

Additional books and e-books in this series can be found on Nova's website under the Series tab.

KEY GOVERNMENT REPORTS

VOLUME 33

BUSINESS AND FINANCE – JUNE 2019

ERNEST CLARK
EDITOR

snova
New York

Library of Congress Cataloging-in-Publication Data

ISBN: 978-1-53616-566-1

Published by Nova Science Publishers, Inc. † New York

CONTENTS

PREFACE

This book is a comprehensive compilation of all reports, testimony, correspondence and other publications issued by the GAO (Government Accountability Office) during the month of June, grouped according to the topic: Business and Finance.

BUSINESS

In: Key Government Reports. Vol. 33
Editor: Ernest Clark
ISBN: 978-1-53616-566-1

Chapter 1

CONSUMER PRIVACY: CHANGES TO LEGAL FRAMEWORK NEEDED TO ADDRESS GAPS*

Alicia Puente Cackley

WHY GAO DID THIS STUDY

Information resellers—companies that collect and resell information on individuals—have dramatically increased the collection and sharing of personal data in recent years, raising privacy concerns. Increasing use of social media, mobile applications, and other technologies have intensified these concerns.

This statement is primarily based on findings from GAO's 2013 report on information resellers (GAO-13-663). It also discusses a 2015 report on facial recognition technology (GAO-15-621), a 2018 report on financial technology (GAO-18-254), and two 2019 reports on internet privacy and consumer data protection (GAO-19-52 and GAO-19- 196, respectively).

---

* This is an edited, reformatted and augmented accessible version of the United States Government Accountability Office Testimony Before the Committee on Banking, Housing, and Urban Affairs, U.S. Senate, Publication No. GAO-19-621T, dated June 11, 2019.

GAO discusses (1) existing federal laws related to the privacy of consumer information held by information resellers and (2) any gaps in this legal framework. For the prior work, GAO analyzed relevant laws, regulations, and enforcement actions and interviewed representatives of federal agencies, trade associations, consumer and privacy groups, and resellers.

WHAT GAO RECOMMENDS

In 2013, GAO recommended that Congress consider strengthening the consumer privacy framework to reflect the effects of changing technologies and markets. In 2019, GAO recommended that Congress consider comprehensive internet privacy legislation. Legislation on these issues has not been enacted to date.

WHAT GAO FOUND

In recent years, GAO issued reports that relate to information resellers and consumer privacy issues. Two central findings from a 2013 GAO report remain current:

- *No overarching federal privacy law governs the collection and sale of personal information among private-sector companies,* including information resellers (data brokers). Instead, a variety of laws are tailored to specific purposes, situations, or entities. For example, the Fair Credit Reporting Act limits use and distribution of personal information collected or used to help determine eligibility for such things as credit or employment. Other laws apply to health care providers, financial institutions, or to online collection of information about children.
- *Gaps exist in the federal privacy framework.* With regard to data that private-sector entities use for marketing, no federal statute

provides consumers the right to learn what information is held about them and who holds it. In many cases, consumers also do not have the legal right to control the collection or sharing with third parties of sensitive personal information (such as their shopping habits and health interests) for marketing purposes. In 2013 and in 2015, GAO also reported that the statutory framework for consumer privacy did not fully address new technologies—such as online tracking and facial recognition—and the vastly increased marketplace for personal information, including the proliferation of information sharing among third parties.

In two 2019 reports, GAO found additional gaps in the federal privacy framework and potential limitations in regulatory authority under current privacy law. Internet content providers and internet service providers collect, use, and share information from customers to enable their services, support advertising, and for other purposes. Although the Federal Trade Commission (FTC) generally has addressed internet privacy through its unfair and deceptive practices authority, and other agencies have used industry-specific statutes, there is no comprehensive federal privacy statute with specific internet privacy standards for the private sector. GAO also reported that the Gramm-Leach-Bliley Act, a key law governing the security of consumer information, does not provide FTC with civil penalty authority for violations of the privacy and data security provisions of the act. New and more advanced technologies and changes in the marketplace for consumer information have vastly increased the amount and nature of personal information collected and the number of parties using or sharing it. Such changes warrant reconsideration of how well the current privacy framework protects personal information.

Chairman Crapo, Ranking Member Brown, and Members of the Committee:

I am pleased to be here today to discuss our prior work on privacy, personal information, and information resellers. Information resellers (also known as data brokers) are companies that collect and resell information on individuals. Privacy concerns about resellers stem, in part, from consumers not always knowing what personal information is collected and how it is used. Moreover, growing use of the internet, social media, and mobile applications has intensified privacy concerns because these media make it much easier to gather personal information, track online behavior, and monitor individuals' locations and activities.

My remarks today are primarily based on our September 2013 report on privacy issues related to the consumer data that information resellers collect, use, and sell, and on our 2015 and 2019 High Risk Reports.[1] In 2013, we found that the framework of federal laws relating to the privacy of consumer information had gaps. We recommended that Congress consider strengthening the consumer privacy framework to reflect changes in technology and the marketplace. In our 2015 High Risk Report, we expanded an area of concern—cybersecurity—to include protecting the privacy of personally identifiable information.[2] We also conducted more recent work in the consumer privacy area on facial recognition technology, financial technology, internet privacy, and consumer data protection.[3] In our 2019 High Risk Report, we reiterated our recommendation that Congress consider what additional actions are needed to protect consumer privacy.[4] My statement will focus on the (1) existing federal laws and regulations related to the privacy of consumer information held by information resellers and (2) any gaps that may exist in this legal framework.

---

[1] GAO, *Information Resellers: Consumer Privacy Framework Needs to Reflect Changes in Technology and the Marketplace*, GAO-13-663 (Washington, D.C.: Sept. 25, 2013).

[2] Every 2 years, we report on federal programs and operations that are vulnerable to waste, fraud, abuse, and mismanagement, or that need broad reform—our High Risk List. See GAO, *High-Risk Series: An Update*, GAO-15-290 (Washington, D.C.: Feb. 11, 2015).

[3] GAO, *Facial Recognition Technology: Commercial Uses, Privacy Issues, and Applicable Federal Law*, GAO-15-621 (July 30, 2015); *Financial Technology: Additional Steps by Regulators Could Better Protect Consumers and Aid Regulatory Oversight*, GAO-18-254 (Mar. 22, 2018); *Internet Privacy: Additional Federal Authority Could Enhance Consumer Protection and Provide Flexibility*, GAO-19-52 (Jan. 15, 2019); and *Consumer Data Protection: Actions Needed to Strengthen Oversight of Consumer Reporting Agencies*, GAO-19-196 (Washington, D.C.: Feb. 21, 2019).

[4] GAO, *High-Risk Series: Substantial Efforts Needed to Achieve Greater Progress on High-Risk Areas*, GAO-19-157SP (Washington, D.C.: Mar. 6, 2019).

For our September 2013 report (GAO-13-663), we reviewed and analyzed relevant laws, regulations, and enforcement actions. We interviewed representatives of federal agencies, trade associations, consumer and privacy groups, and resellers to obtain their views on data privacy laws related to resellers. The work for our 2015 report on facial recognition technology (GAO-15-621), 2018 report on financial technology (GAO-18-254), and January and February 2019 reports on internet privacy and consumer data protection (GAO-19-52 and GAO-19-196) included analyzing laws and regulations and interviewing representatives of federal agencies, regulators in other countries, market participants, consumer advocacy groups, and academia. For this statement, we verified that findings of our previous reports about gaps in the statutory framework for consumer information privacy remain relevant. More details about our scope and methodology can be found in our published reports.

We conducted the performance audit on which the majority of this statement is based from August 2012 through September 2013, in accordance with generally accepted government auditing standards. Those standards require that we plan and perform the audit to obtain sufficient, appropriate evidence to provide a reasonable basis for our findings and conclusions based on our audit objectives. We believe that the evidence obtained provides a reasonable basis for our findings and conclusions based on our audit objectives.

Background

Resellers maintain large, sophisticated databases with consumer information that can include credit histories, insurance claims, criminal records, employment histories, incomes, ethnicities, purchase histories, and interests. As shown in figure 1, resellers largely obtain their information from public records, publicly available information (such as directories and newspapers), and nonpublic information (such as from retail loyalty cards, warranty registrations, contests, and web browsing).

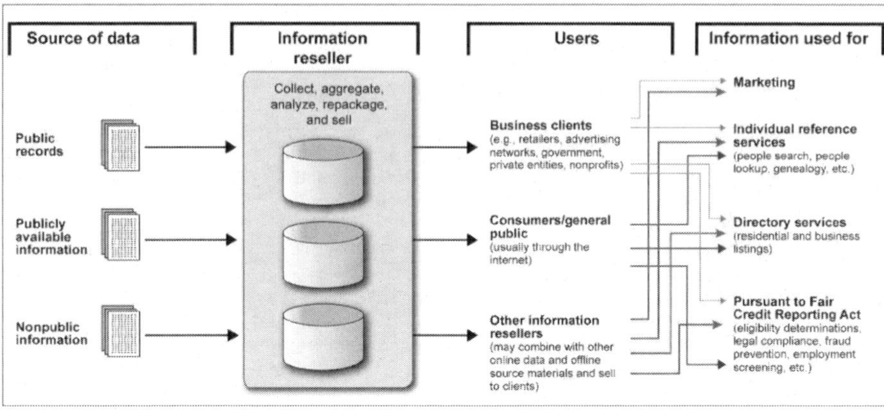

Source: GAO. | GAO-19-621T.

Figure 1. Typical Flow of Consumer Data through Resellers to Third-Party Users.

Consumer information can be derived from mobile networks, devices (including smartphones and tablets), operating systems, and applications. Resellers also may obtain personal information from the profile or public information areas of websites, including social media sites, or from information on blogs or discussion forums. Depending on the context, information from these sources may be publicly available or nonpublic.

In 1973, a U.S. government advisory committee first proposed the Fair Information Practice Principles for protecting the privacy and security of personal information. While these principles are not legal requirements, they provide a framework for balancing privacy with other interests. In 2013, the Organisation for Economic Co-operation and Development (OECD) developed a revised version of the principles (see table 1).[5]

The Fair Information Practice Principles served as the basis for the Privacy Act of 1974—which governs the collection, maintenance, use, and dissemination of personal information by federal agencies.[6] The principles

---

[5] Organisation for Economic Co-operation and Development, *Guidelines on the Protection of Privacy and Transborder Flow of Personal Data* (Paris, France: Sept. 23, 1980). OECD's 30 member countries include the United States. OECD has been considering whether to revise or update its privacy guidelines to account for changes in the role of personal data in the economy and society.

[6] [6]*See* Pub. L. No. 93-579, 88 Stat. 1896 (1974) (codified as amended at 5 U.S.C. § 552a). The act generally prohibits (with a number of exceptions) the disclosure by federal entities of

also were the basis for many Federal Trade Commission (FTC) and Department of Commerce privacy recommendations and for a framework for consumer data privacy the White House issued in 2012.[7]

Table 1. Fair Information Practice Principles

Principle	Description
Collection limitation	The collection of personal information should be limited, obtained by lawful and fair means, and,where appropriate, with the knowledge or consent of the individual.
Data quality	Personal information should be relevant to the purpose for which it is collected, and should be accurate, complete, and current as needed for that purpose.
Purpose specification	The purposes for the collection of personal information should be disclosed before collection and upon any change to those purposes, and the use of the information should be limited to those purposes and compatible purposes.
Use limitation	Personal information should not be disclosed or otherwise used for purposes other than a specified purpose without consent of the individual or legal authority.
Security safeguards	Personal information should be protected with reasonable security safeguards against risks such as loss or unauthorized access, destruction, use, modification, or disclosure.
Openness	The public should be informed about privacy policies and practices, and individuals should haveready means of learning about the use of personal information.
Individual participation	Individuals should have the following rights: to know about the collection of personal information, to access that information, to request correction, and to challenge the denial of those rights.
Accountability	Individuals controlling the collection or use of personal information should be accountable for taking steps to ensure the implementation of these principles.

Source: Organisation for Economic Co-operation and Development. | GAO-19-621T.

records about an individual without the individual's written consent and provides U.S. persons with a means to seek access to and amend their records.

[7] The framework included a consumer privacy bill of rights and encouraged Congress to provide FTC with enforcement authorities for the bill of rights. The White House, *Consumer Data Privacy in a Networked World: A Framework for Protecting Privacy and Promoting Innovation in the Global Digital Economy* (Washington, D.C.: Feb. 23, 2012).

Several Laws Apply in Specific Circumstances to Consumer Data That Resellers Hold

As we reported in 2013 and as continues to be the case, no overarching federal privacy law governs the collection, use, and sale of personal information among private-sector companies, including information resellers. There are also no federal laws designed specifically to address all the products sold and information maintained by information resellers. Federal laws addressing privacy issues in the private sector are generally narrowly tailored to specific purposes, situations, types of information, or sectors or entities—such as data related to financial transactions, personal health, and eligibility for credit. These laws include provisions that limit the disclosure of certain types of information to a third party without an individual's consent, or prohibit certain types of data collection. The primary laws include the following:

Fair Credit Reporting Act (FCRA)[8]

FCRA protects the security and confidentiality of personal information collected or used to help make decisions about individuals' eligibility for credit, insurance, or employment.[9] It applies to consumer reporting agencies that provide consumer reports.[10] Accordingly, FCRA applies to the three nationwide consumer reporting agencies (commonly called credit bureaus) and to any other information resellers that resell consumer reports for use by others. FCRA limits resellers' use and distribution of personal data—for example, by allowing consumers to opt out of allowing consumer reporting agencies to share their personal information with third parties for prescreened marketing offers.

---

[8] Pub. L. No. 91-508, Tit. VI, 84 Stat. 1114, 1128 (1970) (codified as amended at 15 U.S.C. §§ 1681-1681x).

[9] *See* 15 U.S.C. §§ 1681-1681x.

[10] For the definition of "consumer reporting agency," see 15 U.S.C. § 1681a(f). For the definition of "consumer report," see 15 U.S.C. § 1681a(d).

Gramm-Leach-Bliley Act (GLBA)[11]

GLBA protects nonpublic personal information that individuals provide to financial institutions or that such institutions maintain.[12] GLBA sharing and disclosure restrictions apply to financial institutions or entities that receive nonpublic personal information from such institutions.[13] For example, a third party that receives nonpublic personal information from a financial institution to process consumers' account transactions may not use the information or resell it for marketing purposes.

Health Insurance Portability and Accountability Act of 1996 (HIPAA)[14]

HIPAA establishes a set of national standards to protect certain health information. The HIPAA privacy rule governs the use and disclosure of an individual's health information for purposes including marketing.[15] With some exceptions, the rule requires an individual's written authorization before a covered entity—a health care provider that transmits health information electronically in connection with covered transactions, health care clearinghouse, or health plan—may use or disclose the information for marketing.[16] The rule does not directly restrict the use, disclosure, or resale of protected health information by resellers or others not considered covered entities under the rule.

---

[11] Pub. L. No. 106-102, 113 Stat. 1338 (1999) (codified as amended in scattered sections of 12 and 15 U.S.C.).

[12] *See* 15 U.S.C. §§ 6801-6802. Subtitle A of Title V of the act contains the privacy provisions relating to the disclosure of nonpublic personal information. 15 U.S.C. §§ 6801- 6809.

[13] 15 U.S.C. § 6802. A "financial institution" is any institution the business of which is engaging in financial activities as described in section 4(k) of the Bank Holding Company Act (12 U.S.C. § 1843(k)). 15 U.S.C. § 6809(3)(a).

[14] Pub. L. No. 104-191, 110 Stat. 1936 (1996) (codified as amended in scattered sections of 18, 26, 29, and 42 U.S.C.).

[15] 45 C.F.R. Parts 160, 164.

[16] For the definition of "marketing," including exceptions, *see* 45 C.F.R. § 164.501.

Children's Online Privacy Protection Act of 1998 (COPPA)[17]

COPPA and its implementing regulations apply to the collection of information— such as name, email, or location—that would allow someone to identify or contact a child under 13.[18] Covered website and online service operators must obtain verifiable parental consent before collecting such information. COPPA may not directly affect information resellers, but the covered entities are potential sources of information for resellers.

Electronic Communications Privacy Act of 1986 (ECPA)[19]

ECPA prohibits the interception and disclosure of electronic communications by third parties unless an exception applies (such as one party to the communication consenting to disclosure). For example, the act would prevent an internet service provider from selling the content of its customers' emails to a reseller for marketing purposes, unless the customers had consented to disclosure. However, ECPA provides more limited protection for information considered to be "non-content," such as a customer's name and address.

Federal Trade Commission Act (FTC Act), Section 5[20]

The FTC Act prohibits unfair or deceptive acts or practices in or affecting commerce. Although the act does not explicitly grant FTC the specific authority to protect privacy, FTC has interpreted it to apply to

---

[17] Pub. L. No. 105-277, Div. C, Tit. XIII, 112 Stat. 2681-728 (1998) (codified at 15 U.S.C. §§ 6501-6506).

[18] FTC issued regulations implementing COPPA at 16 C.F.R. Part 312.

[19] Pub. L. No. 99-508, 100 Stat. 1848 (1986) (codified as amended in scattered sections of 18 U.S.C.).

[20] 15 U.S.C. § 45. Section 5 of the FTC Act, as originally enacted, only related to "unfair methods of competition." The Wheeler-Lea Act, passed in 1938, expanded the Commission's jurisdiction to include "unfair or deceptive acts or practices." Wheeler-Lea Amendments of 1938, Pub. L. No. 75-447, 52 Stat. 111 (1938).

deceptions or violations of written privacy policies. For example, if a retailer's written privacy policy stated customers' personal information would not be shared with resellers and the retailer later sold information to such parties, FTC could bring an enforcement action against the retailer for unfair and deceptive practices.

Some states also have enacted laws designed to regulate resellers' sharing of personal information about consumers. For example, in 2018, Vermont passed a law that contains, among other requirements, consumer protection provisions related to data brokers.[21] Among other things, the law requires data brokers to register annually and prohibits the acquisition and use of brokered personal information through certain means and for certain uses.

Gaps Exist in the Consumer Privacy Framework

The scope of consumer privacy protections provided under federal law has remained narrow in relation to (1) individuals' ability to access, control, and correct their personal data; (2) collection methods and sources and types of consumer information collected; (3) new technologies; and (4) some regulatory authorities. The examples in the following sections are drawn from our earlier reports and remain pertinent today.

Federal Law Provides Individuals Limited Ability to Access, Control, and Correct Their Personal Data

In our 2013 report, we found that no federal statute that we examined generally requires resellers to allow individuals to review personal information (intended for marketing purposes), control its use, or correct it.

---

[21] VT. STAT. ANN. tit. 9, §§ 2430, 2433, 2446 and 2447. Data broker means a business, or unit or units of a business, separately or together, that knowingly collects and sells or licenses to third parties the brokered personal information of a consumer with whom the business does not have a direct relationship. 9 V.S.A. § 2430(4).

The Fair Information Practice Principles state that individuals should be able to know about and consent to the collection of their information and have the right to access the information, request correction, and challenge the denial of those rights.

We also reported in 2013 that no federal statute provides consumers the right to learn what information is held about them and who holds it for marketing or look-up purposes. FCRA provides individuals with certain access rights, but only when information is used for credit eligibility purposes. And GLBA's provisions allowing consumers to opt out of having their personal information shared with third parties apply only in specific circumstances. Otherwise, under federal law, individuals generally cannot require that their personal information not be collected, used, and shared. Also, no federal law we examined provides correction rights (the ability to have resellers and others correct or delete inaccurate, incomplete, or unverifiable information) for marketing or look-up purposes.

Laws Largely Do Not Address Data Collection Methods, Sources, and Types

Our 2013 report also found that federal privacy laws are limited in addressing the methods by which, or the sources from which, resellers collect and aggregate personal information, or the types of information collected for marketing or look-up purposes. The Fair Information Practice Principles state that personal information should be relevant, limited to the purpose for which it was collected, and collected with the individual's knowledge or consent.

Federal laws generally do not govern the methods resellers may use to collect personal information. For instance, resellers, advertisers, and others use software to search the web for information about individuals and extract and download bulk information from websites with consumer information. Resellers or retailers also may collect information indirectly (by combining information from transactions).

Current federal law generally allows resellers to collect personal information from sources such as warranty registration cards and surveys and from online sources such as discussion boards, social media sites, blogs, and web browsing histories and searches. Current federal law generally does not require disclosure to consumers when their information is collected from these sources.

The federal laws that address the types of consumer information that can be collected and shared are not comprehensive. Under most circumstances, information that many people may consider very personal or sensitive can be collected, shared, and used for marketing. This can include information about physical and mental health, income and assets, political affiliations, and sexual habits and orientation. For health information, HIPAA rule provisions generally apply only to covered entities, such as health care providers.

Privacy Framework Largely Has Not Kept Pace with Changes in Technology

The current privacy framework does not fully address new technologies such as facial recognition technology, privacy issues raised by online tracking and mobile devices, and activities by financial technology firms. The original enactment of several federal privacy laws predates these trends and technologies. But in some instances existing laws have been interpreted to apply to new technologies. For example, FTC has taken enforcement actions under COPPA and revised the statute's implementing regulations to account for smartphones and mobile applications.

Facial Recognition Technology

One example of how privacy law has not kept pace with changes in technology is the use of facial recognition technology, which involves the collection of facial images and may be employed in a wide range of commercial applications. In our 2015 report we concluded that the future trajectory of this technology raised questions about consumer privacy.[22] We found that federal law does not expressly address the circumstances under which commercial entities can use facial recognition technology to identify or track individuals, or when consumer knowledge or consent should be required for the technology's use. Furthermore, in most contexts federal law does not address how personal data derived from the technology may be used or shared. The privacy issues stakeholders raised about facial recognition technology and other biometric technologies in use at the time of our 2015 report served as yet another example of the need to adapt federal privacy law to reflect new technologies. As such, we reiterated our 2013 recommendation that Congress strengthen the current consumer privacy framework to reflect the effects of changes in technology and the marketplace.

Activities by Financial Technology Firms

The rise of financial services provided by nonfinancial firms—often referred to as fintech—is another example of how new technology may create privacy concerns. For example, fintech lenders offer a variety of loans such as consumer and small business loans and operate almost exclusively online. In our 2018 report, we noted that while these lenders may still assess borrowers' creditworthiness with credit scores, they also may analyze large amounts of additional or alternative sources of data to determine creditworthiness.[23] We also found that some fintech firms may collect more consumer data than traditional lenders. For example, fintech lenders may have sensitive information such as consumers' educational background or utility payment information, and according to certain stakeholders, these data may contain errors that cannot be disputed by consumers under FCRA.

Furthermore, some data aggregators may hold consumer data without disclosing what rights consumers have to delete the data or prevent the data from being shared with other parties. A leak of these or other data held by fintech firms may expose characteristics that people view as sensitive.

[22] GAO-15-621.
[23] GAO-18-254.

GLBA generally requires fintech firms and traditional financial institutions to safeguard nonpublic personal information about customers.[24] Our 2018 report discussed that some fintech firms use new technologies or mobile device features to mitigate data privacy risks and that some regulators have issued guidance to consumers publicizing practices that help maintain privacy when using online products and services, including those provided by fintech firms. Regulators also have issued GLBA guidance to businesses, including fintech firms, recommending that they adopt policies and procedures to prevent, detect, and address privacy threats.

Internet Privacy Issues

Online Tracking

In our 2013 report, we found that no federal privacy law explicitly addresses the full range of practices to track or collect data from consumers' online activity. Cookies allow website operators to recall information such as user name and address, credit card number, and purchases in a shopping cart. Resellers can match information in cookies and their databases to augment consumer profiles. Third parties also can synchronize their cookie files with resellers' files. Advertisers can use third-party cookies—placed on a computer by a domain other than the site being visited—to track visits to the websites on which they advertise. While current federal law does not, with some exceptions, explicitly address web tracking, FTC has taken enforcement actions related to web tracking under its authority to enforce the prohibition on unfair or deceptive acts. For example, in 2011, FTC settled charges with Google for $22.5 million after alleging that Google violated an earlier privacy settlement with FTC when it misrepresented to users of Apple's Safari web browser that it would not track and serve targeted advertisements to Safari users.[25] Google agreed to disable its advertising tracking cookies.

---

[24] GLBA restricts, with some exceptions, the disclosure of nonpublic information by companies defined as financial institutions. *See* 15 U.S.C. §§ 6801-6802.

[25] *United States v. Google Inc.*, No. CV 12-04177-SI, 2012 WL 5833994 (N.D. Cal. Nov. 16, 2012).

Mobile Devices

In 2013, we also explained that no federal law comprehensively governs applications software for mobile devices. Application developers, mobile carriers, advertisers, and others may collect an individual's information through services provided on a mobile device. However, FTC has taken enforcement action against companies for use of mobile applications that violate COPPA and FCRA.[26] The agency also has taken action under the FTC Act.[27] We and others have reported that the capability of mobile devices to provide consumer's location engenders privacy risks, particularly if companies use or share location data without consumers' knowledge.[28] ECPA might not apply if location data were not deemed content and would not govern entities that are not covered by ECPA. But FTC could pursue enforcement action if a company's collection or use of the information violated COPPA.

More recently, in January of this year, we issued a report on internet privacy that reinforces what we reported in 2013.[29] To varying extents, internet content providers and internet service providers collect, use, and share information from their customers to enable their services, support advertising, and for other purposes. Consumers access such services through mobile phones and tablets, computers, and other internetconnected devices. However, there is no comprehensive federal privacy statute with specific standards. FTC has been addressing internet privacy through its unfair and deceptive practices authority, among other statutes, and other

---

[26] FTC settled charges that a social networking service deceived consumers when it collected information from children under 13 through its mobile application in violation of COPPA. *See United States v. Path, Inc.*, No. C13-0448 (N.D. Cal. Jan. 31, 2013). FTC also settled charges that a company compiled and sold criminal record reports through its mobile application and operated as a consumer reporting agency, in violation of FCRA. *See In the Matter of Filiquarian Publishing, LLC*, FTC File No. 112 3195 (Apr. 30, 2013).

[27] In addition to the alleged COPPA violation, Path allegedly deceived users by collecting personal information from their mobile address books without their knowledge and consent. *See United States v. Path, Inc.*, No. C13-0448 (N.D. Cal. Jan. 31, 2013).

[28] Risks included disclosure to third parties for unspecified uses, tracking of consumer behavior, and identity theft. See GAO, *Mobile Device Location ID: Additional Federal Actions Could Help Protect Consumer Privacy*, GAO-12-903 (Washington, D.C.: Sept. 11, 2012). A Federal Communications Commission report also noted privacy risks. See Federal Communications Commission, *Location-Based Services: An Overview of Opportunities and Other Considerations* (Washington, D.C.: May 2012).

[29] GAO-19-52.

agencies have been addressing this issue using industry-specific statutes. We concluded that recent developments regarding internet privacy suggest that this is an appropriate time for Congress to consider comprehensive internet privacy legislation. To address such privacy concerns, states and other countries have adopted privacy rules. For example, the European Union's General Data Protection Regulation, which came into force in May 2018, is a set of privacy rules that give consumers control over the collection, use, and sharing of their personal information, and California passed its own privacy law in June 2018 that becomes effective in 2020.[30]

Regulatory Authorities under Current Law May Be Limited

In February of this year, we reported that FTC does not have civil penalty authority for initial violations of GLBA's privacy and safeguarding requirements, which, unlike FCRA, includes a provision directing federal regulators and FTC to establish standards for financial institutions to protect against any anticipated threats or hazards to the security of customer records.[31] To obtain monetary redress for these violations, FTC must identify affected consumers and any monetary harm they may have experienced. However, harm resulting from privacy and security violations (such as a data breach) can be difficult to measure and can occur years in the future, making it difficult to trace a particular harm to a specific breach. As a result, FTC lacks a practical enforcement tool for imposing civil money penalties that could help to deter companies from violating data security provisions of GLBA and its implementing regulations. We recommended that Congress consider giving FTC civil penalty authority to enforce GLBA's safeguarding provisions.

Additionally, in our January 2019 report, we found that FTC had not yet issued regulations for internet privacy other than those protecting

---

[30] California's law generally will require companies to report to customers, upon their request, the categories of personal information they collected about the customer, the business or commercial purpose for collecting and selling such personal information, and what categories of third parties received it.

[31] GAO-19-196.

financial privacy and the internet privacy of children, which were required by law. FTC uses its statutory authority under the FTC Act to protect consumers from unfair and deceptive trade practices. For FTC Act violations, FTC may promulgate regulations but is required to use procedures that differ from traditional notice-and-comment processes and that FTC staff said add time and complexity. In addition, under this authority, FTC can generally only levy civil money penalties after a company has violated an FTC final consent order. In our recommendation that Congress consider developing comprehensive internet privacy legislation, we also suggested that such legislation consider providing rulemaking and civil money penalty authorities to the proper agency or agencies.

In summary, new technologies have vastly changed the amount of personal information private companies collect and how they use it. But our current privacy framework does not fully address these changes. Laws protecting privacy interests are tailored to specific sectors and uses. And, consumers have little control over how their information is collected, used, and shared with third parties for marketing purposes. As a result, current privacy law is not always aligned with the Fair Information Practice Principles, which the Department of Commerce and others have said should serve as the foundation for commercial data privacy. Thus, the privacy framework warrants reconsideration by Congress in relation to consumer interests, new technologies, and other issues.

Chairman Crapo, Ranking Member Brown, and Members of the Committee, this concludes my statement. I would be pleased to respond to any questions you may have.

In: Key Government Reports. Vol. 33 ISBN: 978-1-53616-566-1
Editor: Ernest Clark

Chapter 2

SMALL BUSINESS ADMINISTRATION CONTRACTING PROGRAMS: ADDITIONAL EFFORTS NEEDED TO IMPLEMENT GAO RECOMMENDATIONS*

William B. Shear

WHY GAO DID THIS STUDY

Federal agencies conduct a variety of procurements that are reserved for small business participation through small business set-asides. These set-asides can be for small businesses in general, or they can be specific to small businesses that meet additional eligibility requirements in programs such as those for WOSB or HUBZone. SBA administers both the WOSB and HUBZone programs. SBA also produces an annual Small Business Procurement Scorecard to measure how much contracted spending federal

---

* This is an edited, reformatted and augmented version of the United States Government Accountability Office Testimony Before the Committee on Small Business and Entrepreneurship, U.S. Senate, Publication No. GAO-19-623T, dated June 12, 2019.

agencies allocate to small businesses and whether the federal government is meeting its goals for awarding contracts to small businesses.

GAO issued three reports between September 2018 and March 2019 on SBA contracting programs. This testimony is primarily based on these three reports and discusses prior GAO findings and SBA's progress on implementing GAO's recommendations on (1) the WOSB program, (2) the HUBZone program, and (3) SBA's procurement scorecard.

To update the status of prior recommendations, GAO reviewed updates from SBA and interviewed officials.

WHAT GAO FOUND

The Small Business Administration (SBA) has not fully implemented GAO's prior recommendations to address oversight deficiencies in the Women-Owned Small Business (WOSB) and Historically Underutilized Business Zone (HUBZone) programs and to improve evaluation of its procurement scorecard. GAO maintains that its recommendations should be addressed.

Women-Owned Small Business Program

In its March 2019 report, GAO found that SBA had not addressed WOSB program oversight deficiencies identified in GAO's 2014 report (GAO-15-54). For example, GAO had found that SBA did not have procedures related to reviewing the performance of the four third-party certifers—private entities approved by SBA to certify the eligibility of WOSB firms—as well as information the certifiiers submitted to SBA. GAO recommended that SBA establish procedures to assess the performance of the certifiers and the information they submitted. While SBA conducted a compliance review of the certifiers in 2016, SBA said in June 2018 that it had no plans to conduct further compliance reviews until a final rule implementing a new certification process was completed. SBA officials said that they expected the rule to be implemented by June 2021. By waiting to improve its oversight of the WOSB program, SBA cannot provide reasonable assurance that certifiers are complying with program requirements and cannot improve its efforts to identify ineligible firms or potential fraud.

HUBZone Program

In September 2018, GAO reported that it had reviewed case files for a nongeneralizable sample of 12 firms in Puerto Rico that received HUBZone certification between March 2017 and March 2018 and found that SBA did not consistently document or follow its policies and procedures for certification reviews. For example, SBA did not have complete documentation in nine of 12 cases and did not follow its policy to conduct three levels of review when determining whether to approve or deny a firm in four of 12 cases. As a result, SBA did not have reasonable assurance that firms meet HUBZone criteria. SBA said that it planned to implement GAO's recommendations that SBA (1) update internal policy manuals for certification and recertification and (2) conduct and document reviews of staff compliance with relevant procedures. However, as of May 2019, SBA had not provided documentation showing that it had completed these planned actions.

Small Business Procurement Scorecard

For fiscal year 2017, SBA revised the methodology for its Small Business Procurement Scorecard, which assesses the efforts of federal agencies to support contracting with small businesses. For example, one revision reduced the share of the total scorecard grade devoted to prime contracting achievement (the dollar amount of contracts awarded directly to small businesses). GAO recommended in September 2018 that SBA design and implement a comprehensive evaluation to assess the scorecard revisions. Since that report was issued, SBA has proposed but not yet implemented a two-phase evaluation of the scorecard to include an evaluation of the scorecard's effect on federal agencies achieving small business contracting goals. SBA said that it expects to complete phase one by September 2019 and has not provided a time frame for phase two.

Chairman Rubio, Ranking Member Cardin, and Members of the Committee:

I am pleased to be here today to discuss our recent work on the Small Business Administration's (SBA) contracting programs and SBA's progress in implementing our recommendations. Federal agencies conduct a variety of procurements that are reserved for small business participation through small business set-asides. These set-asides can be for small businesses in general, or they can be specific to small businesses that meet additional eligibility requirements, such as those for SBA's Women-Owned Small Business (WOSB) or Historically Underutilized Business Zones (HUBZone) programs.[1] SBA also produces an annual Small Business Procurement Scorecard (scorecard) to measure how much contracted spending federal agencies allocate to small businesses and whether the federal government is meeting its goals for awarding contracts to small businesses.

My testimony today is based primarily on three reports we issued between September 2018 and March 2019, as well as a report we issued in October 2014.[2] I will discuss SBA's progress on implementing our prior

---

[1] Congress authorized the WOSB program in 2000, allowing contracting officers to set aside procurements to women-owned small businesses in industries in which they are substantially underrepresented. The purpose of the HUBZone program is to provide federal contracting preferences to qualified small businesses located in economically distressed communities (referred to as HUBZones) that employ residents of the areas.

[2] GAO, *Women-Owned Small Business Program: Actions Needed to Address Ongoing Oversight Issues*, GAO-19-168 (Washington, D.C.: Mar. 14, 2019); *Small Business Contracting: Small Business Administration Could Further Strengthen HUBZone Eligibility Reviews in Puerto Rico and Programwide*, GAO-18-666 (Washington, D.C.: Sept. 24, 2018); *Small Business Administration: Actions Needed to Improve Confidence in Small Business Procurement Scorecard*, GAO-18-672 (Washington, D.C.: Sept. 27, 2018); and *Women-Owned Small Business Program: Certifier Oversight and Additional Eligibility Controls Are Needed*, GAO-15-54 (Washington, D.C.: Oct. 8, 2014).

recommendations on (1) the WOSB program, (2) the HUBZone program in Puerto Rico, and (3) SBA's procurement scorecard.

To conduct the work on the WOSB program, we reviewed relevant laws, regulations, and program documents; analyzed federal contracting data from April 2011 through June 2018; and interviewed SBA officials, officials from contracting agencies selected to obtain a range of experience with the WOSB program, and three of the four private third- party certifiers.[3] For our HUBZone report, we analyzed SBA documents and reviewed files of a nongeneralizable sample of 12 firms located in Puerto Rico that received certification between March 2017 and March 2018. We also interviewed SBA officials, representatives from HUBZonecertified firms in Puerto Rico, and local economic development agencies in Puerto Rico. To conduct the work on SBA's procurement scorecard, we analyzed SBA's prior and revised scorecard methodology and results and interviewed officials from SBA, four other federal agencies selected based on small business procurement volume and other attributes, and three groups representing the interests of small businesses. To update the status of recommendations from these reports, we reviewed updates from SBA and interviewed officials. We conducted the work on which this testimony is based in accordance with generally accepted government auditing standards. More details on our methodology can be found in the three reports on which this testimony is based.

SBA Has Not Fully Addressed Deficiencies in Oversight and Implementation for the WOSB Program

SBA has not fully addressed deficiencies we have previously identified for the WOSB program, and these deficiencies are affected by SBA's ongoing implementation of changes to the program authorized by the

[3] To be eligible to participate in the WOSB program, firms have the option to self-certify or be certified by a third-party certifier.

National Defense Authorization Act of 2015 (2015 NDAA). As of early June 2019, SBA had implemented one of the three changes to the program authorized in the 2015 NDAA.[4] Specifically, in September 2015 SBA published a final rule to implement sole-source authority (to award contracts without competition), effective October 2015. The two other changes—authorizing SBA to implement its own certification process for WOSBs and requiring SBA to eliminate the option for firms to self-certify that they are eligible for the WOSB program—had not been implemented.[5] On May 14, 2019, SBA published in the Federal Register a proposed rule that eliminates the self-certification option and describes a potential certification process to be administered by SBA.[6] SBA officials have stated that the agency will not eliminate self-certification until the new certification process for the WOSB program is in place, which they expect to implement by June 2021.

In addition, SBA has not fully addressed WOSB program oversight deficiencies described in our March 2019 report and first identified in our 2014 report.[7] We reported that SBA did not have formal policies for reviewing the performance of its four approved third-party certifiers (private entities approved by SBA to certify the eligibility of WOSB firms), including their compliance with their agreements with SBA. Further, we found that SBA had not developed formal policies and procedures for, among other things, reviewing the monthly reports that certifiers submit to SBA.[8] We recommended that the Administrator of SBA establish comprehensive procedures to monitor and assess the performance of the third-party certifiers in accordance with their agreements with SBA and program regulations. While SBA has taken some steps to address our recommendation, including conducting a

---

[4] GAO-19-168.

[5] The 2015 NDAA expanded the WOSB certification process to include certification by the SBA Administrator, in addition to the previously approved methods of certification by a federal agency, a state government, or a national certifying entity approved by SBA.

[6] Women-Owned Small Business and Economically Disadvantaged Women-Owned Small Business – Certification, 84 Fed. Reg. 21256 (May 14, 2019).

[7] GAO-15-54.

[8] Per their written agreements with SBA, the third-party certifiers are required to submit monthly reports to SBA describing WOSB program performance information.

compliance review of the certifiers in 2016, SBA officials said in June 2018 that SBA had no plans to conduct further compliance reviews until the final rule implementing the new certification process was completed. By waiting to improve its oversight of the WOSB program, SBA cannot provide reasonable assurance that certifiers are complying with program requirements and cannot improve its efforts to identify ineligible firms or potential fraud. In addition, the implementation of sole-source authority in light of these continued oversight deficiencies can increase program risk. Consequently, we maintain that our recommendation should be addressed.

SBA also has not fully addressed deficiencies related to eligibility examinations that we described in our March 2019 report and first identified in our October 2014 report. We found that SBA lacked formalized guidance for its eligibility examination processes and that the examinations identified high rates of potentially ineligible businesses. As a result, we recommended that SBA enhance its examination of businesses that register for the WOSB program to ensure that only eligible businesses obtain WOSB set-asides. Specifically, we suggested that SBA should take actions such as (1) completing the development of procedures to conduct annual eligibility examinations and implementing such procedures; (2) analyzing examination results and individual businesses found to be ineligible to better understand the cause of the high rate of ineligibility in annual reviews and determine what actions are needed to address the causes, and (3) implementing ongoing reviews of a sample of all businesses that have represented their eligibility to participate in the program.

SBA has taken some steps to implement our recommendation, such as including written policies and procedures for WOSB program eligibility examinations in a standard operating procedure and a Desk Guide. However, SBA does not collect reliable information on the results of its annual eligibility examinations. In addition, SBA continues to have no mechanism to look across examinations for common eligibility issues to inform the WOSB program. As we noted in 2014, by not analyzing examination results broadly, the agency is missing opportunities to obtain meaningful insights into the program, such as the reasons many businesses are deemed ineligible.

Further, SBA still conducts eligibility examinations only of firms that have already received a WOSB award. Restricting the samples in this way limits SBA's ability to better understand the eligibility of businesses before they apply for and are awarded contracts, as well as its ability to detect and prevent potential fraud.

We recognize that SBA has made some effort to address our recommendation by documenting procedures for conducting annual eligibility examinations of WOSB firms. However, without maintaining reliable information on the results of eligibility examinations, developing procedures for analyzing results, and expanding the sample of businesses to be examined to include those that did not receive contracts, SBA limits the value of its eligibility examinations and its ability to reduce ineligibility among businesses registered to participate in the WOSB program. Leading fraud risk management practices state that federal program managers should design control activities that focus on fraud prevention over detection and response, to the extent possible.[9] The deficiencies in SBA's oversight of the WOSB program limit SBA's ability to identify potential fraud risks and develop any additional control activities needed to address these risks. As a result, the program may continue to be exposed to the risk of ineligible businesses receiving set-aside contracts. In addition, in light of these continued deficiencies, the implementation of sole-source authority without addressing the other changes made by the 2015 NDAA could increase program risk. For these reasons, we maintain that our previous recommendation that SBA enhance its WOSB eligibility examination procedures should be addressed.

In addition, similar to previous findings from SBA's Office of Inspector General, our March 2019 report found that about 3.5 percent of contracts using a WOSB set-aside were awarded for ineligible goods or

---

[9] GAO, *A Framework for Managing Fraud Risks in Federal Programs*, GAO-15-593SP (Washington, D.C.: July 2015).

services from April 2011 through June 2018.[10] At that time, SBA was not reviewing contracting data that could identify this problem and inform SBA which agencies making awards may need targeted outreach or training. As a result, we found that SBA could not provide reasonable assurance that WOSB program requirements were being met and that the program was meeting its goals. We recommended that SBA develop a process for periodically reviewing the extent to which WOSB program set-asides are awarded for ineligible goods or services and use the results to address identified issues, such as through targeted outreach or training to agencies making awards under the ineligible codes. In early May 2019, SBA said that it had initiated such efforts.

SBA HAS NOT YET IMPLEMENTED RECOMMENDATIONS TO IMPROVE THE HUBZONE CERTIFICATION PROCESS

In September 2018, we found that although SBA had adopted criteria and guidance for a risk-based approach to certifying and recertifying firms for the HUBZone program in March 2017, the extent to which it conducted a risk assessment to inform its approach was unclear.[11] In 2015, we found that SBA lacked key controls for its recertification process and recommended that SBA assess the process.[12] In 2009, SBA increased documentation requirements for certification but not recertification (which determines continued program eligibility every 3 years). In March 2017, SBA changed its recertification criteria and guidance to require firms with $1 million or more in HUBZone contract awards to provide documentation to support continuing eligibility. During our work for the September 2018

---

[10] GAO-19-168. See also Small Business Administration Office of Inspector General, *Improvements Needed in SBA's Management of the Women Owned Small Business Federal Contracting Program*, SBA OIG Report 15-10 (Washington, D.C.: May 14, 2015) and *SBA's Women-Owned Small Business Contracting Program*, SBA OIG Report 18-18 (Washington, D.C.: June 20, 2018).

[11] GAO-18-666.

[12] See GAO, *Small Business Contracting: Opportunities Exist to Further Improve HUBZone Oversight*, GAO-15-234 (Washington, D.C.: Feb. 12, 2015).

report, SBA officials stated they had completed a risk assessment of the HUBZone recertification process, but did not provide us with documentation on when they performed the risk assessment, which risks were identified and considered, or what analysis established the $1 million threshold. As of May 2019, SBA had not provided documentation showing that it had performed the risk assessment, but we maintain that an assessment of the recertification process would help inform a risk-based approach to reviewing and verifying information from firms that appear to pose the most risk to the program. In addition, SBA had not provided documentation showing that a technology-based solution designed to address some of the ongoing challenges with the recertification process had been implemented. SBA officials had previously estimated this solution would be available first in spring 2017 and then by the end of calendar year 2017.[13]

We also found in our September 2018 report that, based on our review of case files for a nongeneralizable sample of 12 firms in Puerto Rico that received HUBZone certification between March 2017 and March 2018, SBA did not consistently document or follow its policies and procedures for certification reviews:

- SBA did not have complete documentation in nine of 12 cases. SBA officials described alternative procedures they used to determine firms' eligibility, but SBA had not updated its internal policy manuals to reflect these procedures, and analysts did not document use of such procedures in the files we reviewed. As a result, SBA did not have reasonable assurance that firms met HUBZone criteria.
- In four of 12 cases, SBA did not follow its policy to conduct three levels of review (by an analyst, a senior analyst, and the program director or deputy) when determining whether to approve or deny a firm.

[13] See GAO, HUBZone Program: Opportunities Exist to Further Improve Oversight, GAO-16-866T (Washington, D.C.: Sept. 7, 2016); and HUBZone Program: Oversight Has Improved But Some Weaknesses Remain, GAO-17-456T (Washington, D.C.: Mar. 2, 2017).

- It was unclear to what extent SBA reviewed staff compliance with certification and recertification review procedures. SBA provided an assurance letter stating that it evaluated the Office of HUBZone's internal controls and concluded the controls were effective, but the letter did not specify what steps SBA took for the evaluation.

We recommended that SBA (1) update its internal policy manuals for certification and recertification reviews to reflect existing policies and procedures not currently in written guidance and (2) conduct and document reviews of staff compliance with procedures associated with HUBZone certification and recertification. In response to our report, SBA said that it planned to update its internal policies on certification and recertification by issuing a procedural notice and to begin reviewing and documenting staff compliance with the updated procedures outlined in the notice. However, as of May 2019, SBA had not provided documentation showing that it had completed these planned actions.

SBA Has Taken Some Steps to Address Recommendations about the Procurement Scorecard

In September 2018, we found that for fiscal year 2017, SBA revised the methodology for its Small Business Procurement Scorecard, which is used to assess federal agencies' progress toward small business procurement goals.[14] SBA made revisions to address requirements specified in the National Defense Authorization Act for Fiscal Year 2016. SBA (1) reduced the share of the total scorecard grade devoted to prime contracting achievement, which is the dollar amount of contracts awarded directly to small businesses, and (2) added an element calculating changes in the number of small businesses receiving prime contracts. SBA made

---

[14] GAO-18-672.

two additional revisions—with input from other agencies' representatives—to increase the share of subcontracting achievement results and the share of the peer review of required activities designed to facilitate small business procurement. In July 2018, officials said they had begun developing a plan to evaluate the effects of the revised scorecard methodology but did not provide a draft plan. Conducting a well-designed and comprehensive evaluation could aid SBA in determining whether the scorecard is an effective tool for helping to achieve the agency's strategic goals.

In our September 2018 report, we also found that the published fiscal year 2017 scorecards originally contained errors, including an incorrect grade and numeric score for one agency, and SBA does not have a process to ensure that scorecard results are published accurately. Although SBA later corrected the errors, it did not initially document that scorecards had been changed, which is inconsistent with SBA's policy on information quality. SBA officials said that errors occurred in the process of formatting scorecards for publication. Errors in the published scorecards—and the initial lack of disclosure about corrections—weaken data reliability and may undermine confidence in scorecard data.

We recommended that SBA (1) design and implement a comprehensive evaluation to assess scorecard revisions and (2) institute a process for reviewing scorecards for accuracy prior to publication and a mechanism for disclosing corrected information. Since our report, SBA has proposed a two-phase program evaluation of the scorecard. SBA officials said that they plan for phase one to include a report to Congress on the impact of the small business procurement goal program for Chief Financial Officers Act agencies and to provide a recommendation on continuing, modifying, expanding, or terminating the scorecard program.[15] SBA plans to provide the phase one report in September 2019. In phase two, SBA plans to conduct a program evaluation that investigates the effectiveness of the small business contracting scorecard on federal agency small business

[15] The Chief Financial Officers Act of 1990, Pub. L. No. 101-576, established chief financial officers to oversee financial management activities at 23 major executive departments and agencies. The list now includes 24 entities, which are often referred to collectively as Chief Financial Officers Act agencies.

contracting goal achievement. SBA has not provided a time frame for phase two. With respect to the second recommendation, SBA officials said that SBA has developed a procedure that includes a prepublication review process for procurement scorecards. The officials said the procedure identifies responsibilities, provides for an independent peer review, and includes supervisory review. Officials said the procedure also includes measures for post-publication review and corrections. We will review supporting documentation for this new procedure to assess whether this recommendation can be closed as implemented.

Chairman Rubio, Ranking Member Cardin, and Members of the Committee, this completes my prepared statement. I would be pleased to respond to any questions that you may have at this time.

FINANCE

In: Key Government Reports. Vol. 33
Editor: Ernest Clark
ISBN: 978-1-53616-566-1

Chapter 3

2017 Disaster Relief Oversight: Strategy Needed to Ensure Agencies' Internal Control Plans Provide Sufficient Information*

United States Government Accountability Office

Abbreviation

DHS	Department of Homeland Security
DOD	Department of Defense
Education	Department of Education
ERM	enterprise risk management
HUD	Department of Housing and Urban Development
IG	inspector general
OMB	Office of Management and Budget

* This is an edited, reformatted and augmented accessible version of the United States Government Accountability Office Report to Congressional Requesters, Publication No. GAO-19-479, dated June 2019.

SBA	Small Business Administration
USACE	U.S. Army Corps of Engineers
USDA	Department of Agriculture

INTRODUCTION

June 28, 2019
Congressional Requesters

The destruction that disasters cause must be addressed immediately, and agencies must deliver disaster relief funding expeditiously. However, the risk of improper payments increases when agencies spend billions of dollars quickly. In 2017, four sequential disasters—Hurricanes Harvey, Irma, and Maria and the California wildfires—created an unprecedented demand for federal disaster response and recovery resources. Congress passed, and the President signed, three supplemental appropriations acts providing for over $120 billion in additional funding for response and recovery activities related to these disasters.[1]

In these supplemental appropriations acts, Congress also provided an oversight framework related to internal control to limit improper payments of these funds. Congress included the following key payment-integrity provisions to help ensure that agencies spend disaster relief funding as efficiently and effectively as possible:

The Office of Management and Budget (OMB) is required to issue criteria for federal agencies to use in designing internal control plans for spending disaster relief funding.

[1] This amount does not include transfers of unobligated balances from prior fiscal years or indefinite appropriations authorized to forgive any outstanding balance owed to the Department of Education under the Historically Black College and University Hurricane Supplemental Loan Program. See Additional Supplemental Appropriations for Disaster Relief Requirements Act, 2017, Pub. L. No. 115-56, div. B, 131 Stat. 1129, 1136 (2017); Additional Supplemental Appropriations for Disaster Relief Requirements Act, 2017 Pub. L. No. 115-72, div. A, 131 Stat. 1224 (2017); and Further Additional Supplemental Appropriations for Disaster Relief Requirements Act, 2018, Pub. L. No. 115-123, div. B, subdiv. 1, 132 Stat. 64, 65 (2018).

Federal agencies are required to submit their plans for ensuring internal control over spending disaster relief funding to GAO, their respective inspectors general (IG), OMB, and Congress.

We have previously reported deficiencies related to OMB's guidance for federal agencies to develop required internal control plans for funds received under the Disaster Relief Appropriations Act of 2013 and federal agencies' creation of those plans in response to Hurricane Sandy.[2]

You requested that we evaluate the federal government's preparedness, response, and recovery efforts related to the three hurricanes and California wildfires in 2017. As part of that effort , this chapter examines the extent to which selected federal agencies' internal control plans for spending disaster relief funds provided timely and sufficient external communication to Congress and others and OMB's strategy for implementing statutory requirements for disaster relief internal control plans. In addition, we are conducting a broader body of work covering various disaster response and recovery issues.

To address our objective, we selected for review six of the 19 agencies that received supplemental appropriations for activities in response to the 2017 hurricanes and wildfires. We selected the six agencies that received the highest amounts of combined supplemental appropriations. Each of the six received in excess of $2 billion in supplemental disaster funding: together they received $115 billion of the approximately $120 billion in supplemental appropriations for activities in response to the 2017 disasters. The six agencies were the Departments of Agriculture (USDA), Defense (DOD), Education (Education), Homeland Security (DHS), and Housing and Urban Development (HUD) and the Small Business Administration (SBA). Because this was a nonprobability sample, our findings cannot be generalized to agencies we did not select.

We identified and reviewed relevant agency criteria included in OMB Memorandum M-18-14 (M-18-14), Implementation of Internal Controls and Grant Expenditures for the Disaster-Related Appropriations, and then evaluated whether the internal control plans submitted by the six agencies

---

[2] GAO, *Hurricane Sandy Relief: Improved Guidance on Designing Internal Control Plans Could Enhance Oversight of Disaster Funding*, GAO-14-58 (Washington, D.C.: Nov. 26, 2013).

we selected included information to demonstrate that those agencies satisfied the OMB criteria.[3] We also evaluated whether the internal control plans satisfied minimum documentation requirements included in Standards for Internal Control in the Federal Government.[4]

We also reviewed whether agencies submitted the internal control plans on or before the statutory deadline of March 31, 2018, and whether agencies submitted the plans as required to OMB, GAO, their respective IGs, and the Committees on Appropriations for the U.S. Senate and House of Representatives. We interviewed OMB staff to understand their strategy for implementing statutory requirements for disaster relief internal control plans and their rationale behind guidance in M-18-14. We also interviewed agency officials to understand their processes for developing the internal control plans, including how they interpreted OMB guidance in M-18-14 and its effect, if any, on helping agencies to meet the statutory requirements.

We conducted this performance audit from April 2018 to June 2019 in accordance with generally accepted government auditing standards. Those standards require that we plan and perform the audit to obtain sufficient, appropriate evidence to provide a reasonable basis for our findings and conclusions based on our audit objective. We believe that the evidence obtained provides a reasonable basis for our findings and conclusions based on our audit objective.

BACKGROUND

Supplemental Appropriations for 2017 Disaster Relief

Congress enacted three supplemental appropriations providing over $120 billion in funding for activities related to the 2017 disasters—

[3] Office of Management and Budget, Implementation of Internal Controls and Grant Expenditures for the Disaster-Related Appropriations, OMB Memorandum M-18-14 (Washington, D.C.: Mar. 30, 2018).

[4] GAO, *Standards for Internal Control in the Federal Government*, GAO-14-704G (Washington, D.C.: September 2014).

Hurricanes Harvey, Irma, and Maria and the California wildfires. Figure 1 shows the distribution of 2017 disaster relief funding by agency.

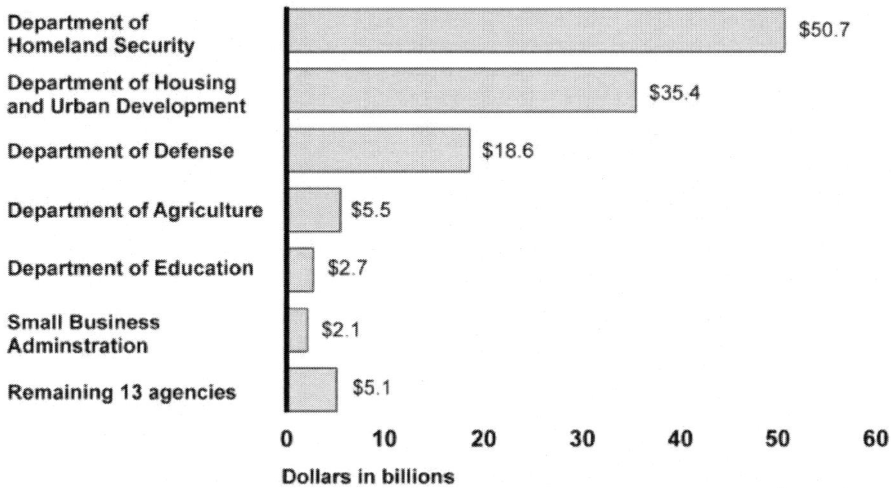

Source: GAO analysis of disaster-related supplemental appropritions acts. | GAO-19-479.

Figure 1. Distribution of Funding Provided by the Supplemental Appropriations for the 2017 Disasters.

The Additional Supplemental Appropriations for Disaster Relief Requirements Act, 2017, as amended by the Further Additional Supplemental Appropriations for Disaster Relief Requirements Act, 2018, required that each federal agency prepare an internal control plan, in accordance with OMB criteria, for funds provided by specified portions of these laws, and submit the plan to GAO, the agency's IG, and the Committees on Appropriations of the U.S. Senate and House of Representatives by March 31, 2018. Congress also required OMB to issue standard guidance for agencies to use in designing internal control plans, leveraging existing internal control review processes, for disaster relief funding. The guidance was to include, at a minimum

- robust criteria for identifying and documenting incremental risks and mitigating controls related to disaster relief funding and

- guidance for documenting the linkage between the incremental risks related to disaster funding and efforts to address known internal control risks.

OMB Guidance

As noted above, the supplemental appropriations acts for 2017 disasters required OMB to establish criteria for agencies to use in developing their 2017 disaster relief internal control plans due March 31, 2018. OMB established the criteria in M-18-14, issued March 30, 2018. This OMB memorandum provides guidance to agencies to implement the internal control provisions of the 2017 disaster relief supplemental appropriations, and in particular, it explains agency responsibilities for managing disaster relief funds. M-18-14 notes that as required by OMB Circular No. A-123, Management's Responsibility for Enterprise Risk Management and Internal Control (Circular A-123), each agency has overall responsibility for establishing internal controls to manage the risk of fraud—one source of improper payments.[5] Additionally, OMB stated that agencies must use a risk-based approach to design and implement financial and administrative controls to identify and mitigate fraud risks.

Standards for Internal Control in the Federal Government

Federal internal control standards provide the overall framework for establishing and maintaining internal control in the federal government.[6] Internal control should be designed, implemented, and operating effectively to provide reasonable assurance that the operations, reporting, and compliance objectives of an entity will be achieved. The five components of internal control are as follows:

---

[5] Office of Management and Budget, Management's Responsibility for Enterprise Risk Management and Internal Control, Circular No. A-123 (Washington, D.C.: July 15, 2016).

[6] GAO-14-704G.

- Control environment: The foundation for an internal control system. It provides the discipline and structure to help an entity achieve its objectives.
- Risk assessment: Assesses the risks facing the entity as it seeks to achieve its objectives. This assessment provides the basis for developing appropriate risk responses.
- Control activities: The actions management establishes through policies and procedures to achieve objectives and respond to risks in the internal control system, which includes the entity's information system.
- Information and communication: The quality information management and personnel communicate and use to support the internal control system.
- Monitoring: Activities management establishes and operates to assess the quality of performance over time and promptly resolve the findings of audits and other reviews.

Documentation is a necessary part of an effective internal control system. The level and nature of documentation vary based on the size of the entity and the complexity of the operational processes the entity performs. Documentation is required to demonstrate the design, implementation, and operating effectiveness of an entity's internal control system. Federal internal control standards' minimum documentation requirements are as follows:

- If management determines that a principle is not relevant, management supports that determination with documentation that includes the rationale of how, in the absence of that principle, the associated component could be designed, implemented, and operated effectively.
- Management develops and maintains documentation of its internal control system.
- Management documents in policies the internal control responsibilities of the organization.

- Management evaluates and documents the results of ongoing monitoring and separate evaluations to identify internal control issues.
- Management evaluates and documents internal control issues and determines appropriate corrective actions for internal control deficiencies on a timely basis.
- Management completes and documents corrective actions to remediate internal control deficiencies on a timely basis.

MAJOR FINDING

Selected Agencies' Internal Control Plans Did Not Communicate Timely and Sufficient Information Because OMB Did Not Employ an Effective Strategy

Selected agencies did not submit their internal control plans timely and the plans lacked necessary information because OMB did not employ an effective strategy for timely submission and sufficient content. OMB issued guidance for agencies to use in designing internal control plans for disaster relief funding on March 30, 2018. This gave agencies 1 day to consult the guidance before their internal control plans were due on March 31, 2018. Only one of the six agencies we reviewed, Education, submitted its internal control plan by the statutory deadline. In addition, OMB did not have an effective strategy to communicate to agencies the information that they had to include in their internal control plans. For the six selected agencies, one had not submitted an internal control plan as of April 2019. For the five that submitted internal control plans, their plans did not include sufficient information for us to determine whether they were consistent with OMB guidance and federal internal control standards' minimum documentation requirements.

Five of Six Selected Agencies Did Not Timely Submit Internal Control Plans

The Additional Supplemental Appropriations for Disaster Relief Requirements Act, 2017, as amended, required that each federal agency receiving funds submit, no later than March 31, 2018, and in accordance with criteria to be established by OMB, an internal control plan for spending funds on activities related to the 2017 disasters. Our review of six selected agencies found that most did not meet this deadline. Specifically, we found the following:

- Education was the only selected agency that submitted its internal control plan by the statutory deadline.
- DOD had not submitted the required internal control plan related to 2017 disaster funding as of April 2019. We inquired with officials at the U.S. Army Corps of Engineers (USACE), a component of DOD that received most of DOD's supplemental appropriations for 2017 disaster response, to determine the status of its internal control plan. USACE officials stated that a review of internal controls for funds received through 2017 disaster supplemental appropriations was incorporated in the financial statement audit that its independent public accountant conducted. However, we do not consider the financial statement audit to constitute an internal control plan for 2017 disaster relief funding because it does not describe the agency's internal controls specific to that funding. Further, USACE officials provided us with a document labeled as an internal control plan for Hurricanes Harvey, Irma, and Maria disaster relief dated March 13, 2019. However, the officials stated that this was an internal document that had not been submitted to OMB or Congress, and that DOD had not requested an internal control plan from USACE for inclusion in a department-level internal control plan for 2017 disaster relief funds.
- The other four selected agencies submitted the required internal control plans after the March 31, 2018, statutory deadline.

> Specifically, SBA, USDA, DHS, and HUD submitted their plans in May 2018, August 2018, October 2018, and November 2018, respectively.

OMB did not have an effective strategy to ensure that agencies submitted their internal control plans by the statutory deadline. Specifically, OMB issued M-18-14, which contains guidance for agencies to use in developing their internal control plans, on March 30, 2018, or 1 day before the agencies' submission deadline. Officials at Education, which submitted its plan on time, stated that they relied on OMB's Hurricane Sandy-related guidance in OMB Memorandum M-13-07 (M-13-07), Accountability for Funds Provided by the Disaster Relief Appropriations Act, to help develop their internal control plan in the absence of more timely guidance from OMB.[7]

Federal internal control standards state that management should externally communicate the necessary quality information to achieve the entity's objectives.[8] As part of this process, management selects the appropriate methods of communication, such as a written document or meetings, to communicate quality information, such as criteria for internal control plans, on a timely basis. Because OMB did not establish an effective strategy for timely communicating requirements for agency reporting in internal control plans, federal agencies lacked the information needed to meet the statutory deadline. As a result, Congress and others did not timely receive agency internal control plans.

Selected Agencies' Internal Control Plans Did Not Include Sufficient Information

As stated previously, five of the six selected agencies submitted the required internal control plans to Congress and others, but these plans did not include sufficient information that would allow us to determine if the agencies met OMB directives and federal internal control standards' minimum documentation requirements. The internal control plans we

---

[7] Office of Management and Budget, Accountability for Funds Provided by the Disaster Relief Appropriations Act, Memorandum M-13-07 (Mar. 12, 2013).

[8] GAO-14-704G.

reviewed varied in completeness and detail. For example, one agency's internal control plan was over 30 pages in length, and it included not just descriptions of risks and mitigation strategies for funded activities but also descriptions of the components of internal control and the agency's strategy for addressing them. Conversely, another agency's internal control plan was just over two pages in length. For its program receiving the largest amount of disaster funding, this agency's description of its internal control plan consisted of one paragraph that identified one incremental risk and mitigation strategy for that program. The agency did not describe other controls it used to ensure the integrity for the payment of funds in this program.

OMB did not provide specific instructions to agencies on what to include in their internal control plans. We reviewed selected agencies' internal control plans to determine whether they contained sufficient information to address the following directives in M-18-14: (1) use a risk-based approach to design and implement financial and administrative controls to identify and mitigate fraud risks, (2) leverage existing enterprise risk management (ERM) processes in assessing risk in disaster situations, (3) weigh operational objectives against the objective of lowering the likelihood of fraud when determining risk tolerances in disaster situations, (4) provide reasonable assurance that the internal control plan specifically addresses disaster relief, and (5) describe how the plan complements existing risk management practices as directed in OMB Circular A-123.

Our review of the internal control plans found that agencies varied in the extent to which their plans communicated how they addressed the directives identified in M-18-14 and federal internal control standards. Specifically, our analysis of internal control plans found the following:

Use of a risk-based approach. M-18-14 states that in disaster situations, fraud risks are higher than under normal circumstances because the need to provide services quickly can hinder the effectiveness of existing controls and create additional opportunities for individuals to engage in fraud. Thus, agencies must use a risk-based approach to design and implement financial and administrative controls to identify and mitigate fraud risks. In four of the five plans we reviewed, agencies addressed elements of using a risk-based approach. Examples of risks the agencies identified included fraud involving construction and related-party transactions, inaccurate grantee data submissions, and misuse of grant funds. Examples of controls agencies described for identifying and mitigating fraud risks included use of data checks to verify eligibility status and conducting regular reviews of grantee performance and financial data. We were unable to determine based on information communicated in the remaining plan whether the agency addressed this directive in developing the plan. The agency did not identify any fraud risks or associated mitigating controls in its plan. Further, M-18-14 does not specify what key information agencies should communicate in their plans in order to demonstrate the use of a risk-based approach to designing and implementing controls to identify and mitigate fraud risks.

Leverage existing ERM processes. M-18-14 states that in assessing risk in disaster situations, agencies should leverage their existing ERM processes, including assessments that contribute to the development of initial risk profiles. In three of the five plans we reviewed, agencies included information related to how the agencies leveraged existing ERM processes to assess risk in disaster situations. For example, one agency's plan listed its relevant existing ERM risks and the potential effect of those risks on disaster programs. The remaining two agencies did not include sufficient information in their plans for us to determine that they addressed the directive in developing their plans. For example, one of the agencies included no reference to or description of ERM processes in its plan. Without such a description included in the plan, we were unable to determine if that agency had leveraged its ERM process to assess risk. Further, M-18-14 does not specify what information agencies should communicate in their plans in order to demonstrate that they leveraged ERM processes.

Weigh operational objectives. M-18-14 states that when determining risk tolerances in disaster situations, managers must weigh the program's operational objectives against the objective of lowering the likelihood of fraud. In two of five plans we reviewed, agencies included information related to how, when determining risk tolerances in disaster situations, they weighed operational objectives against the objective of lowering the likelihood of fraud. For example, one agency's plan included a risk-appetite statement that described accepting higher fraud risk in order to provide more timely assistance to aid recipients. The remaining three agencies did not include sufficient information in their plans for us to determine how they addressed this directive in developing their plans. For example, while one agency included fraud-related risks and mitigation strategies in its plan, it did not include operational objectives or risk tolerances. Without such information included in the plan, we were unable to determine if that agency had weighed operational objectives or risk tolerances. However, M-18-14 does not specify that agencies communicate such information in their plans.

Provide reasonable assurance. M-18-14 states that agencies receiving disaster relief and emergency funding must provide reasonable assurance that their internal control plans specifically address disaster relief. In two of the five plans we reviewed, agencies included information related to providing reasonable assurance that their plans specifically addressed disaster relief. For example, two agencies' plans identified the specific laws that provided these agencies with supplemental appropriations for disaster relief and described how the plans addressed requirements in those laws. The remaining three agencies did not include sufficient information in their plans for us to determine how they addressed this directive in developing their plans. For example, one of these three agencies described incremental risks and mitigation strategies in its plan, but did not communicate how the controls specifically addressed disaster relief. Without such a description, we were unable to determine how that agency would provide assurance that its plan specifically addressed disaster relief. However, M-18-14 does not specify that agencies include in their plans information demonstrating how they will provide reasonable assurance the plans address disaster relief.

Complement existing risk management practices. M-18-14 states that agencies' internal control plans for disaster funds should complement risk-management practices as directed in OMB Circular A-123. In two of the five plans we reviewed, agencies included information that demonstrated that the plans complemented the circular's risk management practices. For example, one agency's plan included a risk-appetite statement and identified program objectives and risks to achieving those objectives, along with mitigating controls. The remaining three agencies did not include sufficient information in their plans for us to determine how the agencies addressed this directive in developing their plans. For example, while one of the agencies described its plan as a risk management plan, the agency did not specify program objectives and risks to achieving the objectives. Without such a description, we were unable to determine how the agency's internal control plan complemented its existing risk management practices. However, M-18-14 does not specify what information agencies should communicate in their plans in order to demonstrate that the plans complement Circular A-123 risk management practices.

Incorporate federal internal control standards. Federal internal control standards provide the overall framework for establishing and maintaining internal control in the federal government and consist of five components and 17 principles that are integral to an entity's internal control system. While three of the five agencies' internal control plans included information that related to most of the 17 principles, none of the agencies provided sufficient descriptions of how their internal control plans met all 17 principles of internal control or rationales for why specific principles were not relevant. For example, none of the internal control plans clearly communicated how the agency's oversight body and management demonstrated a commitment to integrity and ethical values. M-18-14 did not specifically direct agencies to address the five components and 17 principles of internal control. However, M-18-14 states that agencies' internal control plans should complement risk management practices as directed in Circular A-123, which prescribes requirements conforming with federal internal control standards.

OMB did not have an effective strategy to ensure that its guidance for disaster relief internal control plans would help agencies provide sufficient information to Congress and others. OMB issued M-18-14 in response to the statutory requirement to issue standard guidance for federal agencies to use in designing internal control plans.

M-18-14 provided a general description of the process for developing the plans through Circular A-123 ERM requirements; however, the memorandum did not provide clear guidance to federal agencies on the purpose of internal control plans or the type of information that was expected to be included in those written plans.

OMB also did not have an effective outreach strategy to help ensure that agencies had proper assistance in developing and reporting these internal control plans. OMB did not establish an external communication mechanism with an entity such as the Chief Financial Officers Council to determine how agencies could externally communicate key payment-integrity risks that they must address for disaster funds.

OMB staff stated that the current guidance framework was sufficient for the internal control reporting requirements; that Circular A-123 ERM requirements were sufficient for agencies to produce effective internal control plans, because agencies should consider disaster situations as part of their overall consideration of risk. OMB staff also stated that agency managers must be able to prioritize risks, and by implementing ERM, Circular A-123 gives agency managers needed flexibility to address those risks that are most significant. OMB staff stated that risks associated with disaster aid funding may not rise to the same level as other risks that agencies face and thus additional controls may not be warranted. In addition, OMB staff stated that in order to provide flexibility to agencies, their guidance did not specify what key information should be conveyed in the internal control plans.

While it is important that agencies develop effective ERM processes, ERM does not negate the need for assuring effective internal controls over disaster funds. As part of its oversight framework for 2017 disaster funds, Congress specifically required agencies to communicate internal control plans associated with the supplemental funding provided. Congress further specified for the plans to identify and mitigate risks associated with the funding, and for the plans to document the linkage between the incremental risks related to disaster funding and efforts to address known internal control risks.

This requirement served as a mechanism to provide transparency to Congress and others to assure that the agencies have properly evaluated their internal controls to help ensure the proper accountability over their funding. By including this requirement, Congress communicated its view that disaster funding carried specific risks that needed to be addressed by federal agencies. However, with OMB's focus on ERM, it is possible for agencies to determine that disaster funding does not rise to the level of a significant risk; therefore, agencies' internal control plans would not specifically address risks associated with disaster funding.

Further, absent clear reporting guidance, such as criteria specifying plan content or illustrative examples of completed plans, certain federal agencies had difficulties in developing their plans. Officials at Education, HUD, and SBA stated that they consulted OMB's Hurricane Sandy–related guidance in M-13-07, which included an internal control plan template, to help them develop their internal control plans. Also, officials at certain agencies said that it might be helpful to hear from other agencies about the internal control risks they identified for 2017 disaster funds and how they addressed those risks.

Federal internal control standards state that management should externally communicate necessary quality information to achieve the entity's objectives.[9] For example, information communicated to oversight bodies includes significant matters relating to risks, such as with disaster relief spending, that Congress has required be mitigated and reported. This communication is necessary for the effective oversight of internal control. Without a clear OMB strategy for preparing for oversight of future disaster relief funding, there is an increased risk that agencies will not appropriately assess risks associated with disaster funding. Further, Congress and others may not be provided the necessary information about internal controls; this will affect their ability to provide effective oversight.

[9] GAO-14-704G.

OMB Has Not Implemented Our Priority Recommendation on Disaster Funding Guidance

We have previously reported deficiencies related to OMB's guidance for development of internal control plans related to disaster funds. Specifically, in 2013, we reported on several weaknesses in OMB's guidance that limited agencies' effectiveness in providing a comprehensive oversight mechanism for disaster funds.[10] Specifically, the guidance (1) focused on identifying incremental risks without demonstrating that known risks had been adequately addressed; (2) provided agencies with significant flexibility as it did not require documentation or criteria for claiming exceptions, such as why the OMB requirements were not feasible or practicable; and (3) resulted in certain agencies developing their internal control plans at the same time that funds needed to be quickly distributed. We recommended that OMB develop more robust guidance for agencies to design internal control plans for future disaster relief funding. In commenting on the draft report, OMB staff generally agreed with our recommendation. On July 15, 2016, OMB issued the revised Circular A-123. The circular requires agencies to implement ERM, which includes developing a risk profile that analyzes risks to achieving strategic objectives and identifies options for addressing the risks. However, the revised circular did not include specific guidance for identifying risks related to disaster funding; thus, the recommendation remains open. We plan to continue monitoring OMB's progress in implementing this priority recommendation.

CONCLUSION

The destruction that disasters cause must be addressed immediately, and agencies must deliver disaster relief funding expeditiously. However, the risk of improper payments increases when agencies spend billions of

[10] GAO-14-58.

dollars quickly. In mandating that agencies submit internal control plans for spending disaster relief funding in accordance with OMB guidance, Congress underscores the importance of establishing strong internal controls to help ensure that these funds are appropriately safeguarded. These plans serve as a critical transparency tool to provide Congress some assurance that agencies will establish effective and efficient controls over the disaster funds. Selected agencies did not communicate timely or sufficient information related to their internal control plans for disaster relief funds. While OMB directed agencies to use a risk-based approach to internal control in disaster situations, OMB did not have an effective strategy for ensuring that agencies communicated sufficient and timely internal control plans. As a result, Congress and others may not be able to fully assess the extent to which agencies achieve payment integrity objectives for the disaster relief funds.

AGENCY COMMENTS AND OUR EVALUATION

We provided a draft of this chapter to OMB, DOD, DHS, Education, HUD, SBA, and USDA. OMB staff provided comments via email that disagreed with our recommendation, which we summarize below. Education provided comments, which are reproduced in appendix I. SBA provided comments via email, which are summarized below. DOD, DHS, HUD, and USDA informed us that they had no comments.

In its comments, OMB disagreed with our recommendation that it should develop a strategy for ensuring that agencies communicate sufficient and timely internal control plans for effective oversight of disaster relief funds. OMB staff stated that OMB did not believe the sufficiency or timeliness of control plans present material issues that warranted OMB action. While OMB acknowledged that almost all agency control plans were submitted after the statutory deadline, OMB staff stated that this delay in itself neither indicated the absence of controls nor the effectiveness of those controls. Further, OMB staff stated that it is agency management and not OMB that has responsibility for ensuring compliance with applicable laws and regulations.

While agencies were responsible for submitting their internal control plans, federal law placed the responsibility of establishing the criteria for the internal control plans with OMB. We found that OMB provided neither timely nor sufficient guidance to agencies for developing their internal control plans. Specifically, OMB issued M-18-14 1 day before agencies were required to submit their internal control plans. Further, M-18-14 provided a general description of the process for developing the plans through Circular A-123 ERM requirements, but it did not provide clear guidance on the purpose of internal control plans or the type of information that was expected to be included in the written plans. Because OMB did not establish an effective strategy for timely communicating requirements for agency reporting in internal control plans, federal agencies lacked the information needed to meet the statutory deadline. In addition, absent clear reporting guidance, such as criteria specifying plan content or illustrative examples of completed plans, certain federal agencies had difficulties in developing their plans.

OMB staff also stated that OMB believed its guidance, in particular Circular A-123, which OMB said implements GAO's Standards for Internal Control in the Federal Government and GAO's A Framework for Managing Fraud Risks in Federal Programs, provides the guidance needed to prepare agencies' control plans. OMB staff stated that control plans in an effective system of internal control should be operational, iterative, living documents that should be updated in response to emerging risks.[11] According to OMB staff, internal control plans are not developed for external communications and are not the sources of assurances over disaster relief funds, which are published in agencies' annual financial reports.

---

[11] GAO, A Framework for Managing Fraud Risks in Federal Programs, GAO-15-593SP (Washington, D.C.: July 2015).

While it is important that agencies implement Circular A-123, which directs agencies to develop effective ERM processes, we believe that ERM does not negate the need for assuring effective internal controls over disaster relief funds. As we noted in our report, with OMB's focus on ERM, it is possible for agencies to determine that disaster funding does not rise to the level of a significant risk; therefore, agencies' internal control plans would not specifically address risks associated with disaster funding. In addition, while it is important for agencies to update their internal control plans in response to emerging risks, Congress specifically required agencies to communicate internal control plans for the supplemental funds provided for activities related to the 2017 disasters. These plans, when provided timely and with sufficient information, could serve as a critical transparency tool to provide lawmakers some assurance that agencies will establish effective and efficient controls over the disaster funds. Therefore, we believe that our recommendation is warranted.

In its written comments, Education acknowledged that developing and implementing effective internal control plans is essential to assessing the risks associated with federal disaster relief funding. Education disagreed with our assessment that its internal control plan did not provide sufficient information for the following OMB directives in M-18-14:

- weigh operational objectives against the objective of lowering the likelihood of fraud when determining risk tolerances in disaster situations,
- provide reasonable assurance that the internal control plan specifically addresses disaster relief, and
- describe how the plan complements existing risk management practices as directed in OMB Circular A-123.

We did not see sufficient evidence in Education's plan to demonstrate that it addressed the three directives noted above. We acknowledge that in our meetings with them, Education officials discussed with us how the steps described in their plan related to M-18-14 directives.

However, in determining whether agencies' plans communicated sufficient information, we considered for purposes of this chapter only that information that agencies included in the plans themselves.

As previously stated, Education was the only agency in our scope to submit its internal control plan before the March 31, 2018, statutory deadline. Because OMB issued M-18-14 1 day before the plans were due, Education had little time to review directives in M-18-14 and still submit its plan by the due date. As previously mentioned, Education officials stated that in the absence of more timely guidance from OMB, they relied on OMB's previous guidance in M-13-07 to help develop their internal control plan. As discussed in our report, OMB has not developed a strategy for ensuring that agencies, such as Education, communicate sufficient and timely internal control plans for effective oversight of disaster relief funds. Without such a strategy and guidance, Congress and others may not be able to fully assess the extent to which agencies achieve payment integrity objectives for disaster relief funds.

In addition, Education stated that its internal control plan addressed, in part, all five components as outlined in the federal internal control standards, and it believed that our assessment did not take into account the extent to which these components are integrated into its internal control plan. However, federal internal control standards consist of five components, as well as 17 principles, all of which are integral to an entity's internal control system. Our evaluation of internal control plans found that none of the agencies—including Education—provided sufficient descriptions of how their internal control plans met all 17 principles of internal control or rationales for why any particular principles were not relevant. For example, none of the internal control plans clearly communicated how the agencies addressed principle 1, which states the oversight body and management should demonstrate a commitment to integrity and ethical values.

Education also commented that at a meeting held May 8, 2019, we noted that in some cases its plan was deemed insufficient because of either the level of detail or formatting concerns. We disagree with this comment. Our evaluation of the internal control plans focused on whether the plans included sufficient information to demonstrate that they satisfied the OMB directives and federal internal control standards, and not concerns about formatting.

The SBA liaison—Program Manager, Office of Congressional and Legislative Affairs—stated that SBA's Office of Disaster Assistance did not have any comments regarding the content of our draft report. In its email, SBA stated that it has in place a comprehensive, robust system of internal control for its ongoing disaster response operations. SBA stated that its established system of internal control covered the higher risks of improper payments and fraud that come with a larger volume of transactions following a series of large disasters. SBA further stated that its internal control system has proven effective during disasters of all sizes, and that a larger volume of transactions does not fundamentally change its internal control system. In addition, SBA stated that writing a supplementary comprehensive plan on risks and controls for an existing disaster response program would be both duplicative and of low value, and that this would seem to contradict the effort to reduce the burden on federal agencies in order for them to operate more effectively and efficiently to comply with the President's Management Agenda.

As part of our audit, we did not evaluate the extent to which SBA's internal control system was effective in preventing improper payments and fraud. Rather, we evaluated whether selected agencies—including SBA—met Congress's statutory mandate to timely submit internal control plans with sufficient information to demonstrate that agencies met OMB directives and federal internal control standards requirements. Despite SBA's concern that such plans for existing disaster response programs would be duplicative and of low value, Congress, as part of its oversight framework for 2017 disaster funds, specifically required agencies to communicate internal control plans for the supplemental disaster relief funding it provided. This requirement served as an external communication mechanism to provide transparency to Congress and others to assure that the agencies have properly evaluated their internal controls to help ensure accountability over their funding.

We are sending copies of this chapter to the appropriate congressional committees; the Secretaries of Agriculture, Defense, Education, Homeland Security, and Housing and Urban Development; the Administrator of the Small Business Administration; the Director of the Office of Management and Budget; and other interested parties.

Beryl H. Davis Director
Financial Management and Assurance

Congressional Addressees

The Honorable Michael Enzi
Chairman
Committee on the Budget
United States Senate

The Honorable Ron Johnson
Chairman

The Honorable Gary C. Peters
Ranking Member
Committee on Homeland Security and Governmental Affairs
United States Senate

The Honorable Rand Paul, MD
Chairman
Subcommittee on Federal Spending,
Oversight and Emergency Management
Committee on Homeland Security and Governmental Affairs
United States Senate

The Honorable Marco Rubio
Chairman
Committee on Small Business and Entrepreneurship
United States Senate

The Honorable Maxine Waters
Chairwoman
Committee on Financial Services
House of Representatives

The Honorable Sean Duffy
Ranking Member
Subcommittee on Housing, Community Development and Insurance
Committee on Financial Services
House of Representatives

The Honorable Al Green
Chairman
Subcommittee on Oversight and Investigations
Committee on Financial Services
House of Representatives

The Honorable Bennie Thompson
Chairman
Committee on Homeland Security
House of Representatives

The Honorable Elijah Cummings
Chairman

The Honorable Jim Jordan
Ranking Member
Committee on Oversight and Reform
House of Representatives

The Honorable Nydia Velázquez
Chairwoman
Committee on Small Business
House of Representatives

The Honorable Peter DeFazio
Chairman

The Honorable Sam Graves
Ranking Member
Committee on Transportation and Infrastructure
House of Representatives

The Honorable Emanuel Cleaver, II
House of Representatives

The Honorable Michael McCaul
House of Representatives

The Honorable Gary J. Palmer
House of Representatives

The Honorable Ann Wagner
House of Representatives

Appendix I: Comments from the Department of Education

UNITED STATES DEPARTMENT OF EDUCATION
OFFICE OF ELEMENTARY AND SECONDARY EDUCATION

May 21, 2019

Ms. Beryl H. Davis
Director, Financial Management and Assurance
Government Accountability Office
Washington, DC 20548

Dear Ms. Davis:

Thank you for the opportunity to provide comments on the Government Accountability Office (GAO) draft report, *2017 Disaster Relief Oversight: Strategy Needed to Ensure Agencies' Internal Control Plans Provide Sufficient Information to Congress and Others*. I am providing comments on behalf of the U.S. Department of Education (Department) regarding some of the limitations of the GAO draft report and its conclusions.

The Department appreciates the importance of looking at federal agencies' internal control plans and the guidance provided by the Office of Management and Budget (OMB) to develop them. As the GAO draft report notes, Hurricanes Harvey, Irma, and Maria and the California wildfires created an unprecedented demand for federal disaster response and recovery resources. Developing and implementing effective internal control plans are essential to assessing the risks associated with federal disaster relief funding. As discussed below, we recommend that GAO acknowledge more fully the Department's efforts to ensure effective internal control planning and implementation both in the summary and in the body of the report.

On pages 9-10 of the report, GAO suggests that the Department's plan does not provide sufficient information to address the requirement that managers weigh the program's operational objectives against the objective of lowering the likelihood of fraud when determining risk tolerances in disaster situations. As discussed at the exit conference, the Department's plan does address this element of an internal control system. As stated in the plan, the Department uses an internal entity risk tool to identify any current or recurring issues, such as A-133 single audit findings, that may be impacting existing grant funds and that might impact the disaster relief funds for relevant recipients. The results of this review inform us of specific fiscal management areas requiring attention by the grantees prior to or after receipt of disaster relief funds. In addition, a key program objective—providing disaster relief in an expeditious and minimally burdensome manner—was a factor that the Department "weighed" and one that mitigated against any extraordinary (and potentially burdensome) additional internal control measures.

On page 10 of the report and during the May 8, 2019, meeting, GAO stated the Department's plan does not communicate sufficient information for GAO to determine whether the plan specifically addresses disaster relief. GAO's determination fails to take into account the title of the Department's plan, *2018 Disaster Relief, Initial Draft Internal Control Plan*, which clearly states the plan is specific to disaster relief. In addition, the plan itself includes funded activities, risks associated with funded activities, and mitigation strategies for the five new disaster relief programs authorized by the Bipartisan Budget Act of 2018: Immediate Aid to Restart School Operations (K-12 Restart program); Emergency Impact Aid for Displaced Students; Assistance for Homeless Children and Youths; Emergency Assistance to Institutions of Higher Education; and Defraying Costs of Enrolling Displaced Students in Higher Education.

On pages 10-11 of the report, GAO suggests that the Department's plan does not include sufficient information for GAO to determine whether the plan complements risk-management practices as directed in OMB Circular A-123. The Department developed its internal control plan by identifying existing strategies currently used by the Department to assess possible grantee risks and by incorporating disaster-specific considerations. This includes an assessment of grantees' current audit findings and their efforts to resolve the findings, as well as any issues identified through program monitoring activities of current grantees. The Department also included in its internal control plan existing strategies to address risks previously identified with certain grantees who demonstrated high or elevated risks, most notably Puerto Rico and the U.S. Virgin Islands.

On page 11 of the report, GAO suggests that the Department's plan does not include sufficient information for GAO to determine whether the plan includes all of the Federal Internal Control Standards. These standards provide the overall framework for establishing and maintaining internal controls in the federal government and consist of 5 components and 17 principles that are integral to an entity's internal control system. The Department's internal control plan addresses, in part, all five components as outlined in the Federal Internal Control Standards and that GAO's assessment does not take into account the extent to which these components are integrated into the Department's internal control plan. We are addressing all five components, and we would be glad to discuss it further.

At the May 8, 2019, meeting, GAO noted that in some cases, ED's internal control plan was deemed insufficient, due to either the level of detail or formatting concerns. The substantive soundness of the Department's internal control plan outweighs any concerns about the format of the plan. However, we are willing to consider other formatting options should GAO choose to provide examples of an "appropriate format or level of detail" from which the Department might learn.

The Department appreciates the opportunity to provide these comments on the GAO draft report. We are available to respond to any questions.

Sincerely,

Frank T. Brogan

Frank Brogan
Assistant Secretary
Office of Elementary and Secondary Education

In: Key Government Reports. Vol. 33 ISBN: 978-1-53616-566-1
Editor: Ernest Clark

Chapter 4

U.S. TERRITORIES: PUBLIC DEBT OUTLOOK – 2019 UPDATE*

United States Government Accountability Office

ABBREVIATIONS

CDL	Community Disaster Loan
COFINA	Puerto Rico Sales Tax Financing Corporation
CNMI	Commonwealth of the Northern Mariana Islands
FEMA	Federal Emergency Management Agency
GASB	Governmental Accounting Standards Board
GDB	Government Development Bank for Puerto Rico
GDP	Gross Domestic Product
GNP	Gross National Product
Interior	U.S. Department of the Interior
PPACA	Patient Protection and Affordable Care Act

* This is an edited, reformatted and augmented version of United States Government Accountability Office; Report to Congressional Committees, Accessible Version, Publication No. GAO-19-525, dated June 2019.

PROMESA	Puerto Rico Oversight, Management, and Economic Stability Act
USVI	United States Virgin Islands
Treasury	U.S. Department of the Treasury

WHY GAO DID THIS STUDY

The five U.S. territories—Puerto Rico, USVI, American Samoa, CNMI, and Guam—borrow through financial markets. Puerto Rico, in particular, has amassed large amounts of debt, and began to default on debt payments in 2015. In 2017, Hurricanes Irma and Maria caused widespread damage and destruction in Puerto Rico and USVI, placing additional financial pressures on their already strained economies.

In June 2016, Congress passed and the President signed the Puerto Rico Oversight, Management, and Economic Stability Act (PROMESA). It contains a provision for GAO to review the public debt of each of the five territories every two years. GAO issued the first report on the territories' public debt in October 2017, reporting on trends in public debt between fiscal years 2005 and 2015.

In this chapter, for each U.S. territory, GAO updates (1) trends in public debt, its composition, and drivers; (2) trends in revenue and its composition, and overall financial condition; and (3) what is known about the ability to repay public debt.

GAO analyzed the territories' single audit reports for fiscal years 2016 and 2017, as available; reviewed relevant documentation and analyses; and interviewed officials from the territories' governments, federal agencies, credit rating agencies, and subject matter experts.

In commenting on a draft of this chapter, the governments of Puerto Rico and Guam raised concerns about some aspects of the analysis of their debt. GAO maintains its analysis is correct, as discussed in the report.

What GAO Found

Puerto Rico

Puerto Rico has finalized two out of six total debt restructuring agreements to date. Through this restructuring process, Puerto Rico's bonds are replaced by bonds with new repayment terms. Public debt was 93 percent of Gross National Product in fiscal year 2016, the most recent fiscal year for which audited financial statements were available. Puerto Rico's general revenue decreased by 11 percent and longstanding deficits persisted during this period. Puerto Rico's capacity for debt repayment depends primarily on the outcomes of the ongoing debt restructuring process and its ability to generate sustained economic growth. While federal hurricane recovery grants are likely to stimulate the economy in the short term, it is unclear whether the resulting economic benefits will be sustainable.

United States Virgin Islands (USVI)

USVI has not been able to access capital markets at favorable interest rates since early 2017 and it has not issued any new bonds. It has, however, received federal loans for hurricane recovery, which may contribute to its overall debt burden if they are not forgiven. Public debt decreased from 72 to 68 percent of Gross Domestic Product (GDP) between fiscal years 2015 and 2016, the most recent year for which audited data were available. While general revenue increased by 40 percent during this time period, longstanding deficits persisted. USVI's continued ability to repay public debt depends primarily on whether it can access capital markets at favorable rates in the future, its ability to create economic growth, and its ability to address its pension liabilities and the pending insolvency of its public pension system.

American Samoa

American Samoa's public debt increased from 13 to 19 percent of GDP between fiscal years 2015 and 2017. This increase was due largely to a single bond issued in early 2016 to fund various infrastructure projects. General revenue fluctuated during this period and the territory had a deficit in 2017. The territory continues to face fiscal risks that may affect repayment of public debt, such as a reliance on the tuna canning and processing industry and significant pension liabilities.

Commonwealth of the Northern Mariana Islands (CNMI)

CNMI has not issued any new debt since fiscal year 2007, and as such, public debt decreased from 16 to 8 percent of GDP between fiscal years 2015 and 2017. During this period, CNMI's general revenue increased by 48 percent and it operated with a surplus. CNMI's potential labor shortages due to federal restrictions on foreign workers have been mitigated. However, pension liabilities and future reductions in revenue from recent typhoons present fiscal risks that may affect repayment of public debt in the future.

Guam

Guam's public debt increased by 6 percent between fiscal years 2015 and 2017, growing from 44 to 45 percent of GDP. New debt has primarily been used to refinance existing debt and fund infrastructure projects. Guam's general revenue increased by 12 percent during this period and it operated with a surplus. Pension liabilities continue to present a fiscal risk that may affect repayment of public debt in the future.

June 28, 2019

The Honorable Lisa Murkowski
Chairman

The Honorable Joe Manchin
Ranking Member
Committee on Energy and Natural Resources
United States Senate

The Honorable Raúl Grijalva
Chairman

The Honorable Rob Bishop
Ranking Member
Committee on Natural Resources
House of Representatives

The United States has five permanently inhabited territories: Puerto Rico, the United States Virgin Islands (USVI), American Samoa, the Commonwealth of the Northern Mariana Islands (CNMI), and Guam. The territories, like U.S. states in some cases, borrow through financial markets. Puerto Rico, in particular, has amassed large amounts of debt, and began to default on debt payments in 2015. In June 2016, Congress passed and the President signed the Puerto Rico Oversight, Management, and Economic Stability Act (PROMESA), which contains a provision for us to review the public debt of each U.S. territory every two years.[1] We issued our first report on the territories' public debt in October 2017, reporting on trends in public debt between fiscal years 2005 and 2015.[2] Since our first report, Puerto Rico and USVI continue to face significant financial challenges and vulnerability to natural disasters. In September 2017, Hurricanes Irma and Maria, two back-to-back hurricanes, significantly

[1] Pub. L. No. 114-187, § 411, 130 Stat. 549, 594–595 (June 30, 2016).
[2] GAO, *U.S. Territories: Public Debt Outlook*, GAO-18-160 (Washington, D.C.: Oct 2, 2017).

impacted USVI and Puerto Rico, causing widespread damage to and destruction of critical infrastructure, livelihoods, and property, which placed additional financial pressures on their already strained economies. American Samoa, CNMI, and Guam are also vulnerable to natural disasters.

For Puerto Rico, USVI, American Samoa, CNMI, and Guam, this chapter updates (1) trends in public debt, its composition, and drivers; (2) trends in revenue and its composition, and in overall financial condition; and (3) what is known about the ability to repay public debt.

To describe trends and composition of each territory's public debt, revenue, and composition, we reviewed the audited financial statements included within each territory's single audit reporting packages, hereinafter referred to as the single audit report, for the most recent fiscal years available as of early May, 2019—fiscal years 2016 and 2017 for American Samoa, Guam, and CNMI, and fiscal year 2016 for USVI.[3] For Puerto Rico, audited financial statements were not available for fiscal year 2017, but we included information for fiscal year 2015, which was not available when we issued our last report in 2017, in addition to fiscal year 2016. We analyzed data on public debt—specifically, bonds, loans, and notes for both the primary government and component units[4]—for those years.[5] In addition, for each territory, we obtained and reviewed the independent

[3] The Single Audit Act, as implemented by guidance issued by the Office of Management and Budget (OMB), requires nonfederal entities that expend above a dollar threshold in federal awards in a fiscal year to have a single audit. Recipient organizations are required by the act to submit their single audits reports to the Federal Audit Clearinghouse (FAC). The single audit reporting package sent to the FAC includes (1) the auditor's reports; (2) the entity's audited financial statements and related notes; (3) the schedule of expenditures of federal awards, related notes, and the auditor's report on the schedule; (4) a schedule of findings and questioned costs; (5) reports on internal controls over financial reporting, and compliance with laws and regulations; and (6) a summary schedule of prior audit findings. Puerto Rico provides audited financial statements but does not submit single audit report packages to FAC. Puerto Rico's and USVI's audited financial statements for fiscal year 2017 were not available as of May 2019.

[4] Component units are legally separate entities for which a government is financially accountable.

[5] Bonds are the written evidence of debt, which upon presentation entitles the bondholder or owner to a fixed sum of money plus interest. Bonds generally have maturities greater than the short-term range. Notes differ from bonds in that they are short-term obligations of an issuer to repay a specified principal amount on a certain date, together with interest at a stated rate, usually payable from a defined source of anticipated revenue. Notes usually mature in 1 year or less, although notes of longer maturities are also issued.

auditor's report corresponding to each single audit report, when available, and noted the type of opinion expressed by the independent auditor on the financial statements and accompanying note disclosures.

To determine the drivers of public debt and what is known about the territories' ability to repay, we interviewed officials from each of the territories' governments. In addition, we interviewed representatives of the three major credit rating agencies and officials at the U.S. Department of the Treasury and Department of the Interior's Office of Insular Affairs (OIA). We also obtained and reviewed relevant documentation, reports, and analyses from the territorial governments and ratings agencies. To determine the effects of Hurricanes Irma and Maria on the economies and public debt of Puerto Rico and USVI, we interviewed officials from government agencies, including departments of finance or treasury, the agencies responsible for issuing and marketing bonded debt, the agencies responsible for economic development, the Offices of Management and Budget, and the Offices of the Inspectors General. We also conducted interviews with experts on Puerto Rico and USVI's economies, municipal securities markets, and select industry groups. We selected the experts we interviewed based on their professional knowledge closely aligning with our engagement objectives, as demonstrated through published articles and referrals from other experts. We also analyzed a non-generalizable sample of Bloomberg data on secondary market trading prices of USVI and Puerto Rico bonds to illustrate the possible effects of market events, such as the 2017 hurricanes, on bond prices.

We conducted this performance audit from April 2018 to June 2019 in accordance with generally accepted government auditing standards. Those standards require that we plan and perform the audit to obtain sufficient, appropriate evidence to provide a reasonable basis for our findings and conclusions based on our audit objectives. We believe that the evidence obtained provides a reasonable basis for our findings and conclusions based on our audit objectives.

Background

U.S. Territories

The five territories are permanently inhabited and have elected governors, territorial legislatures, and non-voting members in the U.S. House of Representatives.[6]

Puerto Rico

Puerto Rico, with a population of 3.3 million as of 2017, is the largest U.S. territory. Puerto Rico consists of a main island and several smaller ones—a total of 3,425 square miles. The economy of Puerto Rico is mainly driven by manufacturing goods such as pharmaceuticals, textiles, petrochemicals, and electronics. The service industry is also a key contributor to the economy, and includes finance, insurance, and the tourism sector. The government of Puerto Rico began to default on its debt in August 2015 and has been operating with austerity measures in place, such as hiring freezes and budget cuts.

PROMESA, enacted on June 30, 2016, temporarily prevented creditors from suing Puerto Rico over missed debt payments.[7] PROMESA established a Financial Oversight and Management Board (FOMB) with broad powers of budgetary and financial control over Puerto Rico. In addition, it created procedures for adjusting debts accumulated by the government of Puerto Rico and its component units. On May 3, 2017, after the termination of the original stay preventing creditors from suing the territory, the FOMB filed a petition under Title III of PROMESA beginning a broad-based debt restructuring process. PROMESA provides two mechanisms for restructuring debt of a territory or territorial instrumentality. First, Title III, which follows a bankruptcy-like procedure, and second, Title VI, a mechanism to formalize agreements negotiated between the territory and its creditors.

---

[6] For the purpose of this report we present the Caribbean territories first and the remaining territories in alphabetical order.

[7] Pub. L. No. 114-187, § 405, 130 Stat. 549, 587–592 (June 30, 2016).

USVI

USVI, with a population estimated at 104,500 in 2017, is composed of three main islands—St. Croix, St. John, and St. Thomas—and many other surrounding islands, comprising 134 square miles. Most of the population of USVI resides on St. Thomas and St. Croix. Tourism remains the territory's leading industry. On the island of St. Croix, the Hovensa oil refinery was the island's largest private employer; however, it shut down in 2012 and approximately 2,000 jobs were lost. The Hovensa refinery facility was purchased by Limetree Bay, and in 2018 the government entered into an agreement to restart refinery operations and expand storage operations at the facility. According to territory officials, the refinery is expected to resume operations in late 2019.

American Samoa

American Samoa, with a population estimated at 58,700 in 2017, lies about 2,600 miles southwest of Hawaii and consists of seven islands covering a land area of 76 square miles. American Samoa's main island of Tutuila has little level land and is mostly rugged. Tourism is limited by the island's remote location and lack of tourist-rated facilities. Most of American Samoa's economic activity—primarily tuna canning—and government operations take place on Tutuila in the Pago Pago harbor area. American Samoa admits foreign workers to the territory, many of whom are employed by the tuna cannery.

CNMI

CNMI, with a population estimated at 50,300 in 2017, lies in the western Pacific Ocean just north of Guam and about 5,500 miles from the U.S. mainland. Part of the Mariana Islands Archipelago, the territory is a chain of 14 islands with a total land area of 183 square miles. CNMI's population resides primarily on the island of Saipan, with additional residents on the islands of Rota and Tinian. CNMI's economy depends on tourism. The United States admits foreign workers to CNMI under a special work program, which affects the territory's access to labor.[8]

Guam

Guam, with a population estimated at 162,500 in 2017, is located about 50 miles south of the southernmost island of CNMI, 3,700 miles west of Hawaii, and has a total land area of 212 square miles. Guam has long been a strategic location for the U.S. military. Guam's economy depends largely on U.S. military spending and tourism. As of 2017, Department of Defense bases cover about 30 percent of the island. Most of the military service members and their dependents are attached to one of the two major military installations on the island—U.S. Naval Base Guam and Andersen Air Force Base.

2017 and 2018 Natural Disasters

On September 6, 2017, Hurricane Irma struck St. John and St. Thomas, USVI, and less than 2 weeks later, Hurricane Maria struck St. Croix, USVI, and the main island of Puerto Rico. Hurricanes Irma and Maria severely damaged the territories' critical infrastructure and reduced their short-term economic activity.

In response to the hurricanes, the federal government provided disaster assistance grant funding to both territories.

- According to the most recent publically available data from the Federal Emergency Management Agency (FEMA), it had obligated $5.6 billion in Public Assistance grants to Puerto Rico.[9] As of March 31, 2019, it had obligated $1.69 billion in Public

[8] GAO, *Commonwealth of the Northern Mariana Islands: Implementation of Federal Minimum Wage and Immigration Laws,* GAO-17-437 (Washington, D.C.: May 18, 2017).

[9] Also see GAO, *Puerto Rico Hurricanes: Status of FEMA Funding, Oversight, and Recovery Challenges*, GAO-19-256 (Washington, D.C.: Mar 14, 2019).

Assistance grants to USVI.[10] FEMA's Public Assistance Program provides grant funding to state, territorial, local, and tribal governments to assist with responding to and recovering from major disaster or emergencies.

- As of February 2019, the U.S. Department of Housing and Urban Development awarded $19.9 billion in Community Development Block Grant Disaster Recovery funding to Puerto Rico and $1.9 billion to USVI.[11] These flexible grants are intended to help cities, counties, states, and territories recover from presidentially declared disasters, especially in low-income areas.

In addition to hurricane-related grant funding, the governments of Puerto Rico and USVI have also received federal loans for disaster recovery.

FEMA manages the Community Disaster Loan (CDL) program, the purpose of which is to provide financial assistance to local and territorial governments that are having difficulty providing government services because of a loss in tax or other revenue following a disaster. While both Puerto Rico's and USVI's central governments were approved for CDLs after the hurricanes, Puerto Rico's government will not be permitted to access this funding unless its cash levels fall below a set amount that would make it eligible to receive the approved funding.[12]

The Pacific territories have also recently experienced natural disasters that caused significant destruction. Tropical Cyclone Gita hit American Samoa in February 2018, Super Typhoon Mangkhut struck Guam and the island of Rota in CNMI in September 2018, and Super Typhoon Yutu made landfall across the islands of Saipan and Tinian in CNMI in October

---

[10] Also see GAO, *U.S. Virgin Islands Recovery: Status of FEMA Public Assistance Funding and Implementation*, GAO-19-253 (Washington, D.C.: Feb 25, 2019).

[11] GAO, *Disaster Recovery: Better Monitoring of Block Grant Funds is Needed*, GAO-19-232 (Washington, D.C.: Mar. 25, 2019).

[12] According to officials from the U.S. Department of the Treasury, if Puerto Rico's cash balance drops below $1.1 billion, a loan disbursement would be available to the central government. Although the central government of Puerto Rico has not used CDLs, some Puerto Rican municipalities have been approved for and received CDL funding. Municipalities are the highest level of local government under the central level government and each municipality has the legal authority over all matters of a municipal nature.

2018. FEMA has obligated funding for Public Assistance grants for both Typhoon Mangkhut and Typhoon Yutu.

Medicaid in the Territories

All five territories receive federal funding through Medicaid — a joint federal-state health financing program for low-income and medically needy individuals. There are notable differences in the funding and operation of this program between the territories as compared to the states. For example, federal Medicaid spending in the territories is subject to an annual cap that does not apply to the states.[13]

In recent years, the territories have been provided temporary increases of up to $10.6 billion in Medicaid funding. Specifically, the Patient Protection and Affordable Care Act (PPACA) appropriated $7.3 billion for the territories in additional Medicaid funding, the majority of which is available only through fiscal year 2019.[14] The Consolidated Appropriations Act, 2017, provided an additional $296 million in Medicaid funding for Puerto Rico ending September 30, 2019.[15] Additionally, the Bipartisan Budget Act of 2018 authorized increases in Medicaid funding for Puerto Rico of $3.6 billion and for USVI of $106.9 million through September 30, 2019; Puerto Rico and USVI can also receive another $1.2 billion and $35.6 million, respectively, if they meet certain conditions related to data reporting and program integrity.[16]

We previously reported that territory officials cited positive effects of the additional funding, such as the ability to enroll more providers and cover more services; however, some officials also expressed concerns about the temporary nature of the funding, noting that they may have to

---

[13] 42 U.S.C. § 1396d(b).

[14] Pub. L. No. 111-148, §§ 1323, 2005(a), 124 Stat. 119, 283 (Mar. 23, 2010), as amended by the Health Care and Education Reconciliation Act of 2010, Pub. L. No. 111-152, § 1204(a)-(b), 124 Stat. 1029, 1055 (Mar. 30, 2010).

[15] Pub. L. No. 115-31, div. M, § 202, 131 Stat. 135, 805 (May 5, 2017).

[16] Pub. L. No. 115-123, § 20301(a), 132 Stat. 64, 118–119 (Feb. 9, 2018).

make program cuts once the funding is exhausted at the end of fiscal year 2019.[17]

Previous GAO Findings

In 2017 we reported that:[18]

- Puerto Rico's debt grew from 71 to 99 percent of Gross National Product (GNP) between fiscal years 2005 and 2014.[19] When we issued our report, 2015 financial statements had not yet been released, the territory was in default, and its financial future was unclear, pending debt restructuring.
- USVI's debt grew from 34 to 72 percent of Gross Domestic Product (GDP) between fiscal years 2005 and 2015, and USVI was unable to issue new debt at favorable rates, essentially barring the territory from the financial markets through which it traditionally raised capital. In 2017, USVI was beginning to undergo fiscal reform and we reported that its outcome was uncertain.
- American Samoa's debt remained small relative to the size of its economy between fiscal years 2005 and 2015, increasing from 5 to 11 percent of GDP. We reported that disruptions in the tuna processing and canning industry could affect its ability to repay debt.
- CNMI's debt decreased from 23 to 16 percent of GDP between fiscal years 2005 and 2015. We reported that labor shortages, if unaddressed, may impede repayment.

---

[17] GAO, *Medicaid and CHIP: Increased Funding in U.S. Territories Merits Improved Program Integrity Efforts.* GAO-16-324 (Washington, D.C.: April 8, 2016).

[18] GAO-18-160.

[19] GNP is generally a more representative measure of Puerto Rico's economic activity than GDP. In Puerto Rico, GDP has consistently been greater than GNP, which means that income from foreign companies and residents in Puerto Rico is higher than income from Puerto Rican companies and residents abroad. We do not present information on debt as a share of GNP for the other four territories.

- Guam's debt increased from 24 to 44 percent of GDP between fiscal years 2005 and 2015. We reported that large pension liabilities, if unaddressed, may hamper repayment.

Gross National Product

Gross National Product (GNP) measures the values of goods and services produced by a territory's residents. GNP includes production from residents abroad and excludes production by foreign companies in a territory.

Source: GAO-18-160 | GAO-19-525.

Gross Domestic Product

Gross Domestic Product (GDP) measures the value of goods and services produced inside a country, or for the purposes of this chapter, a territory.

Source: GAO-18-16 | GAO-19-525.

PUERTO RICO

Puerto Rico's First Two Debt Restructuring Agreements Finalized without Audited Fiscal Year 2016 and 2017 Financial Statements

Puerto Rico is in the process of restructuring its outstanding debt, which it began defaulting on in August 2015. PROMESA established two debt restructuring processes under Titles III and VI respectively. Title III is similar to municipal bankruptcy and Title VI provides a process by which the debtors and creditors can negotiate and vote on an agreement with less of a role played by a court. In 2018, Puerto Rico reached its first debt restructuring agreement through the Title VI restructuring process established by PROMESA, and replacement bonds were issued according to the terms of the agreement, which have reduced the total amount in debt payments owed by Puerto Rico to creditors as of May 3, 2019.

In November 2018, the first case was settled, which restructured bonds issued by the Government Development Bank for Puerto Rico (GDB), reducing the amount originally owed to creditors by 45 percent.[20] In February 2019, a second debt restructuring agreement was finalized under Title III of PROMESA for bonds issued by the Puerto Rico Sales Tax Financing Corporation (Spanish acronym COFINA)[21] resulting in an overall reduction of the total current amount owed to creditors.[22] As of May 3, 2019, four cases involving petitions under Title III for debt restructuring had not yet been settled. According to Puerto Rico government officials, there is no predetermined order in which the remaining restructuring agreements will be negotiated.

There is no current audited information on Puerto Rico's public debt and revenue. Prior to initiating a restructuring under Title III of PROMESA, the Financial Oversight and Management Board for Puerto Rico (FOMB) is required, at its sole discretion, to make certain determinations.[23]

---

[20] The Government Development Bank (GDB) was a public corporation acting as the bond issuer, fiscal agent, intragovernmental bank, and financial advisor of the government of Puerto Rico. Under the terms of the settlement, claims of GDB's bondholders, municipal and private depositors, and certain other contingent creditors have been resolved by exchanging such claims for new bonds. Each $1,000 of affected claims have been exchanged for new bonds having a face amount equal to $550. The new bonds will have a 7.5 percent annual coupon rate, payable each February 20 and August 20 with the final scheduled payment date expected August 20, 2040.

[21] In 2006, the Puerto Rico government created the Puerto Rico Sales Tax Financing Corporation (known by its Spanish acronym COFINA) as a means to issue bonds backed by a new sales and use tax –imposed on the sale, use, consumption, and storage of taxable items such as personal property–that originally was intended to repay debt, but by 2009 was used to finance operations.

[22] The terms of repayment and structure of the COFINA bonds were changed as part of the debt restructuring agreement. Under the plan, holders of senior COFINA bond claims have received a 93.01 percent recovery on their bonds while holders of junior COFINA bond claims have received a 56.41 percent recovery. Senior bonds have priority over junior bonds, and must be repaid first. Under the plan, new COFINA bonds are to be issued with fixed interest rates. All COFINA bonds accrue interest beginning as of August 1, 2018.

[23] The FOMB was established by PROMESA and has broad powers of budgetary and financial control over Puerto Rico.

These include determining the entity whose debt is to be restructured "has adopted procedures necessary to deliver timely audited financial statements and made public draft financial statements and other information sufficient for any interested person to make an informed decision with respect to a possible restructuring."[24] With respect to the five Title III cases, the FOMB made these determinations in 2017. At the time, Puerto Rico did not have audited financial statements and had not made public draft financial statements for fiscal year 2016, and it continues not to have audited financial statements and has not made public draft financial statements for fiscal year 2017.

The timely release of audited financial information has been a long-standing problem for Puerto Rico. On May 3, 2019, Puerto Rico's government released its financial statements for fiscal years 2016, marking 1,037 days past the end of that fiscal year. Puerto Rico's 2015 financial statements were released 1,095 days after the end of that fiscal year. As of May 3, 2019, the Puerto Rico government had not yet released its financial statements for fiscal year 2017, marking 670 days after the end of that fiscal year. According to a 2017 Municipal Securities Rulemaking Board report, between 2010 and 2016, municipal issuers issued their audited financial statements an average of 200 days after the end of their fiscal years.[25] According to Puerto Rico Treasury officials, challenges in complying with new accounting standards, decentralized accounting systems, as well as the loss of time and evidence that resulted from Hurricane Maria have contributed to delays in the timely release of these financial statements. Officials told us that efforts are underway to consolidate the various government accounting systems, which will make the compilation of audited financial statements easier in the future. Officials said that financial statements for fiscal year 2017 will be released sometime in calendar year 2019.

---

[24] 48 U.S.C. § 2146(a)(2).

[25] Municipal Securities Rulemaking Board, *Timing of Annual Disclosures by Issuers of Municipal Securities* (Washington, D.C.: February 2017). The Municipal Securities Rulemaking Board is a regulating body that creates rules and policies for investment firms and banks in the issuing and sale of municipal bonds, notes, and other municipal securities.

Total Public Debt Outstanding

Total public debt outstanding refers to the sum of bonds and other debt held by and payable to the public, as reported in the territories' single audit reports. Marketable debt securities, primarily bonds with long-term maturities, are the main vehicle by which the territories access capital markets. Other debt payable may include shorter term marketable notes and bills issued by territorial governments, non-marketable intragovernmental notes, notes held by local banks, federal loans, intragovernmental loans, and loans issued by local banks.

Source: GAO-18-160 | GAO-19-525.

As we reported previously, Puerto Rico's total public debt outstanding increased continuously between fiscal years 2005 and 2014, prior to the default in 2015.[26] In fiscal year 2016, the last year for which audited financial statements are available, total public debt outstanding decreased by more than four percent, from $68.1 billion in fiscal year 2014 to $65.2 billion at the end of fiscal year 2016. This decrease was due to a reduction in component unit debt. Of the total amount of public debt outstanding, Puerto Rico's primary government owes $40.8 billion, while component units owe $24.3 billion. (See Figure 1.)

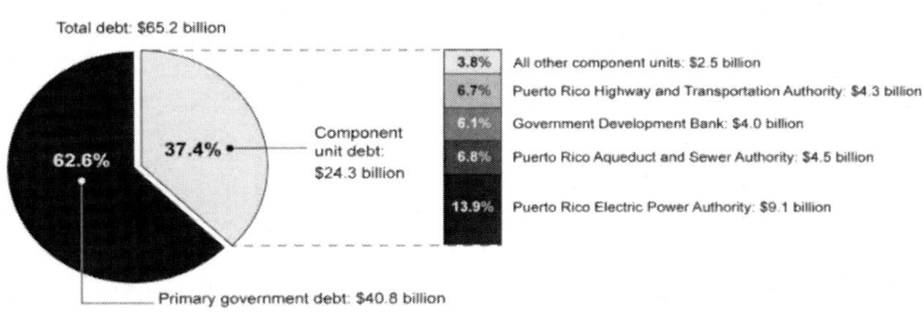

Source: GAO analysis of Puerto Rico's fiscal year 2016 audited financial statements. | GAO-19-525.

Note: Totals may not equal the sum of their parts due to rounding.

Figure 1. Composition of Puerto Rico's Public Debt, Fiscal Year 2016.

[26] GAO-18-160.

Primary Government

The primary government is generally comprised of governmental activities (generally financed with taxes and intergovernmental aid) and business-type activities (generally financed with charges for goods and services).

Source: The Governmental Accounting Standards Board | GAO-19-525.

Component Units

Component units are legally separate entities for which a government is financially accountable.

Source: The Governmental Accounting Standards Board | GAO-19-525.

General Revenue

General revenue includes all tax revenues as well as unrestricted aid from other governments and investment earnings. Tax revenues typically represent the largest component of general revenues and include both derived tax revenues (resulting from assessments imposed on exchange transactions, such as income taxes and sales taxes) and imposed revenues (resulting from assessments imposed on non-exchange transactions, such as property taxes and fines).

Source: The Governmental Accounting Standards Board | GAO-19-525.

Between fiscal years 2014 and 2016, both total public debt outstanding and bonded debt outstanding as a share of GNP decreased slightly, from 99 and 85 percent, respectively, to 93 and 81 percent of GNP. Per capita, this was a decrease of close to one percent, from $19,356.7 in fiscal year 2014 to $19,224.7 in fiscal year 2016.

Puerto Rico first defaulted on its debt in August of 2015. Prior to defaulting, Puerto Rico used public debt as a means to finance general government operations—a major driver of its public debt.

Puerto Rico's General Revenue Decreased between Fiscal Years 2014 and 2016, and Longstanding Deficits Persisted

In fiscal year 2016—the latest year for which audited financial data are available—Puerto Rico collected $30.0 billion in total revenue, a decrease of almost 8 percent since fiscal year 2014. Puerto Rico's total revenue includes both general revenue and program revenue. (See Figure 2.) Puerto Rico's general revenue decreased from $13.8 billion to $12.3 billion between fiscal years 2014 and 2016, a decrease of about 11 percent. General revenue is the primary source of funds for the repayment of debt issued by Puerto Rico's primary government. The decrease in general revenue was mainly due to reductions in non-tax revenue and income tax collections between fiscal years 2014 and 2016. Tax revenue represented 85 percent of fiscal year 2016 general revenue, with income and excise taxes representing 77 percent of all taxes collected. Program revenue for Puerto Rico's primary government and component units are generated from grants and contributions to fund governmental activities and from charges for services. From fiscal years 2014 to 2016, Puerto Rico's program revenue decreased by $1.1 billion, or close to 6 percent.

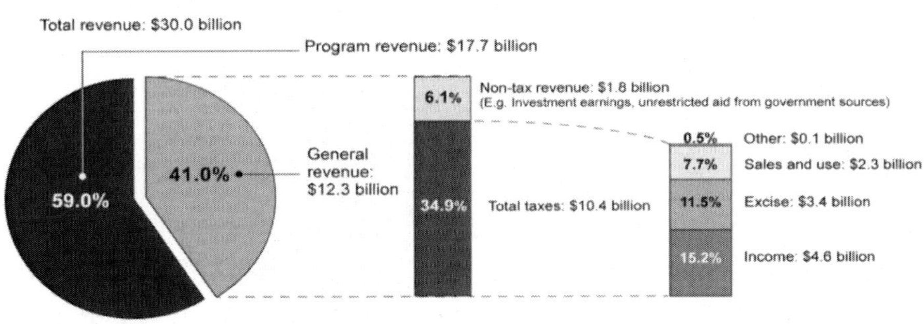

Source: GAO analysis of Puerto Ricco's fiscal year 2016 audited financial statements. | GAO-19-525.

Note: Totals may not equal the sum of their parts due to rounding.

Figure 2. Composition of Puerto Rico's Revenue, Fiscal Year 2016.

Puerto Rico's government has operated with a deficit—where expenses exceed revenue—in each fiscal year since 2002. Puerto Rico's longstanding deficits persisted in 2016, as expenses exceeded revenue by $5 billion. That year Puerto Rico's government spent $34.9 billion, of which $24.2 billion was spent directly by the primary government and $10.8 billion was spent by the government's various component units. Education and general government expenses were the largest expense categories for the primary government.

Program Revenue

Program revenue is revenue that is directly linked to functions or programs and includes charges for services, such as electricity fees, and grants. While program revenues are generated by the associated functions or programs, such revenues are not always restricted to use in those functions or programs.

Source: The Governmental Accounting Standards Board | GAO-19-525.

Puerto Rico's Prospects for Debt Repayment Depend on Several Factors, Including Outcomes of the Current Debt Restructuring Process

Two significant factors will determine Puerto Rico's future capacity for repaying its restructured debt: 1) the outcome of the ongoing debt restructuring process, and 2) Puerto Rico's ability to generate sustained economic growth. Territory officials also identified other fiscal risks that could hamper Puerto Rico's fiscal health and jeopardize prospects for debt repayment in the future, such as shortfalls in federal healthcare funding.

Debt Restructuring Process

Puerto Rico's future ability to repay its restructured debt will ultimately depend on the outcome of all outstanding debt restructuring agreements and on the terms of repayment established with creditors, including interest rates and debt repayment schedules. As noted previously, as of May 3, 2019, two debt restructuring agreements have been reached to date out of six total cases that have been initiated.[27]

Fiscal Risks

Fiscal risks refer to responsibilities, programs, and activities that may legally commit or create the expectation for future government spending. Fiscal risks may be explicit in that the government is legally required to fund the commitment, or implicit in that an exposure arises not from a legal commitment, but from current policy, past practices, or other factors that may create the expectation for future spending.

Source: GAO. | GAO-19-525.

Although the two debt restructuring agreements finalized as of May 3, 2019 reduce the total amount of principal owed by Puerto Rico to creditors, two of the experts we interviewed on Puerto Rico's economy expressed concern that they do not reflect Puerto Rico's limited capacity for repayment and were based on estimated economic growth that seems unlikely over the next 5 years. If the agreements were based on economic growth estimates that were overly optimistic, Puerto Rico may again face difficulty meeting its financial obligations as restructured debt payments become due. A recent study found that Puerto Rico will need to reduce debt by more than what has been negotiated as of May 3, 2019 to ensure it can fully repay restructured debt moving forward.[28] Puerto Rico government officials agreed with experts that the economic growth and revenue estimates in the FOMB's version of fiscal plan that was certified in October 2018 and in place until May 2019 were overly optimistic. This

[27] On June 16, 2019, the FOMB announced that it reached an agreement with certain bondholders on the framework for a plan of adjustment to resolve $35 billion worth of debt and non-debt claims. This debt includes general obligation and Public Building Authority bonds.

[28] National Bureau of Economic Research, *An Analysis of Puerto Rico's Debt Relief Needs to Restore Debt Sustainability*. (Cambridge, MA: November, 2018). The authors of this study state that, if all public debt of Puerto Rico's debt is considered, then a cancellation of all interest payments and up to 80 percent of the total face value of debt included in the fiscal plan may be necessary. The study does not take funding for hurricane recovery into account.

fiscal plan was a revision of a September 2018 fiscal plan developed by the government of Puerto Rico. In the FOMB's October 2018 fiscal plan, the FOMB revised the government's proposed plan according to its projections for economic growth and analyses of the outcomes of structural reform. However, there is no public documentation available to explain why the FOMB's economic growth estimates in that plan were higher than those provided in the government of Puerto Rico's September 2018 version of the fiscal plan. The debt restructuring agreements as of May 3, 2019 were based on the more optimistic growth estimates in the October 2018 plan. The growth estimates contained in the May 2019 version of the FOMB's certified fiscal plan are considerably more conservative—half of what was projected in the prior plan by 2019—and will inform future debt restructuring agreements going forward.

Puerto Rico officials and experts on Puerto Rico's economy that we interviewed said they do not have information about the methodology and assumptions used by the FOMB in the 2018 version of the fiscal plan to develop forecasts of revenue and economic growth.[29] Without this information, external parties cannot verify the sustainability of repayment terms established under the recently finalized debt restructuring agreements. According to officials involved in the development of the Puerto Rico government's fiscal plan, ongoing legal proceedings related to Puerto Rico's debt restructuring process restrict the FOMB's ability to publically release information about economic growth and revenue estimates in its version of the fiscal plan. They told us parties involved in the debt restructuring process, however, such as creditors, have access to this information. While the FOMB did provide us with some information on other matters for this chapter, the FOMB did not respond to our requests for information on the 2018 version of the fiscal plan. We have previously reported that transparency is a key element of economic analysis.[30] An important benefit of transparency is that the public can assess the structure

[29] While the FOMB provides some information on the methodology of its fiscal plan, it does not include enough detail for an external party to assess or verify its revenue and economic growth forecasts.

[30] GAO, *Assessment Methodology for Economic Analysis,* GAO-18-151SP (Washington, D.C.: April 10, 2018).

of an analysis and, in particular, how much of an analytic result hinges on the specific choices made by those who developed the analysis. This transparency allows the implication of choices, related risks, and any uncertainties factored into economic analyses to be readily assessed.

Economic Growth

Puerto Rico's economy is in a prolonged period of contraction. According to data from Puerto Rico's government, Puerto Rico's economy grew in the 1990s and early 2000s. However, between 2005 and 2018, Puerto Rico's economy experienced year-over-year declines in real output in all but 4 years, as measured by real GNP.[31] Between 2015 and 2018, Puerto Rico's economy contracted by 9 percent, as measured by real GNP.

Federal officials, current and former Puerto Rico officials, and other experts on Puerto Rico's economy previously told us that Puerto Rico's continued economic decline contributed to its recurring deficit and the resulting debt crisis. Going forward, Puerto Rico's ability to create sustained economic growth is essential to its fiscal health and ability to repay debt. Puerto Rico's economic growth depends largely on the following factors – the extent to which it implements structural reforms and fiscal measures, the effects of federal hurricane recovery funding, its ability to attract and retain industry, outmigration, and investor confidence.

Structural Reforms and Fiscal Measures

In the FOMB's prior and current fiscal plans, it outlines a series of structural reforms and fiscal measures that it describes as key for restoring growth in Puerto Rico, as detailed in Table 1 below.

Through implementation of these reforms, the FOMB initially projected savings and increased revenue, resulting in real GNP growth of almost 8 percent in 2019 followed by three years of GNP increases, growth that was built into the FOMB's projections of Puerto Rico's prospects for debt repayment under the first two debt restructuring agreements. According to the FOMB, these structural reforms are integral to Puerto

[31] GNP data obtained from Puerto Rico Planning Board.

Rico's economic recovery. However, municipal market analysts, Puerto Rico government officials, and experts on Puerto Rico's economy expressed doubt about the feasibility of the reforms proposed by the FOMB in the 2018 version of the fiscal plan and the extent to which they will yield projected economic benefits. In May 2019, the FOMB certified a new fiscal plan, which replaced the October 2018 plan, and includes the same structural reforms with more conservative estimates of their financial impact. The current version of the fiscal plan also includes significantly more conservative GNP growth rates, of 4 percent in 2019, followed by less growth in 2020, and negative growth by 2021. According to the FOMB, relative to the prior fiscal plan, the current plan includes a revised macroeconomic forecast in light of slower disaster recovery funding rollout.

The FOMB aims to promote workforce participation by instituting work requirements for food assistance programs and by establishing a local version of the federal Earned Income Tax Credit for working people with low to moderate incomes. It is a refundable tax credit, which means that the taxpayer receives the full amount of the credit regardless of whether they have a tax liability.

Table 1a. Strategies for restoring economic growth in Puerto Rico, Financial Oversight and Management Board (FOMB)

Structural Reform *Measures proposed in the recent fiscal plan to "improve the trajectory of Puerto Rico's economy and drive growth."*
Human capital and welfare: Increase labor force participation through a Puerto Rico version of the Earned Income Tax Credit (EITC)[a] benefits and reforms to Nutritional Assistance Program (NAP)[b] as well as providing other workforce development opportunities.
Ease of doing business: Promoting economic activity and reducing the obstacles to starting and sustaining a business in Puerto Rico through comprehensive reform to improve ease of paying taxes, registering property, and obtaining permits.
Power sector: Providing low-cost and reliable energy through the transformation of the Puerto Rico Electric Power Authority and the establishment of an independent, expert, and well-funded energy regulator.
Infrastructure: Prioritizing economically transformative capital investments with federal funds.

Table 1b. Strategies for restoring economic growth in Puerto Rico, Financial Oversight and Management Board (FOMB)

Fiscal Measures *A set of measures proposed in the fiscal plan that the Government of Puerto Rico "must take to increase Government revenues and reduce Government expenditures."*
Creation of Office of the Chief Financial Officer: Instituting fiscal controls and accountability, reducing special revenue fund deficits, and improving governance, accountability, and transparency.
Agency efficiencies: Consolidating agencies and deploying new management tools and practices to deliver better governmental services for substantially lower cost.
Healthcare reform: Reducing healthcare cost inflation through a comprehensive new health care model that prioritizes high quality, cost-effective care.
Enhanced tax compliance and optimized taxes and fees: Employing new technology and other innovative and now commonly used practices in other jurisdictions to broaden the tax base, reduce fraud, and improve fairness to boost overall tax revenues; adjusting existing taxes and fees to capture revenues from under-leveraged sources.
Reduction of appropriations: Lowering the fiscal burden on the Commonwealth and encouraging sound fiscal self-management by reducing appropriations to municipalities and the University of Puerto Rico, while instituting an independent scholarship fund for low- income students.
Comprehensive pension reform: Improving the financial stability of public employees' retirement funds and ensuring payment of pensions.

Source: FOMB data from October 2018 and May 2019 Fiscal Plans. I GAO-19-525.

[a]The Earned Income Tax credit is a benefit for working people with low to moderate incomes. It is a refundable tax credit, which means that the taxpayer receives the full amount of the credit regardless of whether or not they have a tax liability.

[b]Puerto Rico does not have access to the federal Supplemental Nutrition Assistance Program (SNAP) but has received funding for its Nutrition Assistance Program (NAP) since 1982 in the form of a block grant. Like SNAP, NAP provides nutrition assistance to households that meet certain eligibility criteria, such as income and resources, though Puerto Rico households receive fewer benefits than SNAP eligible households. A family of four in Puerto Rico receives a maximum monthly benefit of $410 compared to around $668 for a family of four living in the continental United States.

The volume of growth projected by the FOMB in the October 2018 version of the fiscal plan, which was used to inform the first two debt restructuring agreements, represented a significant departure from economic trends seen in Puerto Rico in recent years, as shown in Figure 3. In its September 2018 version of the fiscal plan, the government of Puerto Rico projected slightly less optimistic growth figures, particularly from 2019 to 2020. As noted previously, the current version of the FOMB's fiscal plan includes economic growth rates that are considerably more conservative, and predict less growth by 2023 than the Puerto Rico government in its version of the fiscal plan.

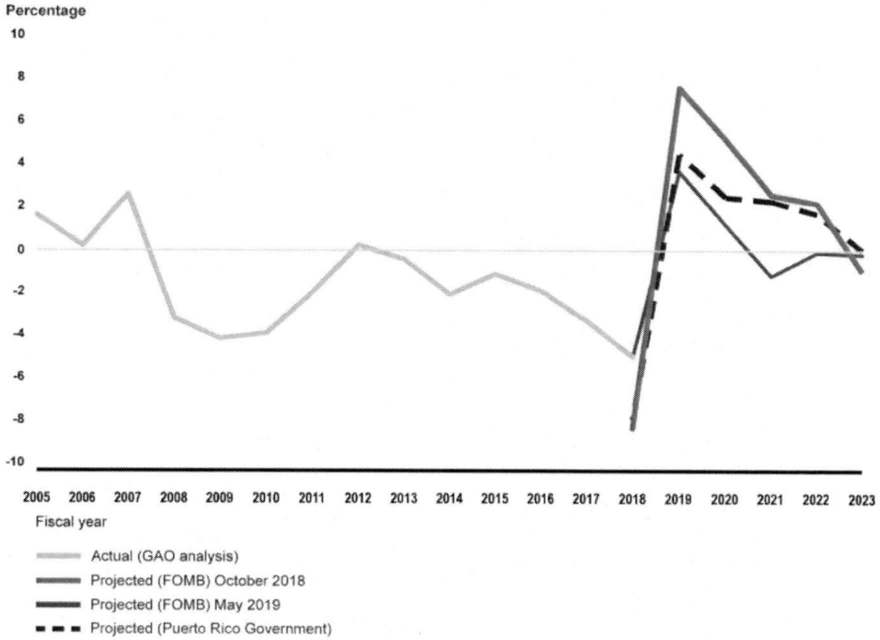

Source: GAO analysis of Puerto Rico Planning Board for actual data, 2005 to 2018 and Financial Management and Oversight projected data, 2018 to 2023. | GAO-19-525.

Figure 3. Actual vs. Projected Growth in Puerto Rico Gross National Product (GNP), 2005-2023.

Federal Hurricane Recovery Funding

According to Puerto Rico government officials, though hurricane recovery is likely to stimulate the economy in the short term, it is not yet clear whether the economic benefits resulting from federal hurricane recovery funding will be sustainable in the longer term. Generally, federal hurricane recovery funding cannot be used to pay debt service directly. It may, however, stimulate the economy and thereby indirectly make funding available for other government spending.

This stimulus, which Puerto Rico officials attributed in part to construction contracts and related economic activity, will in turn increase tax revenue.

Two of the experts on Puerto Rico's economy we interviewed told us that they felt that the FOMB overestimated the volume and timeliness of federal hurricane recovery funding in its October 2018 version of the fiscal plan. Since economic growth estimates are based, in part, on revenue generated through recovery activity, delayed or incomplete funding may make the achievement of projected economic growth rates more challenging.

The Puerto Rico government and the FOMB differ in their estimates of pass through rates, or the portion of funding for recovery projects that will remain in the territory rather than benefiting multinational or U.S. mainland corporations. The economic stimulus Puerto Rico is likely to experience as a result of this funding depends on the volume of funds received for recovery and the pass through rate of these funds. In the October 2018 version of its fiscal plan, the FOMB predicted pass through rates ranging from 15.5 percent to 100 percent depending on the type of funding. Two of the experts on Puerto Rico's economy that we interviewed estimated a pass through rate closer to 13 percent. In its current version of the fiscal plan, the FOMB did not adjust its prediction of pass through rates.

Attraction and Retention of Industry

Puerto Rico's ability to attract and retain companies that plan to remain in the territory long-term is important for sustained economic growth. According to Puerto Rico Treasury officials, 24 large multinational companies generate one-third of Puerto Rico's corporate tax revenue. Officials noted the importance of these companies to Puerto Rico's economic health, and told us that the government will continue to offer these companies tax incentives to encourage them to stay in the territory.

Officials from associations representing the private sector in Puerto Rico also said that, in addition to tax incentives, it is important that Puerto Rico improve its energy infrastructure and decrease energy costs in order to attract and retain business in the long term. Puerto Rico is taking steps to overhaul the structure and management of the Puerto Rico Electric Power Authority, which operates the territory's electricity generation and distribution infrastructure. According to officials, this includes retaining a private sector entity to operate the transmission and distribution system by the end of 2019, with further plans to privatize generation by 2020.

Outmigration

Outmigration results in a diminished workforce and tax base, which strains a territory's economy and finances. As we reported previously, outmigration in Puerto Rico increased between 2005 and 2016. Since then, the territory has continued to lose residents. Between July 2009 and July 2016, Puerto Rico's population decreased by 14 percent.[32] In the same year as the 2017 hurricanes, Puerto Rico experienced an accelerated outmigration, losing 4 percent of its total population between July 2017 and July 2018, according to Census Bureau estimates. Puerto Rico government officials, municipal market analysts, and recent studies have noted that reversing outmigration is essential to Puerto Rico's economic future.[33]

Investor Confidence

According to municipal market analysts, a rebound in Puerto Rico's bond prices since the hurricanes may indicate that certain investors have increased confidence in Puerto Rico's short-term economic outlook. Based on our analysis of a non-representative sample of 24 bonds issued by the Puerto Rico government since 2010, 22 bonds experienced a price drop of between 41 and 68 percent from the end of August 2017 to the end of

---

[32] GAO-18-160.

[33] Estudios Tecnicos, Inc. *Balance of the Economy Post Hurricane Maria,* (San Juan, Puerto Rico: Sept. 19, 2018) and Federal Reserve Bank of New York, *The Causes and Consequences of Puerto Rico's Declining Population*, Current Issues in Economics and Finance, Volume 20, Number 4, (New York, New York: 2014).

December 2017, and the prices of all 22 had rebounded higher than pre-hurricane levels by September 2018.

Other Fiscal Risks

Pension Liabilities

Puerto Rico's three main public pension systems are nearly insolvent and Puerto Rico reported a net pension liability of approximately $44.9 billion as of the end of fiscal year 2016, the most recent year for which data were available. Pension liabilities are similar to other kinds of debt because they constitute a promise to make a future payment or provide a benefit. Puerto Rico's pension systems are currently funded through "pay as you go" pension payments, at a rate of close to $2 billion a year payable from the general fund.[34] Although reforms proposed by the FOMB are intended to stabilize Puerto Rico's pension system in the long term, officials and experts said that Puerto Rico government agencies' payments to cover pension amounts due to current retirees have already begun crowding out spending for other government services.

Healthcare Funding

In recent years, Puerto Rico has been provided temporary increases of up to $10.2 billion in Medicaid funding. Given its current fiscal condition and inability to access capital markets, the Puerto Rico government may not be able to cover future funding gaps when expanded federal funding for the Medicaid program expires. As a result, according to a recent statement by the Governor, some of Puerto Rico's projected 1.3 million Medicaid enrollees are at risk of losing benefits in fiscal year 2020.

---

[34] "Pay as you go" is a pension system in which retirement benefits for current pensioners are paid on an ongoing basis by organizations rather than from a funded system in which benefits are financed by prior investments in a pension fund.

U.S. VIRGIN ISLANDS (USVI)

USVI Has Been Unable to Access Capital Markets at Favorable Rates since 2017, and Has Not Issued Any New Debt

USVI has not been able to access capital markets at favorable interest rates since January 2017, when investors began to demand higher rates to compensate for what they perceived as increased risks.[35] As such, USVI has not issued any new bonds since before 2017. Territory officials told us USVI has not attempted to access capital markets since January 2017, and does not plan to do so in the near future.

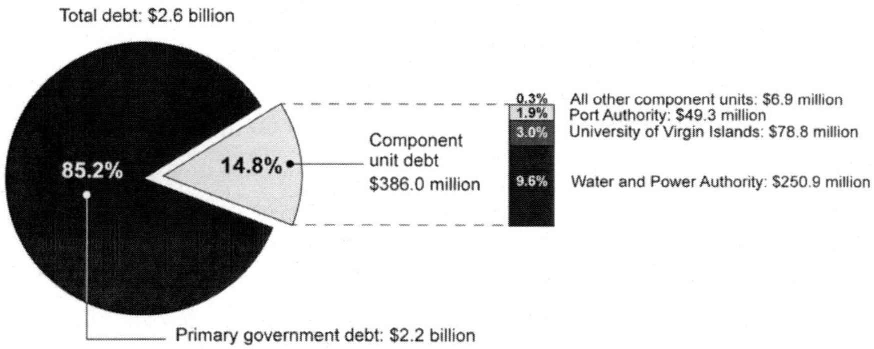

Source: GAO analysis of United States Virgin Islands' fiscal year 2016 audited financial statements. | GAO-19-525.

Note: Totals may not equal the sum of their parts due to rounding.

Figure 4. Composition of United States Virgin Islands' Public Debt, Fiscal Year 2016.

USVI's total public debt outstanding increased between fiscal years 2005 and 2015 from $1.4 billion to $2.7 billion, and subsequently declined to $2.6 billion in fiscal year 2016—the most recent year for which data were available—due to the repayment of existing debt. The majority of USVI's public debt is owed by the primary government. (See Figure 4.)

[35] In late January 2017, USVI cancelled a new bond issuance because the offer was not adequately subscribed. The new bond would have provided financing for government operations. USVI subsequently lost market access to new debt.

Total public debt outstanding as a share of GDP declined from 72 percent of GDP in fiscal year 2015 to 68 percent of GDP in fiscal year 2016.

Similarly, total public debt outstanding per capita decreased during this period, from $25,468.8 in fiscal year 2015 to $24,853.7 in fiscal year 2016.

While USVI has not issued any new bonds since before 2017, it has received federal loans for hurricane recovery, which may contribute to its total debt burden if they are not forgiven.[36] In 2018, the territory was approved for $309.5 million in Community Disaster Loans (CDL) from the federal government to bridge the loss in revenue from the hurricanes and provide funding for essential operations of the primary government and its component units. According to territory officials, as of March 2019, the primary government had drawn down $145 million in CDL funding and the two major hospitals in the territory and the USVI Water and Power Authority had also drawn down funding. According to territory officials, USVI was able to access CDL funding until the end of March 2019.

USVI officials told us they are treating the CDLs as if they will need to be repaid. However, according to officials from Treasury and FEMA,[37] CDLs become eligible for cancellation in full or part 3 fiscal years after a disaster if the government's revenue is insufficient to meet operating expenses, including disaster related expenses.[38] According to Treasury officials, historically 40 to 50 percent of these loans have been forgiven. USVI is scheduled to begin repaying the CDLs in October 2019. These loans are not included in USVI's single audit reports that we analyzed, since the fiscal year 2018 report has not yet been issued.

As of May 3, 2019, USVI had not released its single audit report for fiscal year 2017. According to officials from the U.S. Department of the Interior, USVI has received an extension for completion of the fiscal year 2017 single audit report due to the hurricanes. It is due on June 30, 2019. Territory officials told us they expect to release the fiscal year 2017 single

---

[36] As we reported previously, USVI's bonded debt has primarily been used for general government operations since 2010 – the major driver of its public debt. GAO-18-160.

[37] While the CDL program is typically administered by FEMA, Treasury and FEMA officials told us they are jointly managing the loans for USVI.

[38] 42 U.S.C. § 5184(c)(1); 44 C.F.R. § 206.376.

audit report by the June 30, 2019 deadline and the fiscal year 2018 single audit report by December 2019.

USVI's General Revenue Increased between Fiscal Years 2015 and 2016 and Longstanding Deficits Persisted

In fiscal year 2016—the latest year for which audited financial data are available—USVI collected $2.3 billion in total revenue, an increase of 21 percent from $1.9 billion in 2015. USVI's total revenue includes both general revenue and program revenue. (See Figure 5.) USVI's general revenue increased by 40 percent during the same period, from $919.4 million to $1.3 billion. This growth was due to a one-time payment for refinery operations in lieu of taxes totaling $283.8 million, and increased tax collections. Tax revenue represented almost 70 percent of fiscal year 2016 general revenue. Program revenue for USVI's primary government and component units is generated from grants and contributions to fund governmental activities, and from charges for services. From fiscal years 2015 to 2016, USVI's program revenue generally remained constant, increasing by $37.3 million, or almost 4 percent.

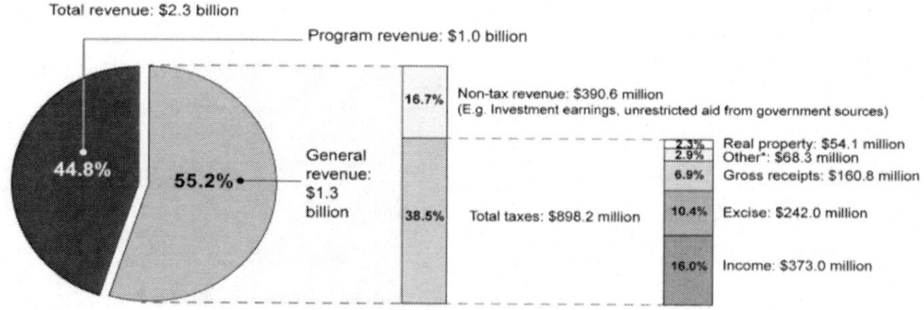

* Other Taxes includes an adjustment for tax revenue not recognized on the full accrual basis.

Source: GAO analysis of United States Virgin Islands' fiscal year 2016 audited financial statements. | GAO-19-525.

Note: Totals may not equal the sum of their parts due to rounding.

Figure 5. Composition of United States Virgin Islands' Revenue, Fiscal Year 2016.

USVI operated with a deficit in 8 of the last 12 years, including in fiscal year 2016. In fiscal year 2015, USVI's expenses exceeded its revenues by $310.7 million. In fiscal year 2016, increases in revenue reduced the deficit to approximately $45.0 million. In fiscal year 2016, USVI's government spent $2.4 billion, of which $1.6 billion was spent by the primary government and the remainder by the government's various component units, such as the Water and Power Authority.

USVI's Continued Ability to Repay Its Outstanding Debt Depends on Several Factors, Including its Ability to Access Capital Markets in the Future to Rollover Debt

Six factors may contribute to USVI's continued ability to repay public debt moving forward: 1) the integrity of USVI's "lockbox" provisions for repaying debt, 2) USVI's ability to access capital markets at favorable interest rates in the future, 3) USVI's ability to create sustained economic growth, 4) USVI's ability to address its pension liabilities and the pending insolvency of its public pension system, 5) USVI's ability to address potential reductions in tax revenue due to recently enacted federal tax changes, and 6) USVI's ability to mitigate shortfalls in Medicaid funding.

Lockbox Provisions

While territory officials expressed confidence that USVI's "lockbox" provisions prevent the territory from defaulting on its public debt, municipal market analysts we spoke with had differing opinions about the security of the lockbox structure and its ability to protect against default. USVI's bonds are backed by the tax collected from some individuals and entities doing business in USVI, and by excise taxes collected by the federal government and remitted to USVI as required by federal statute.[39] As required by USVI law, these tax collections and excise taxes go directly to an escrow account in a private bank, and an escrow agent not affiliated

---

[39] 26 U.S.C. § 7652.

with the territory's government makes debt service payments twice a year from the account. A year's worth of payments is held in reserve at all times in the escrow account.[40]

Territory officials told us that the lockbox structure is still in place, is secure, and continues to protect investors against the possibility of default. Two municipal market analysts we spoke with confirmed that having the receipts designated for debt service payment bypass the USVI government, with payments made through an intermediary, adds security and provides investors additional confidence. Others told us that such a lockbox structure does not offer significant additional protection since there are no legal provisions preventing the government from recalling the funds if needed for essential government operations. Territory officials confirmed that there are no legal provisions that explicitly prevent the government from accessing the lockbox funds in a stress situation, however they do not anticipate such a need arising. Officials also noted that the lockbox has not been breached to date.

Repayment of the federal CDLs may also test the security of the lockbox structure. CDLs are backed by the same revenue streams as previously issued bonds and have senior lien status, according to an agreement between the government of USVI and FEMA. As noted previously, CDLs become eligible for cancellation 3 years after a disaster and, moreover, federal officials told us some of these loans have been forgiven in the past. However, if cash flow is limited, the senior status of the CDLs could provide the federal government access to revenue already dedicated for bond repayment, which could jeopardize the repayment of bonded debt.

Market Access and Rollover Risk

In August 2017, USVI announced it would no longer provide financial information to the three major credit rating agencies.[41] Officials said they

---

[40] 2016 V.I. Sess. Laws 7951, § 1(D) (Nov. 7, 2016).

[41] Credit rating agencies are independent companies that evaluate the financial condition of issuers of debt securities and then assign ratings that reflect their assessment of the issuers' ability to repay debt. The three major rating agencies are Moody's, Standard & Poor's, and Fitch.

felt the rating agencies were treating USVI unfairly by instituting downgrades and comparing it with Puerto Rico, despite USVI never having missed a debt service payment. The rating agencies subsequently withdrew their ratings of USVI's debt due to a lack of information. This came on the heels of the failed attempt to bring a new bond to market in January of 2017. After ceasing to provide information to the rating agencies, the government launched a website through an investor relations platform in October 2017 to provide information to investors. Although market analysts noted that certain investors—such as investors looking to invest in bonds with noninvestment grade ratings for the potential of a high yield—may rely on their own internal analyses to determine the credit-worthiness of bond issuances, large retail investors rely heavily on credit ratings. Officials from the current gubernatorial administration in USVI told us the government intends to reinstate relationships with the credit rating agencies to increase fiscal transparency and eventually regain access to the larger, traditional municipal bond market.[42]

Territory officials expressed confidence that USVI will be able to re-access capital markets at favorable rates in the future. However, if it is unable to do so, its susceptibility to rollover risk may be high. Specifically, if USVI cannot pay the principal on outstanding bonds as they mature, it must refinance, or rollover the bonds into new debt, using the proceeds to repay the maturing debt. The inability to do this could lead to default.

Economic Growth

While federal hurricane recovery funding and restarting refinery operations may bolster USVI's economy in the short term, some municipal market analysts we spoke with told us that it is critical for USVI to engage in longer-term economic planning in the wake of the hurricanes to sustain any economic growth.

In September 2016, under the prior administration, USVI released a 5-year economic plan to reduce government expenditures and generate

---

[42] USVI held gubernatorial elections in November 2018. A new governor was elected and took office in January 2019.

additional revenues.[43] The government began implementing the measures included in that plan prior to the hurricanes, although officials stated that full implementation of the plan was effectively interrupted by the hurricanes and its effect on revenue was unclear. Officials from the current administration told us they are in the process of developing a new long-term economic plan that will likely include provisions for sustaining growth beyond the hurricane recovery period, addressing deficits, achieving economic diversification, and addressing high energy costs. However, it is not year clear when the plan will be released or when its provisions may be implemented.

According to a post-hurricane recovery report published by the government of USVI, the total estimated negative economic impact of the hurricanes was $1.5 billion, and about 11 percent of jobs on the islands were lost.[44] The tourism industry, in particular, was hard hit by the hurricanes, with 5 of USVI's largest hotels closing in the wake of the disaster. According to the report, there was a 78 percent drop in hotel reservations in December 2017 compared to the year before. A representative from a tourism association told us that in the long term, tourism to the islands may increase if the major hotels update and enhance their facilities as they rebuild. Similarly, territory officials said additional investment in the territory's hotels and other tourist infrastructure could help strengthen the industry and make USVI a more attractive tourist destination relative to its neighbors.

Municipal market analysts and subject matter experts we spoke with told us that the federal funding USVI received in the wake of the hurricanes has improved the territory's liquidity, or available cash, in the short term and has also had a stimulative effect on the economy. In a recent statement, the Governor stated that USVI would not have been able to meet its day to day expenses in the prior 12 months without the CDLs.

While generally federal hurricane recovery funding cannot be used to pay debt service directly, USVI's improved liquidity may stimulate the

[43] GAO-18-160.

[44] United States Virgin Islands, First-Year Progress Report – Hurricanes Irma and Maria, (October, 2018).

economy in the short term and thereby generate some additional revenue for other government spending.

The longer-term impact of federal funding on USVI's economy, however, is not yet clear. Territory officials and municipal market analysts mentioned various factors that could contribute to long-term economic growth in USVI, including the territory practicing good financial management and transparency, reducing energy costs to attract and retain business, and implementing structural economic reforms and achieving economic diversification.

In 2018, the government entered into an agreement to restart refinery operations and expand storage facilities at the former Hovensa facility. In 2012, when it shut down operations, Hovensa was the largest private employer on St. Croix. Territory officials told us refining operations are expected to resume in late 2019 at the facility under new ownership.

While the new facility represents an opportunity to generate revenue and create jobs, the extent of the refinery's contributions to the economy is not yet clear.

Municipal market analysts noted USVI's bond prices have rebounded since the hurricanes, which may signal increased investor confidence in the territory's short-term ability to repay its outstanding debt. Based on our analysis of a non-representative sample of five bonds issued by the USVI government since 2010, four bonds experienced a price drop of between 22 and 41 percent from the end of August 2017 to the end of December 2017, and the prices of all four had rebounded higher than pre- hurricane levels by September 2018.

Pension Liabilities

At the end of fiscal year 2016, the most recent year for which data were available, USVI's public pension system had a net pension liability for the primary government and component units of $4.0 billion, which was 105 percent of GDP in that year. The USVI government has projected that the pension system will reach insolvency by 2024 or 2025. Officials from the previous gubernatorial administration told us they were planning to propose earmarking revenues from operations at the Limetree Bay refinery for the pension system and were also considering other measures to prolong the solvency of the fund, such as increasing employer contributions and reducing benefits. Officials from the current administration said they are reviewing the prior administration's plans and evaluating the best way to restructure the pension system going forward.

Federal Tax Reform

USVI's territorial income tax is required to mirror the federal income tax code.[45] In other words, USVI taxpayers must comply with federal income tax law but the proceeds are paid into the treasury of USVI rather than the U.S. Treasury. As such, any changes to the U.S. Internal Revenue Code have a direct impact on USVI's income tax revenue. As a result of changes to the federal tax code, officials anticipate that USVI's individual and corporate tax revenue will fall by 24 percent in fiscal year 2019.[46] Territory officials told us they are in the process of assessing how to mitigate the effect of these changes on revenue going forward.

Healthcare Funding

According to a recent statement by the Governor, up to 30,000 USVI residents, or 30 percent of the total population, could lose access to Medicaid after certain expanded PPACA and other federal funding for the program expires on September 30, 2019. Given USVI's current fiscal condition and inability to access capital markets, it is unclear how this funding shortfall will be addressed in order to make up these healthcare benefits. According to territory officials, the government is currently

---

[45] 48 U.S.C. § 1397. U.S. law restricts the territories' authority to impose certain territorial taxes. Three territories—Guam, CNMI, and USVI—are required by U.S. law to have a mirror tax code. 48 U.S.C. §§ 1397 (USVI), 1421i (Guam), 1801 note (CNMI). In general this means that these territories must use the U.S. Internal Revenue Code (IRC) as their territorial income tax law. In contrast, American Samoa and Puerto Rico, which are not bound by a mirror tax code, have established and promulgated their own income tax regulations.

[46] Enacted in December 2017, Public Law 115-97—commonly referred to by the President and many administrative documents as the Tax Cuts and Jobs Act—included significant changes to corporate and individual tax law. In particular, for individual taxpayers, for tax years 2018 through 2025, tax rates were lowered for nearly all income levels, some deductions from taxable income were changed (personal exemptions set to zero, while the standard deduction was increased), and certain credits, such as the child tax credit, were expanded.

assessing how it will mitigate the effect of this loss of federal Medicaid funding on the population.

AMERICAN SAMOA

American Samoa's Public Debt Increased by 42 Percent between Fiscal Years 2015 and 2017, and Infrastructure Projects Remain the Primary Driver

American Samoa's total public debt outstanding grew from $85.9 million in fiscal year 2015 to $122.2 million in fiscal year 2017, an increase of 42 percent. In fiscal year 2017, the majority of American Samoa's public debt was owed by the primary government. (See Figure 6.) Total public debt outstanding as a share of GDP increased from 13 percent in fiscal year 2015 to 19 percent in fiscal year 2017. Total public debt outstanding per capita increased from $1,482.2 in fiscal year 2015 to $2,081.9 in fiscal year 2017. The increase in debt was due largely to a single bond issued in January 2016 for $23.0 million to fund various infrastructure projects, which remains the major driver of American Samoa's public debt.

American Samoa also issued a series of general revenue bonds in December 2018 totaling another $50.3 million, which will be reflected in future single audit reports. The proceeds from these new bonds will be used to fund infrastructure projects, including constructing a new legislature building and expanding broadband and telecommunications services in the territory. Territory government officials told us the intent of this expansion is to diversify American Samoa's economy by making the territory a regional telecommunications hub.

In November 2018, Moody's affirmed American Samoa's noninvestment grade rating and assigned the same rating to its 2018 bond series, citing the territory's reliance on substantial assistance from the federal government, low income levels, and financial management challenges. Moody's also assigned a negative outlook to the 2018 bond series, noting the territory's stagnant revenues, underfunded retirement system, and need to service an increasing debt burden.[47] Moody's also noted that American Samoa's financial position is weak but improving, and stated that its rating incorporated the territory's recent positive financial trends and enhanced fiscal discipline. According to government officials, there are no plans to issue any additional bonds for the next 3 to 5 years.

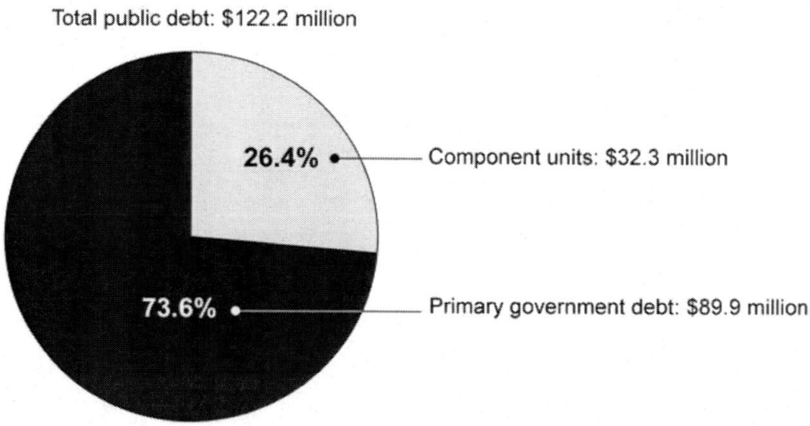

Source: GAO analysis of American Samoa's fiscal year 2017 audited financial statements. | GAO-19-525.

Figure 6. Composition of American Samoa's Public Debt, Fiscal Year 2017.

In addition to bonded debt, American Samoa carries loans from the U.S. government, including 1993 and 1994 CDLs from FEMA for disaster recovery.[48] These balances remained relatively constant between fiscal

---

[47] A noninvestment grade rating is any credit rating "BB" or lower on a scale that runs from AAA to either C or D, depending on the rating agency. Noninvestment grade ratings deem the likelihood that the debt will be repaid as "speculative". A Moody's rating outlook is an opinion regarding the likely rating direction over the medium term. Rating outlooks fall into four categories Positive, Negative, Stable, and Developing. A stable outlook indicates a low likelihood of a rating change over the medium term. A negative, positive, or developing outlook indicates a higher likelihood of a rating change over the medium term.

[48] In May 2000, FEMA cancelled $8,638,009 of principal and $3,227,779 of interest on these loans and the government of American Samoa expects the remaining amounts of these loans plus interest to be cancelled in the future.

years 2015 and 2017, decreasing slightly from $14.3 million to $13.8 million.

American Samoa's General Revenue Fluctuated between Fiscal Years 2015 and 2017, and it Operated with a Deficit in 2017

American Samoa's total revenue (i.e., general revenue and program revenue combined) decreased slightly from $436.4 million in fiscal year 2015 to $418.3 million in fiscal year 2017, a decrease of 4 percent.

American Samoa's general revenue increased 14 percent from $116.5 million in fiscal year 2015 to $132.8 million in fiscal year 2016 and subsequently decreased to $116.6 million in fiscal year 2017, a total increase of less than 1 percent during this time period. Between fiscal years 2015 and 2017, income and excise taxes combined represented an average of 56 percent of general revenue. Income and excise tax collection decreased by 9.6 percent, or $6.8 million, between fiscal years 2015 and 2017. This decrease was mainly driven by income tax collection, which declined by 23 percent, or $10.5 million, within the same period.

American Samoa operated with a deficit of $24.1 million in fiscal year 2017, the third deficit since fiscal year 2005. While total revenue declined, government expenses increased by 5 percent, or from $420.7 million to $442.4 million between fiscal years 2015 and 2017. Of total government expenses in fiscal year 2017, $281.0 million was spent by the primary government, while $161.4 million was spent by the government's various component units. Education was one of largest categories of primary government spending.

American Samoa Continues to Face Fiscal Risks, Such as Significant Pension Liabilities

American Samoa's public debt has grown and the territory continues to face fiscal risks that may affect repayment, such as a reliance on a single industry and significant pension liabilities. American Samoa's economy relies heavily on the tuna processing and canning industry, and since one of the two companies with cannery operations in American Samoa closed in December 2016, only one cannery is now in operation. Six hundred jobs were lost as a result of the cannery closure, and hundreds of more jobs were lost in related and support industries.[49] Officials told us that federal laws, such as the Clean Water Act and a minimum wage increase, may hamper the long-term sustainability of the industry. The closure of the remaining cannery, without economic growth elsewhere in the economy, may further reduce revenues available for repaying outstanding debt.

In fiscal year 2017, American Samoa reported a net pension liability for the primary government and components units of $213.1 million, which was 33 percent of GDP in that year.[50] If the territory is unable to make annual contributions to the pension fund, then the fund's condition may continue to deteriorate. According to territory officials, the government is exploring options to reduce the unfunded pension liability, including increasing the employee and employer contribution rates over a period of 3 years.

In addition, territory officials told us that while they do not plan to issue to debt to cover the shortfall in federal Medicaid funding after certain expanded PPACA funding for the program expires on September 30, 2019, the effect of this loss in funding on the territory will be significant.

---

[49] According to territory officials, the cannery currently in operation leased the space previously occupied by the closed cannery. Of the workers who lost their jobs as a result of the cannery closure, 333 individuals received government assistance such as paid work experience. The remaining 211 individuals either returned to their home countries, were employed by the remaining cannery, obtained other employment on their own, and/or enrolled in higher education.

[50] According to territory officials, the unfunded pension liability has decreased since reaching a low in 2016. When a pension is unfunded, it does not have enough assets to cover its liabilities.

Commonwealth of the Northern Mariana Islands (CNMI)

CNMI's Public Debt Decreased by 20 Percent between Fiscal Years 2015 and 2017

CNMI has not issued any new bonded debt since fiscal year 2007, and its total public debt outstanding declined from $144.7 million in fiscal year 2015 to $116.3 million in fiscal year 2017, a decrease of nearly 20 percent, due to repayment of existing debt.[51] In fiscal year 2017, the majority of CNMI's debt was owed by the primary government. (See Figure 7) Total public debt outstanding as a share of GDP declined from 16 percent in fiscal year 2015 to 8 percent in fiscal year 2017. Total public debt outstanding per capita declined from $2,844.7 in fiscal year 2015 to $2,307.8 in fiscal year 2017.

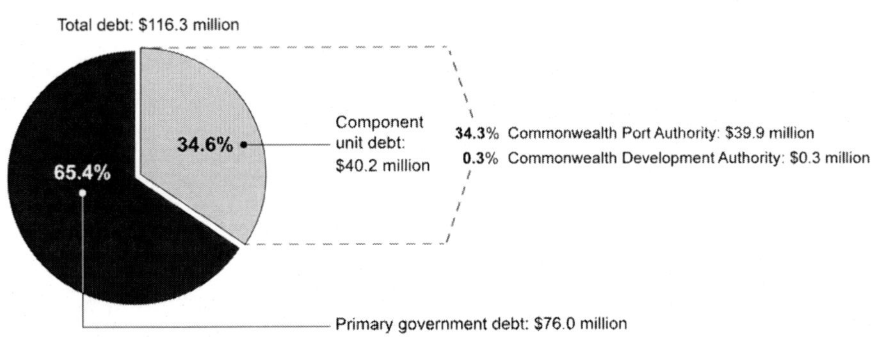

Source: GAO analysis of Commonwealth of the Northern Mariana Island's fiscal year 2017 audited financial statements. | GAO-19-525.

Note: Totals may not equal the sum of their parts due to rounding.

Figure 7. Composition of CNMI's Public Debt, Fiscal Year 2017.

[51] In 2007, the primary government of CNMI issued one general obligation bond to refinance two bonds originally issued in 2000 and 2003. Both the 2000 and 2003 bonds were issued to finance various infrastructure improvement projects. The 2003 issuance was also used for a onetime payment to settle land claims for the appropriation of private lands for public use.

Since CNMI has not issued any new debt, the major drivers of its public debt have not changed. As we reported previously, CNMI's constitution prohibits the government from using debt to pay for government operations, and bonds issued prior to fiscal year 2015 were used to refinance existing debt, fund various infrastructure improvements projects, and settle legal claims.[52]

While Program Revenue Decreased, CNMI's General Revenue Increased Significantly between Fiscal Years 2015 and 2017 and It Operated with a Surplus

CNMI's total revenue (i.e., general revenue and program revenue combined) decreased from $573.8 million in fiscal year 2015 to $516.6 million in fiscal year 2017, a decrease of 10 percent. CNMI's general revenue, however, increased from $226.3 million in fiscal year 2015 to $334.4 million in fiscal year 2017, an increase of 48 percent. Territory officials attributed the growth in general revenue to fees generated from casino operations and related businesses, growth in tourism driven from the construction of new hotels, and increased tax collections. A decrease in program revenue—from $347.5 million to around $182.2 million between fiscal years 2015 and 2017—was the main driver of the decline in total revenue, and was mainly due to a drop in charges for services generated by component units. On average, taxes comprised 75 percent of total revenue from fiscal years 2015 to 2017. Business taxes were a key contributor to tax revenue growth, with increases in this category of around $82.7 million between fiscal years 2015 and 2017.

CNMI has operated with a surplus—where revenue exceeds expenses— for each of the last 6 fiscal years.[53] In fiscal year 2017 CNMI

---

[52] CNMI Const., art. X, §§ 3, 4.

[53] CNMI received an adverse opinion on its governmental activities in fiscal years 2016 and 2017. CNMI has not recorded pension expense or the related net pension asset or liability, deferred inflows of resources and deferred outflows of resources as of and for the years ended September 30, 2016 and 2017. Additionally, CNMI received an adverse opinion and a disclaimer of opinion on its aggregate discretely presented component units in fiscal years

reported a surplus of $86.5 million, a decline from $94.4 million the prior year. While total revenue declined in CNMI between fiscal years 2015 and 2017, expenses also declined by 20 percent during the same period, from $536.6 million to $430.1 million, driven mainly by declines in component unit expenses. Of the total government expenses in fiscal year 2017, $374.9 million was spent by CNMI's primary government and the remainder, $55.3 million, by component units.

CNMI's Labor Shortages Have Been Mitigated, however Pension Liabilities and Reductions in Revenue due to Natural Disasters Present Fiscal Risks

CNMI's public debt has declined and, for the time being, potential labor shortages have been addressed. However, pension liabilities continue to present a fiscal risk that may affect the repayment of public debt. In addition, Typhoons Yutu and Mangkhut may have an adverse effect on CNMI's future revenue, which may affect funds available for repaying public debt. As we previously reported, CNMI's economy relies heavily on a foreign workforce. The temporary work permit program established by the Department of Homeland Security pursuant to the Consolidated National Resources Act of 2008 was scheduled to phase out temporary work permits for foreign workers by 2019, and we previously reported that with no permitted workers, CNMI's GDP in 2015 would have declined.[54] Congress passed and in July of 2018, the President signed, the Northern Mariana Islands U.S. Workforce Act of 2018, which extended the temporary work permit program by 10 years and increased the number of permits for foreign workers from 4,999 in fiscal year 2019 to 13,000

2016 and 2017, respectively. In fiscal year 2016, CNMI did not include significant component unit data in the discretely presented component units column of its government-wide financial statements. In fiscal year 2017, significant component unit data included on CNMI's government-wide financial statements had not been audited. The amounts by which the corresponding departures from U.S. Generally Accepted Accounting Principles would affect the reported assets, liabilities, revenues, expenses, and net position on the government-wide financial statements has not been determined.

[54] GAO-17-437.

beginning on October 1, 2018.[55] The number of permits allowed will subsequently decrease each year from 13,000 to 5,000 in fiscal year 2029 and to 1,000 in the first quarter of 2030.

CNMI also has pension liabilities, which are not included in the territory's fiscal year 2016 and 2017 single audit reports because the government continues not to comply with accounting standards that require it to do so. As such, CNMI's total net pension liability remains unclear. CNMI has received adverse opinions on its fiscal years 2016 and 2017 single audit reports as a result of its continued noncompliance with accounting standards requiring it to report pension liabilities. CNMI continues to make annual payments to its pension settlement fund. In fiscal years 2016 and 2017 payments of $30 million and $33 million, respectively, were made to the fund.[56] Officials told us that, as of March 2019, they were considering whether to issue a bond to finance additional payments to the settlement fund.

Typhoons Yutu and Mangkhut caused considerable damage to homes, businesses, and infrastructure in CNMI. They also adversely impacted the tourist industry, which CNMI's economy is dependent upon. As a result of the typhoons, the government is projecting a 5 percent reduction in revenue in fiscal year 2019, and is planning to implement reductions in spending to help offset the shortfall. Territory officials told us that, as of January 2019, CNMI has expended $62 million for typhoon recovery, most of which is expected to be reimbursed by the federal government.

In addition, territory officials told us CNMI has already run out of certain expanded PPACA funding for the Medicaid program, which is set to expire on September 30, 2019. Officials said that while they do not plan to issue debt to cover this shortfall in federal Medicaid funding, they may have to either cut benefits for current enrollees or incur budget deficits to fund the program going forward.

---

[55] Pub. L. No. 115-218, § 3, 132 Stat. 1547, 1547, 1550 (July 24, 2018), *codified at* 48 U.S.C. § 1806(a)(2), (d)(3)(B).

[56] In 2013, a U.S. district court approved a settlement agreement with the territory's government pension plan, which applied for bankruptcy in 2012. As part of the settlement, CNMI agreed to make minimum annual payments to the fund to allow members to receive 75 percent of their full benefits. *Johnson v. Inos*, No. 09-00023 (D.N. Mar. I. Aug. 6, 2013) (final amended stipulation and agreement of settlement).

GUAM

Guam's Public Debt Increased by Six Percent between Fiscal Years 2015 and 2017, due to Refinancing and Infrastructure Projects

Guam's total public debt outstanding increased slightly from $2.5 billion in fiscal year 2015 to $2.6 billion in fiscal year 2017, an increase of 6 percent. In fiscal year 2017, the majority of Guam's public debt was owed by component units. (See Figure 8.) Total public debt outstanding as a share of GDP remained fairly constant, increasing slightly from 44 to 45 percent between fiscal years 2015 and 2017. Total public debt outstanding per capita increased from $15,334.9 in fiscal year 2015 to $16,106.2 in fiscal year 2017.

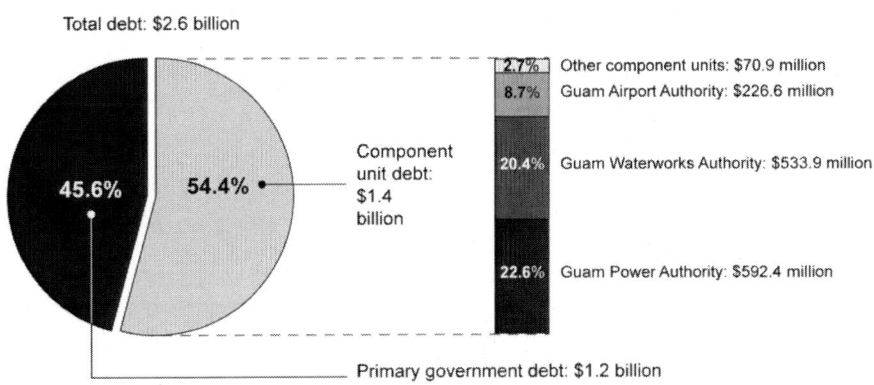

Source: GAO analysis of Guam's fiscal year 2017 audited financial statements. | GAO-19-525.

Note: Totals may not equal the sum of their parts due to rounding.

Figure 8. Composition of Guam's Public Debt, Fiscal Year 2017.

Since fiscal year 2015, the major drivers of new public debt issued by Guam's primary government and its component units have been refinancing existing debt—originally issued to comply with federal requirements and court orders[57]—and funding infrastructure projects. Since fiscal year 2015, the government of Guam and its component units have issued five bonds and entered into two federal loan agreements with the U.S. Department of Agriculture (USDA). Proceeds from the USDA loans were used to finance the construction and renovation of Guam Community College and University of Guam buildings. Collectively, the amount of new bonds issued since fiscal year 2015 is about $190 million and the amount of refinanced debt is approximately $844 million. Two of the refinanced bonds were issued in November and December of 2017 totaling about $260 million, which will be reflected in the fiscal year 2018 single audit report, which will be released in June 2019. According to officials, the government does not plan to issue debt for government operations moving forward, although it may continue to do so to refinance existing debt or fund infrastructure projects as needed.

Guam's General Revenue Increased between Fiscal Years 2015 and 2017, and It Operated with a Surplus

Guam's total revenue (i.e., general revenue and program revenue combined), remained relatively constant between fiscal years 2015 and 2017 at approximately $2.2 billion. Guam's general revenue increased from $862.7 million in fiscal year 2015 to $970.2 million in fiscal year 2017, an increase of 12 percent. On average, taxes comprised 83 percent of general revenue over this period. Income taxes were a key contributor to

---

[57] In 2006, the Superior Court of Guam held that a territorial statutory provision required the retirement fund for government employees to pay past due annual lump sum Cost of Living (COLA) payments plus interest to eligible retirees and survivors. In February 2004 the U.S. Environmental Protection Agency (EPA) and the Department of Justice filed a consent decree in the U.S. District Court of Guam. The consent decree set forth the settlement terms agreed to by the federal government and Guam settling a lawsuit alleging Guam violated the Clean Water Act. The consent decree included deadlines for opening a new landfill and adopting a dump closure plan. In response to a 2009 District Court order that Guam comply with the terms of the consent order, the territory chose to issue a $202.4 million limited obligation bond to fund closing the Ordot dump and constructing a new landfill to meet the terms of the settlement agreement.

tax revenue growth, with increases of around $46.0 million dollars for income tax collection between fiscal year 2015 and 2017.

Guam operated with a surplus of $134.0 million in fiscal year 2017 and $3.8 million in fiscal year 2016. The surplus in fiscal year 2017 was due to revenue growth in that year, as well as spending reductions in some areas like healthcare and other general government expenses. Guam last experienced a deficit in fiscal year 2014. Guam's expenses remained relatively constant between fiscal years 2015 and 2017, increasing by only $31.2 million over this period. In fiscal year 2017, Guam's government expenses totaled about $2.1 billion, of which 58 percent was spent by the primary government and the remainder by the component units.

Guam Continues to Face Fiscal Risks, Including Significant Pension Liabilities

Guam's fiscal risks for repaying public debt remain largely unchanged since our prior report, and pension liabilities continue to pose a fiscal risk that may affect repayment of public debt. Guam's net pension liability for the primary government and components units was $1.2 billion, or 22 percent of GDP, in fiscal year 2015. In fiscal year 2017, Guam reported a net pension liability for the primary government and component units of more than $1.6 billion, or 28 percent of GDP in that year. Territory officials told us they made several changes to the government retirement system that took effect January 1, 2018, including increasing the contribution rate and creating a new defined benefit plan for existing employees.[58] Officials said the government is still on track to eliminate the funding deficit by 2033, as required by territory law.[59]

Guam's territorial income tax code is generally required to mirror the federal income tax code.[60] In other words, Guam taxpayers must comply

---

[58] Guam Pub. L. 33-186 (Sept. 14, 2016).

[59] 4 Guam Code. Ann. § 8137(b). We did not independently verify this estimate.

[60] 48 U.S.C. § 1421i. Although Guam is mirror-code jurisdictions, it is authorized under the Tax Reform Act of 1986 to delink from the Internal Revenue Code if certain conditions are met. Pub. L. No. 99-514, § 1271, 100 Stat. 2085, 2591–2592 (Oct. 22, 1986).

with federal income tax law but the proceeds are paid into the treasury of Guam rather than the U.S. Treasury. As such, any changes to the U.S. Internal Revenue Code can have a direct effect on Guam's income tax revenue. Officials expressed concern that federal tax reform would decrease Guam's individual and corporate tax collections. However, Guam officials told us that steps have been taken to address revenue shortfalls, such as increasing certain taxes and decreasing expenditures, and that these measures will offset the effect of changes to the tax code on revenues in fiscal years 2018 and 2019. While Standard and Poor's placed Guam under a credit watch and Moody's changed its outlook from stable to negative in March 2018 as a result of the potential effect of changes in federal tax law on Guam's revenue, Standard and Poor's subsequently lifted the credit watch in light of Guam's improved cash flow and success in balancing its fiscal year 2019 budget.[61]

In addition, according to a recent statement by the Governor, 50 percent of current Medicaid enrollees are at risk of losing benefits after certain expanded PPACA funding for the program expires on September 30, 2019. Territory officials told us that while they do not plan to issue debt to cover this shortfall in federal Medicaid funding, it will cost Guam approximately $39 million to fund the program in fiscal year 2020.

Agency Comments, Third Party Views, and Our Evaluation

We provided a draft of this chapter to the Department of the Interior and the Department of the Treasury for review and comment. We also provided, to the governments of Puerto Rico, the United States Virgin Islands (USVI), American Samoa, the Commonwealth of the Northern Mariana Islands (CNMI), and Guam, and to the Financial Oversight and

---

[61] A credit watch is a notice from a credit rating agency to a bond issuer that a negative factor has arisen in the agency's review of the issuer's credit rating. If the issuer does not take steps to explain or alleviate the factor, the credit watch may be the first step toward a reduction in the issuer's rating.

Management Board for Puerto Rico (FOMB), portions of the draft that were relevant to them for review and comment. We received technical comments from the Department of the Interior, Puerto Rico, USVI, American Samoa, and Guam, which we incorporated as appropriate. We did not receive any comments from the Department of the Treasury or the FOMB. We also received written comment letters from each of the five territories' governments, some of which expressed their viewpoints and concerns on broader federal actions, programs, or policies that might affect their territory's financial condition. The comment letters from Puerto Rico, USVI, American Samoa, CNMI, and Guam are reprinted in appendixes II, III, IV, V, and VI, respectively. The letters from the governments of Puerto Rico and Guam raised some issues to which we respond below.

The letter from the government of Puerto Rico notes that the government has concerns about our statement that the first two debt restructuring agreements (i.e., the GDB and COFINA agreements) were based on optimistic economic growth estimates in the prior October 2018 version of the certified FOMB Fiscal Plan. The letter also notes that those agreements were based on separate fiscal plans specific to those entities. The economy-wide growth estimates, as measured by real GNP growth, included in the COFINA fiscal plan are nearly identical to those included in the prior version of the FOMB's fiscal plan. While we acknowledge the inclusion of the other financial projections specific to COFINA contained in its fiscal plan, we maintain that the economy-wide growth projections included in both the FOMB and COFINA fiscal plans are important, as Puerto Rico's ability to generate sustained economic growth will be a key determinant for repaying restructured debt.

In addition, pursuant to the Title VI Qualifying Modification, we recognize that GDB's restructured debt will be repaid using GDB's liquidated assets that have been placed into a statutory public trust. However, general economic health is important for repaying municipal bonds, and therefore we reiterate that economic growth is relevant and that the pertinent economic growth estimates at the time the Qualifying Modification was made were those estimates in the prior version of FOMB's fiscal plan.

The letter also states that information pertaining to the prior version of the FOMB's fiscal plan in our draft is "academic" because the FOMB certified a new fiscal plan in May 2019. However, we reiterate here that information from the prior version of the fiscal plan is relevant because that plan was in place when the first two debt restructuring agreements were made and at the time we conducted our audit work.

The letter from the Governor of Guam states that tax-supported debt (i.e., primary government debt) reflects the core of Guam's outstanding debt obligations, and takes issue with our inclusion of public enterprise or revenue bonds (i.e., component unit debt) in our calculation of Guam's total public debt outstanding. We believe that by including component unit debt, we provide the most comprehensive metric of Guam's total public debt, and therefore it would be incorrect for us to exclude public enterprise and revenue bond debt (i.e., component unit debt) in our report.

While it is our objective to provide the most comprehensive metric of Guam's public debt, we do, however, show how much debt is owed by Guam's primary government versus component units. In addition, we include both primary government and component unit revenue in our calculations of general revenue and total revenue; as such, an equivalent comparison can be made to our total public debt figure, which includes primary government and component unit debt.

Further, consistent with our prior work, including our 1994 report, which is mentioned in Guam's letter, we do not compare Guam's public debt with any other territory, state, county, or locality. Moreover, our calculations are consistent with this prior work in that our calculation of total public debt includes debt related to functions carried out by different levels of government.

We are sending copies of this chapter to the appropriate congressional committees, the Governor of each territory, the Secretary of the Interior, and the Secretary of the Treasury.

Tranchau (Kris) T. Nguyen
Acting Director,
Strategic Issues

David Gootnick
Director,
International Affairs and Trade

Appendix I: Objectives, Scope and Methodology

To describe trends in each territory's public debt, revenue, and composition, we reviewed the audited financial statements included within each territory's single audit report for the most recent fiscal years– fiscal years 2016 and 2017, if available, as of early May, 2019.[62] We analyzed data on public debt—bonds, loans, and notes for both the primary government and component units—for each of those years. For the purposes of this chapter, total public debt outstanding refers to the sum of bonds and other debt held by and payable to the public, as reported in the territories' single audit reports. Marketable debt securities, primarily bonds with long-term maturities, are the main vehicle by which the territories access capital markets. Other debt payable may include marketable notes issued by territorial governments, non-marketable intragovernmental notes, notes held by local banks, federal loans, intragovernmental loans, and loans issued by local banks. Although pension liabilities and other post-employment benefits are similar to other kinds of debt because they constitute a promise to make a future payment or provide a benefit, they are not included in our definition of total public debt.

---

[62] The Single Audit Act, as implemented by guidance issued by the Office of Management and Budget (OMB), requires nonfederal entities that expend above a dollar threshold in federal awards in a fiscal year to have a single audit. Recipient organizations are required by the act to submit their single audits reports to the Federal Audit Clearinghouse (FAC). The single audit reporting package sent to the FAC includes (1) the auditor's reports; (2) the entity's audited financial statements and related notes; (3) the schedule of expenditures of federal awards, related notes, and the auditor's report on the schedule; (4) a schedule of findings and questioned costs; (5) reports on internal controls over financial reporting, and compliance with laws and regulations; and (6) a summary schedule of prior audit findings. Puerto Rico provides audited financial statements but does not submit single audit report packages to FAC. Puerto Rico's and USVI's audited financial statements for fiscal year 2017 were not available as of May 2019.

In addition, we obtained and reviewed data on each of the territories' revenue from single audit reports for each fiscal year for both the primary governments and component units.[63] Revenues are amounts that result from governments' exercise of their sovereign power to tax or otherwise compel payment. Revenues also include income generated by the territories' component units. The primary government is generally comprised of governmental activities (generally financed with taxes and intergovernmental aid) and business-type activities (generally financed with charges for goods and services). Component units are legally separate entities for which a government is financially accountable. For the purposes of this chapter, any reference to total government activity and balances includes both the primary government and component units.

For each territory, we obtained and reviewed the independent auditor's report corresponding to each single audit and noted the type of opinion that was expressed on the financial statements and accompanying note disclosures. We reviewed each of these opinions and determined that, despite the modified opinions, the data we obtained from each of the single audit reports was reliable for the purpose of describing trends in debt and revenue and their composition for the fiscal years included in our analysis.[64] Where appropriate, we included cautionary language in our report for instances in which a modified opinion could affect the reliability of data included in our report.

To determine the drivers of public debt and what is known about the territories' ability to repay public debt, we interviewed officials from each of the territories' governments. In addition, we interviewed representatives of the three major credit rating agencies—Fitch, Moody's and Standard

---

[63] In addition to revenue levels, another measure of fiscal health is net position. Net position represents the difference between the primary government's assets (including the deferred outflow of resources) and the primary government's liabilities (including the deferred inflow of resources.) In other words, the net position for primary government activities reflects what the primary government would have left after satisfying its liabilities. Since it is difficult to draw conclusions about trends in net position over the short period covered by this update, we did not include net position in our analysis.

[64] Auditors express modified opinions when (1) the auditors conclude that, based on the audit evidence obtained, the financial statements as a whole are materially misstated or (2) the auditors are unable to obtain sufficient appropriate audit evidence to conclude that the financial statements as a whole are free from material misstatement.

and Poor's—that provide ratings for the territories' securities. We also interviewed officials at the U.S. Department of the Treasury and Department of the Interior's Office of Insular Affairs, which provides grant aid and technical assistance and support to the territories.[65] In addition, we obtained and reviewed relevant documentation, reports, and analyses from the territorial governments and ratings agencies. We also obtained and reviewed information on territorial bond issuances for debt issued since fiscal year 2015 from the Electronic Municipal Market Access database of the Municipal Securities Rulemaking Board, the primary regulator of the municipal securities market.

To determine the effects of Hurricanes Irma and Maria on the economies and public debt of Puerto Rico and USVI, we interviewed officials from government agencies, including departments of finance or treasury, the agencies responsible for issuing and marketing bonded debt, the agencies responsible for economic development, the Offices of Management and Budget, and the Offices of the Inspectors General. We also conducted interviews with experts on Puerto Rico and USVI's economies, municipal securities markets, and select industry groups. We selected the experts we interviewed based on their professional knowledge closely aligning with our engagement objectives, as demonstrated through published articles and referrals from other experts. In addition, we analyzed a non-generalizable sample of Bloomberg data on secondary market trading prices of USVI and Puerto Rico bonds to illustrate the possible impact of market events, such as the 2017 hurricanes, on bond prices.

We conducted this performance audit from April 2018 to June 2019 in accordance with generally accepted government auditing standards. Those standards require that we plan and perform the audit to obtain sufficient, appropriate evidence to provide a reasonable basis for our findings and conclusions based on our audit objectives. We believe that the evidence obtained provides a reasonable basis for our findings and conclusions based on our audit objectives.

---

[65] The Office of Insular Affairs does not exercise any responsibilities in relation to Puerto Rico.

Appendix II: Comments from the Government of Puerto Rico

GOVERNMENT OF PUERTO RICO

Puerto Rico Fiscal Agency and Financial Advisory Authority

June 10, 2019

Hon. Gene L. Dodaro
Comptroller General of the United States
U.S. Government Accountability Office
441 G Street, N.W.
Washington, DC 20548

Dear Mr. Dodaro:

I am writing with regards to the U. S. Government Accountability Office (**"GAO"**) report (the "**Report**"), GAO 19-525, *U.S. Territories Public Debt Outlook*. I would like to thank you for the opportunity to review and provide feedback on the Report in its draft form. This report will inform the public policy debate surrounding critical issues to Puerto Rico and other U.S. Territories.

Below are the official comments and feedback of the Government of Puerto Rico ("**Government**").

Progress Toward Meaningful Change

- **Successful Restructurings.** As noted in the Report, the Government has achieved successful restructurings of $6.96 billion of debt of two government entities: the Government Development Bank (**"GDB"**) and Puerto Rico Sales Tax Financing Corporation ("**COFINA**"). These restructurings were achieved through agreements with creditors and created new municipal bonds for Puerto Rico intended to promote Puerto Rico's ongoing market access. The Legislature of Puerto Rico enacted new legislation in connection with both restructurings in support of the new bond structures, demonstrating the support of the Government for debt restructurings that further the interests of both its creditors and the people of Puerto Rico.

- **Action by Current Administration to Achieve Transparency.** Although the Government's audited financial statement have been delayed, Governor Ricardo Rosselló's administration is making every effort to be current and timely regarding the completion of the fiscal year 2017 and 2018 financial statements. Furthermore, in order to provide more transparency and timely information, the Puerto Rico

Fiscal Agency and Financial Advisory Authority ("**AAFAF**", for its Spanish acronym) continues to publish monthly bank account balances for the Government and its instrumentalities and weekly cash flow of the Treasury Single Account of the Government. Moreover, the Puerto Rico Planning Board has continued to publish economic data annually. Official Government revenue data is released by the Puerto Rico Treasury Department on a monthly basis. It is also important not to conflate any lack of transparency in the Financial Oversight and Management Board for Puerto Rico's ("**FOMB**") Fiscal Plan with a lack of transparency by the Government. The Government has been fully transparent regarding the assumptions and sources for its fiscal plan submissions. Detailed letters explaining methodology submitted alongside the Fiscal Plans and Supplemental Economic Information showing the economic model and assumptions are available publicly on AAFAF's website (http://aafaf.pr.gov/other-documents.html#fiscalplanspin).

Comments Regarding Certain Assumptions in the Report

- **Fiscal Plan Assumptions.** The certification of the Commonwealth fiscal plans is an extensive process that includes several iterations of a plan that is first submitted by the Government to the FOMB. Ultimately, the FOMB has certified their own version of the Fiscal Plan; however, it is important to note where the Government and the FOMB are not aligned. The most recent Government Fiscal Plan submission has an assumed pass-through rate of 18% for most federal funding. The aggregate pass-through rate used by FOMB is higher and is at times arbitrarily assigned to certain categories of uses of the funds. We feel it is important to clarify that during the Report's draft process and in our comments to the GAO, we indicated that certain information found therein was academic as a result of the certification by the FOMB of a new Fiscal Plan on May 9, 2019.

- **Debt Restructurings.** In multiple places the Report assumes that the GDB and COFINA restructuring agreements were based on, or informed by, "more optimistic growth estimates" in the previously certified (October 2018) Fiscal Plan for the Commonwealth. While we respect the GAO's methodology, we have concerns that these statements are based on an incorrect premise. The Title VI qualifying modification for GDB was premised on a separate fiscal plan for GDB, and the payment of the GDB bonds is based only on a fixed set of collateral and was not otherwise based on the Commonwealth Fiscal Plan and the estimates contained therein. The GDB creditors do not have recourse to the Commonwealth and bear the risk of the economics on the Title VI qualifying modification. Further, the Title III restructuring agreement for COFINA is a securitized plan and was based on the projections set forth in the certified fiscal plan for COFINA.

Federal Actions that Impact Puerto Rico's Prospects for Repayment of Debt

The Report states that two significant factors will determine Puerto Rico's capacity for repaying its restructured debt: (1) the outcomes of the ongoing debt restructuring process, and (2) Puerto Rico's ability to generate sustained economic growth. The GAO must also recognize the impact that the undemocratic, unequal and oftentimes arbitrary federal legal, regulatory and constitutional frameworks that apply to the island as a U.S. territory have had on Puerto Rico's situation. The Government believes that certain federal actions are central to addressing Puerto Rico's economic and fiscal viability.

- **Triple Tax Exempt Status.** The Government of Puerto Rico is strongly opposed to the possible modification of the triple tax-exempt status for Puerto Rico's municipal debt. Indeed, obtaining tax-exempt treatment for the COFINA bonds is a key element to the success of that restructuring. Given all the improvements in fiscal and budgetary controls, transparency and economic structural balance that are currently being implemented, the Government is confident that the triple tax-exempt bonding capacity can and will be used responsibly in the future when Puerto Rico is eventually able to return to the capital markets. Finally, although the triple tax-exempt status can be considered a benefit that the federal government grants the territories, its existence is attributable to some extent to the understanding by federal policymakers that the territory is subject to an unfair legal framework, particularly in terms of reduced levels of funding and various other areas of disadvantageous federal treatment. For this reason, until the federal government provides for Puerto Rico full equality under federal laws and programs, it should not remove one of the most important economic development tools and advantages that they have granted us.

- **Congressional & Executive Actions to Address Critical Challenges.** The report issued by the Congressional Task Force on Economic Growth in Puerto Rico in December 2016 identified a variety of policy recommendations for Congress and the federal Executive that could help address critical challenges in Puerto Rico and support the restoration of economic growth on the island. Whether Congress and the Executive work with the Government of Puerto Rico to act on the challenges and opportunities identified by the Task Force could make a very big difference in improving the conditions for economic growth to take place in the territory. Some of these challenges are well known in Congress and in the Executive and both have an immense impact on Puerto Rico's economic and fiscal prospects for the future. Among the most notable is the unequal treatment of Puerto Rico in Federal Medicaid funding which periodically puts the stability of the island's entire healthcare system at risk and has contributed to a mass exodus of medical and health professionals which cannot be easily replaced. In this case Congress should work with Puerto Rico to establish a sustainable funding structure for our Medicaid program in a way that is tied to the levels of need, is means-tested and provides the same or better levels of care than the current unequal funding structure. Another notable challenge is the imposition of the Global Intangible Low-Taxed Income Tax (GILTI) on Puerto Rico as if we were foreign jurisdiction, whose impact on the manufacturing sector is projected to cause a very substantial reduction in local tax revenues. Congress should treat Puerto Rico as a domestic jurisdiction for purposes of GILTI in any upcoming legislative vehicle with tax provisions or technical fixes before the end of this year, and should work to improve upon Opportunity Zones to attract new private sector investment to the island. Other examples of policies that Congress could change to significantly improve Puerto Rico's economy and therefore our fiscal and debt outlook would be the full extension of the Child Tax Credit and the Earned Income Tax Credit to families on the island.

- **Resolution of Undemocratic & Unequal Territorial Status**. The question of Puerto Rico's ultimate political status and relationship with the Federal Government is intimately linked to the island's prospects for economic growth, and therefore its capacity to repay its debts. By allowing Congress and the federal Executive Branch to treat Puerto Rico differently and in ways that discriminate against the island and its residents, the current territorial status inherently limits economic growth. It does this by allowing the propagation of federal laws and policies toward the territory that lack the coherence and consistency required to provide for the island's sustained economic development and growth. The democratic deficit generated by the lack of voting representation at the federal level results in an inability of the elected officials from Puerto Rico to exert sufficient influence in the federal policy and regulatory making process to be able to ensure that the island's needs, conditions and aspirations are duly considered and accounted for. Unfortunately, federal policy towards the island is oftentimes executed as an afterthought and without a proper understanding of the circumstances of the island and its residents. There are countless examples of federal policies and practices that harm or limit Puerto Rico's economic development potential. Among these are the disparate treatment and sometimes-outright exclusion of Puerto Rico from a variety of federal programs, the island's exclusion from a multitude of federal studies and statistics, the disproportionately low level of federal procurement from businesses in Puerto Rico, and unnecessary regulations that limit interstate commerce such as the Electronic Export Information requirement. Another factor that negatively impacts the island's economy is the significant levels of political and policy uncertainty and risk created by the territorial status at both the local and federal levels. For businesses making investment decisions this political and policy risk decreases the desirability of making investments on the island and it also increases the borrowing cost for the government and private businesses on the island. The current reform process happening in Puerto Rico under PROMESA, and the post disaster reconstruction, present an ideal opportunity to finally define the ultimate political future of Puerto Rico, and to begin a transition toward that end. Congress must act definitively to resolve Puerto Rico's future political status, because extending the failed

120-year-old territory status will only further delay the island's full economic, fiscal and demographic recovery as well as its reconstruction. Congress must resolve Puerto Rico's status to unleash its full potential, and should implement the democratically expressed will of voters who have expressed twice in the last six years a clear desire to end the current territory status and to achieve statehood for Puerto Rico. Indeed, for America and Puerto Rico both, statehood is the best possible answer and the best path forward out of this century old issue and into a new century of economic growth and prosperity.

In closing, I want to thank GAO for its efforts in preparing the Report. I hope that the comments contained here are helpful.

Sincerely,

Christian Sobrino Vega
CEO and President

Appendix III: Comments from the Government of the United States Virgin Islands

The Virgin Islands Of The United States
OFFICE OF THE GOVERNOR
GOVERNMENT HOUSE

1105 King Street
Christiansted, St. Croix, U.S.V.I. 00820

Ms. Tara Carter
Assistant Director for Federal Budget Analysis – Strategic Issues
U.S. Government Accountability Office
441 G Street., NW
Washington, DC 20548

Dear Ms. Carter:

The Government of the Virgin Islands would like to express our sincere appreciation to you and your team, led by Senior Analyst Divya Bali, for the opportunity to comment on the draft report entitled U.S. Territories: Public Debt Outlook – 2019 Update (GAO-19-525), as required by the Puerto Rico Oversight Management and Economic Stability Act (PROMESA).

We were able to provide some technical comments to Ms. Bali and her team, however, our overarching comment is that the information appears to be presented negatively in the report. In addition to presenting negative information, the report also fails to look at the underlying circumstances or provide any assistance (either technical or financial) to improve the Territories public debt outlook.

For instance, in our comments on last year's report, we discussed at length how the unequal treatment of the Territories in most federal programs, including Medicaid and other federal healthcare funding, has contributed to our budget deficits, which, in turn, resulted in borrowing to fund government operations. We also commented on how other mandatory federal programs, such as the Earned Income Tax Credit and the Child Tax Credit, impose additional burdens on the finances of the Territory.

Yet, to our knowledge, there has been no discussions in Congress on how changes to these programs can help to reduce budget deficits and the debt burden of the Territory. We believe that the reason these reports are required by PROMESA is so that Congress can look at ways to assist the Territory **before** getting into a situation like Puerto Rico.

The current report lists six factors that may contribute to USVI's continued ability to repay public debt moving forward: 1) the integrity of USVI's "lockbox" provisions for repaying debt, 2) USVI's ability to access capital markets at favorable interest rates in the future, 3) USVI's ability to create sustained economic growth, 4) USVI's ability to address its pension liabilities and the pending insolvency of its public pension system, 5) reduced tax revenue due to recently enacted federal tax changes, and 6) shortfalls in Medicaid funding.

Items 5 and 6 were discussed above, and I highlight our continued concerns over the unequal treatment of the Territory in federal funding. We continue to hope that these reports will establish how to assist the Territory in reducing its debt burden.

Moreover, the USVI has made multiple efforts on its own accord to reduce the debt burden, through the implementation of the following:

1) Lockbox Provisions. We maintain that the "lockbox" provision is secure and provides investors confidence that the loans will be repaid. This has been in place for many years and has now been codified in Virgin Islands law.

2) Market Access. The USVI has not attempted any bond financings since January 2017 when a proposed sale was withdrawn. For my first Executive Budget, I submitted a balanced Fiscal Year 2020 Budget to the Legislature based on increased revenue without any debt financing or tax increases to include $5 million in reserves to the Budget Stabilization Fund.

3) Economic Growth. The economy continues its recovery, fueled by the rebuilding after the storms and federal funding for hurricane recovery activities. Additionally, tourism is expected to increase as the larger hotels come back online and additional flights are added to the Territory.

4) Pension Liabilities. My administration will work tirelessly with GERS and other stakeholders on a strategic plan to address the unfunded liability of the pension system. Recent legislation increased the additional contribution to the GERS from $7 million to $10 million annually.

Once again, with your assistance the USVI can continue to reduce its debt, and we thank you and your team for your ongoing cooperation and assistance to facilitate this process.

Sincerely,

Albert Bryan, Jr.
Governor

APPENDIX IV: COMMENTS FROM THE GOVERNMENT OF AMERICAN SAMOA

LOLO M. MOLIGA
GOVERNOR

OFFICE OF THE GOVERNOR
AMERICAN SAMOA GOVERNMENT
Telephone: (684)633-4116 Fax: (684)633-2269

LEMANU P. MAUGA
LIEUTENANT GOVERNOR

June 3, 2019

Serial: 441

Thomas Melito
Managing Director
U.S. Government Accountability Office
Internal Affairs and Trade (IAT)
441 G St. N.W.
Washington, DC 20548

Dear Mr. Melito:

Aligned with the previous engagement in 2017 facilitating the issuance of the subsequent report that year, the collaboration between my staff and the GAO Team headed by Ms. Divya Bali Senior Analyst and her staff was seamless and effective thus enabling the compilation of this comprehensive final report on the public debt status of the American Samoa Government. Our staff's review of the 2019 report generated the following responses relative to the important issues highlighted in the report.

Increase in Public Debt

The American Samoa Government has a duty to provide public goods and services to our people so the private sector can flourish with reciprocal improvement in the quality of their lives. This responsibility requires that we continually maintain, repair and upgrade public infrastructure such as roads, public utilities, port and airport facilities, education facilities, and all other physical infrastructure, not only to meet the needs of the people, but also to forge the creation and sustainment of a conducive economic climate for continual bolstering of the territory's economy. While we are grateful for the US Department of the Interior for providing $10 million annually toward these capital projects, this funding is woefully insufficient to pay for all required capital needs.

Our government has embarked on a strategic financial plan inclusive of the use of publicly issued debt to not only supplement but also maximize the use of local funds to advantageously and broadly address our capital project needs. Our finance plan also includes public-private partnerships propelled by new Federal Incentive Schemes such as New Market Tax Credit, Opportunity Zones, and other operating strategies such power purchase agreements. We will continue to vigilantly balance the needs of the Territory with the financial constraints and finance tools available. Our commitment to be fiscally responsible cannot be overstated or underscored. We will never issue new debt without identifying the long-term repayment source to fully liquidate any debt to its maturity.

Fiscal and Economic Risks

The economy of American Samoa is narrow and fragile consequential to its sole dependence on one major industry (fishing) and the American Samoa Government which also heavily depends on this one economic pillar. Our administration has determined to use public debt to create additional opportunities to expand and to diversify our economy. This has included bolstering the local banking sector by investing in the establishment of a Territorial Bank with the long-term goal to transition this bank back to the private sector. The Territory has also issued bonds to invest in building high-speed broadband capacity to the island. This investment significantly shores up the territory's economic environment which not only improves local business operations but it is also attracting the attention of mainland business who want to do business in the Pacific under US Law. The Territory of American Samoa's pathway to social and economic self-reliance and self-sufficiency is embedded its steadfast and unwavering commitment to continual and steady economic development progress.

Our administration is committed to fiscal responsibility and it neither unafraid nor will it side step making difficult decisions. In 2018, due to projected revenue shortfalls, a reduction in working hours for the American Samoa Government was implemented for months to align expenses with actual revenues collected. We are also very mindful and concerned with the rising level of the unfunded liability of our pension plan; actions are being taken with the introduction of legislation to increase employee contribution along with others, which are being considered. While these measures are socially and economically painful decisions, they had to be made.

US Government Policies

The American Samoa Government, since transfer of administrative responsibilities from the Department of the Navy to the Department of the Interior in 1951, has had its efforts to develop its economy stymied and stifled by prohibitive federal policies that do not match the facts on the ground. These federal impediments are documented herein.

The Territory of American Samoa's economy is defined by just one industry engaged in the production of can tuna fish and other fish related products destined for the US Market. Withdrawal of federal incentives, automatic imposition of federal minimum wage hikes, prohibition of fishing in the high seas by NOAA, reduction of fishing grounds by Presidential Ocean Monuments expansion, grossly insensitive enforcement of United States Coast Guard rules and regulations, and stiff competition from foreign low wage can tuna fish producing foreign countries severely threaten the continued viability of this industry. StarKist Samoa is the only remaining company in the Territory. Two others, Van Camp Samoa Packing and Tri-Marine's Samoa Tuna Processing both terminated their can packing operations and departed the Territory because of impractical federal economic policies.

American Samoa's economy is still going through recovery and the potential eminent loss of StarKist Samoa attributed to the above enumerated factors, will cause the Territory of American Samoa to emulate the financial crisis being experienced by the Territory of Puerto Rico and the Territory of the Virgin Islands. American Samoa will be at the Federal Government's doorstep requesting a bailout if our remaining fish cannery StarKist is forced to relocate its facilities to a low wage can tuna fish producing country.

The above discourse highlights American Samoa's total vulnerability due to its dependence on one industry (one company) and emphasizes the absolute need for economic diversification. Many of the island microstates in the Pacific are aggressively pushing the development of their tourism industries. American Samoa has struggled for a very long time to diversify its economy by developing its tourism industry. These efforts have been exercises in futility because the basic component of the tourism infrastructural system is air transportation. Regrettably, the federal "Cabotage Policy" created a monopolistic air transportation environment and placed American Samoa in a hostage situation subjecting visitors and residents alike to the payment of exorbitant airfares with only two flights a week except for the Summer and Christmas holidays.

Conclusion

The American Samoa Government will continue to provide a conducive business climate to foster private sector success so our peoplecan access opportunities to improve their quality of lives by lifting themselves and their families out of poverty. We are committed and resolved to continually pursue this pathway in a fiscally responsible manner. We will continue to refine our economic development and capital deployment plans to ensurethat the proper balance is continuously struck between fiscal discipline and economic expansion. It is abundantly clear that the future of American Samoa is directly affected by policy declarations issued by the Congress of the United States and enforced by the Federal Government. It is also with clarity that we recognize that our needs are dwarfed and overshadowed by the needs of the 50 States, thus we are aggressively and feverishly struggling to assume responsibility for the needs of our people through the exploration of other financing options. Notwithstanding, we will continual reach out to the US Government to straighten and to affectively affirm partnership dedicated to establishing a pathway aided by federal incentives, proactive federal policies, and financial investment which will finally fulfill the United States' political vision for American Samoa articulated by the United States Department of the Interior of full self-reliance and economic self-sufficiency.

Sincerely,

LEMANU P. MAUGA
Acting Governor of American Samoa

cc: Honorable Aumua Amata Radewagen, Member of Congress
Honorable David Bernhardt, Secretary, US Department of the Interior
Honorable Douglas W. Domenech, Assistant Secretary, Insular and International Affairs
Honorable Nikolao Pula, Director, Office for Insular and International Affairs

Appendix V: Comments from the Government of the Commonwealth of the Northern Mariana Islands

RALPH DLG. TORRES
Governor

ARNOLD I. PALACIOS
Lieutenant Governor

COMMONWEALTH of the NORTHERN MARIANA ISLANDS
OFFICE OF THE GOVERNOR

June 3, 2019

Mr. David Gootnick
Director, International Affairs and Trade
United States Government Accountability Office
411 G Street, N.W.
Washington, DC 20548

Dear Mr. Gootnick,

Thank you for the time and effort you have spent in drafting the report "U.S. Territories: Public Debt Outlook – 2019 Update." The findings are critical toward illustrating the Commonwealth of the Northern Mariana Islands' (CNMI) efforts toward its public debt. We certainly appreciate the opportunity to be a part of the GAO's final report and hope that our contribution helps depict an accurate understanding of the Commonwealth's current economic standing.

The GAO findings, as discussed in the draft, report that the CNMI's total public debt outstanding has declined from $144.7 million in fiscal year 2015 to $116.3 million in fiscal year 2017, effectuating a decrease in its public debt by 20%. Per capita, the CNMI's total debt has declined from about $2,844.7 in fiscal year 2015, to about $2,307.8 in 2017. These numbers reflect the CNMI's economic growth in the past decade and supports the Commonwealth's assertion that it is both financially prudent and secure.

The draft report gives merit to the CNMI's steady increase in revenue after 2015 from revenues generated from casino operations and related businesses. The report further supports a boost in CNMI in tourism as a result of construction of new hotels, and increased tax collections.

Although the CNMI's public debt has improved across the board with its Gross Domestic Product (GDP) increasing, the GAO draft report notes that pension liabilities, coupled with the adverse impacts of Typhoons Mangkhut and Yutu on the Commonwealth's revenue present a fiscal risk that may affect the repayment of future public debt. As a result of the typhoons and projected reduction in revenue in fiscal year 2019, the Commonwealth has implemented cost-containment measures and reductions in spending to help offset the shortfall. The Commonwealth is hopeful that much needed financial reprieve will be provided through Congressional appropriation of funds from the disaster relief legislation for areas affected by major natural disasters.

Furthermore, as previously reported by the GAO, the Commonwealth still faces challenges with access to skilled workers. However, in 2018, Congress passed and the President enacted the Northern Mariana Islands U.S. Workforce Act, extending the temporary work permit program by ten years and increasing the number of work permits from 4,999 in fiscal year 2019 to 13,000 beginning on October 1, 2018, along with required decreases annually to 5,000 permits in fiscal year 2029, and then 1,000 permits in the first quarter of 2030. The enactment of the NMI U.S. Workforce Act provides the Commonwealth with a greater opportunity to exert efforts to build upon its workforce capacity over the ten-year period.

Thank you again for your hard work and diligence in putting this report together. I appreciate GAO's willingness to work collaboratively with the CNMI to produce a precise and detailed work product for implementation in the territories' financial planning processes. The discussed data is essential to the CNMI's self-assessments as well as our goal of enhancing the Commonwealth's financial standing in the coming years. I anticipate that the final report will assist us in meeting this objective.

I am hopeful that this report will shed light on the CNMI's dire need for Congressional action in our efforts to sustain and continue to grow our islands' economy.

Sincerely,

RALPH DLG. TORRES
GOVERNOR

APPENDIX VI: COMMENTS FROM THE GOVERNMENT OF GUAM

UFISINAN I MAGA'HÅGA
OFFICE OF THE GOVERNOR

LOURDES A. LEON GUERRERO
MAGA'HÅGA • GOVERNOR

JOSHUA F. TENORIO
SIGUNDO MAGA'LÅHI • LIEUTENANT GOVERNOR

June 3, 2019

Tranchau Kris Nguyen
Acting Director, Strategic Issues
United States Government Accountability Office
441 G. Street, N.W., Washington DC 20548

Re: Guam's Response to U.S. Territories: Public Debt Outlook – 2019 Update (GAO-19-525)

Dear Acting Director Nguyen,

Hafa Adai! Thank you for allowing the government of Guam the opportunity to review and respond to the Government Accountability Office (GAO) *U.S. Territories: Public Debt Outlook – 2019 (GAO-19-525)*. We appreciate the collaborative approach the GAO has taken to ensure the accuracy from which Guam is represented in its report. The government of Guam's comments below have been prepared by my Fiscal Discipline Team and it is my hope that the GAO considers the suggestions, recommendations, and explanations provided toward continuing to enhance these reports for the general public.

Public Debt Outstanding, Public Debt per Capita, & Public Debt as a Share of GDP

The government of Guam recommends that the methodology utilized by the GAO in determining public debt be revisited and reconsidered. In the draft GAO-19-525 Report and the prior U.S. Territories Public Debt Outlook (GAO-18-160), the GAO identified public debt to include both the primary government and component unit debt.

As was previously stated in the government of Guam's comments to the GAO-18-160 Report and as is the practice in the Municipal Finance Market, tax-supported debt (or the primary government debt) truly reflects the core of Guam's outstanding debt obligations. The inclusion of public enterprise or revenue bonds issued by the Guam Waterworks Authority (GWA), the Guam Power Authority (GPA), the A.B. Won Pat Guam International Airport Authority (GIAA), and the Jose D. Leon Guerrero Commercial Port (Port) does not take into consideration the unique differences the government of Guam as well as the U.S. territories have in relation to states, which may include school districts, cities, counties, and transportation districts.

RICARDO J. BORDALLO GOVERNOR'S COMPLEX · HAGÅTÑA, GUAM 96910
P.O. BOX 2950 · HAGÅTÑA, GUAM 96910
671.472.8931 · 671.472.8932/6

The GAO previously understood the uniqueness of a jurisdiction that has similar circumstances as those in the U.S. Territories in its November 1994 GAO/AIMD-95-19, District of Columbia Information on the District's Debt Report. In the GAO/AIMD-95-19 Report, the GAO calculated the District of Columbia's public debt per capita and stated the following:

> The District of Columbia's overall net debt per capita was $6,315, and the ratio of net debt to taxable real property was 8.1 percent. Although both ratios are high when compared with other cities, counties, or states, **comparing the District's debt limitations and amount of debt with other jurisdictions is problematic because of the unique nature of the District**. For example, **debt limits for state, counties, and cities would only affect the debts incurred to finance the functions carried out by the specific jurisdiction. In contrast, the District has a single debt limit applicable to carry out all its governmental functions, whether these functions are representative of those carried out by states, counties, or cities. Thus, comparing the District's ratios to state, county, or city debt ratios may not be a meaningful comparison to the extent the District's debt is used to finance functions that may overlap functions financed by state, county and city debt.** For example, the District's debt would include debt related to typical city functions (for example, police and fire protection) as well as debt associated with typical state and county functions (for example, motor vehicle and driver licensing). District officials also pointed out that other unique factors make comparing the District to other jurisdictions difficult. They noted that unlike most cities and counties, sales and income tax provide a substantial portion of the District's tax revenue. Therefore, the debt/taxable real property ratio is not meaningful to compare the District to other jurisdictions[1]. *Emphasis added*

Further to the discussion of the calculation of debt per capita, in the GAO/AMID-95-19 Report, the GAO relied upon Moody's Investors Service's calculation of "Overall net debt per capita[2]." The government of Guam highlights that the "Overall net debt per capita" noted:

> Amount of debt for a jurisdiction used in this calculation refers only to debt of that jurisdiction. For example, the debt per capita for a city would not include any debt of the state. In contrast, calculations of debt per capita of the District include debt that covers both city and state functions[3].

The GAO was keenly aware of the differing levels of governments found in states and local jurisdictions that may provide sufficient justification for the government of Guam's recommendation of calculating debt per capital less component unit debt or, a variation of calculating public debt per capita and public debt to nominal Gross Domestic Product (GDP) as discussed below.

---

[1] See GAO/AIMD-95-19 *District of Columbia Information on the District's Debt* published in November 1994: pages 10 – 11.
[2] See GAO/AIMD-95-19 *District of Columbia Information on the District's Debt* published in November 1994: Table 3 page 10.
[3] See GAO/AIMD-95-19 *District of Columbia Information on the District's Debt* published in November 1994: Footnote (a) on Table 3 page 10.

The government of Guam understands that the report does not intend to compare or rank the U.S. Territories[4] as it relates to its total public debt, its public debt per capita, or public debt as a percent of GDP nor does it attempt to compare such ratios to other U.S. states or jurisdictions. Given the lack of such comparisons and the apparent flexibility in the GAO's ability to represent such data and ratios, the government of Guam recommends that the report differentiate between primary government and component unit debt and the two separate "types" of public debt per capita and public debt to GDP as found in Tables 1 and 2.

Table 1.

Primary Government Debt, Primary Government Debt Per Capita, & Primary Government Debt to GDP FYs 2015 - 2017

	Primary Government	FY 2015	FY 2016	FY 2017
(a)	**Total Primary Government Debt[5]**	**1,075,112,614**	**1,115,052,231**	**1,096,752,318**
(b)	Population[6]	161,500	162,000	162,500
(a)/(b)	**Primary Government Debt Per Capita**	**6,657**	**6,883**	**6,749**
(c)	GDP[6]	5,710,000,000	5,793,000,000	5,859,000,000
(a)/(c)	**Primary Government Debt to GDP**	**18.8%**	**19.2%**	**18.7%**

Based on the government of Guam's calculations specific to tax-supported or primary government debt at the end of FY 2017, the debt per capita was **$6,749** and the Debt to GDP is **18.7%**.

Table 2.

Component Unit Debt, Component Unit Debt Per Capita, & Component Unit Debt to GDP FYs 2015 - 2017

	Component Units	FY 2015	FY 2016	FY 2017
(a)	**Total Component Units Debt[5]**	**1,321,848,825**	**1,408,949,539**	**1,387,701,636**
(b)	Population[6]	161,500	162,000	162,500
(a)/(b)	**Component Unit Debt Per Capita**	**8,185**	**8,697**	**8,540**
(c)	GDP[6]	5,710,000,000	5,793,000,000	5,859,000,000
(a)/(c)	**Component Unit Debt to GDP**	**23.1%**	**24.3%**	**23.7%**

Based on the government of Guam's calculations specific to public enterprise or component unit debt at the end of FY 2017, the debt per capita was **$8,540** and the Debt to GDP is **23.7%**.

[4] See GAO-18-160 *U.S. Territories Public Debt Outlook* published in October 2017: GAO Comment # 8 to Guam, page 77.

[5] Data taken from the *Schedule of Outstanding Debt* found in the FYs 2015 through 2017 Government-Wide Audited Financial Statements; pages 206 (FY15), 211 (FY16), and 217 (FY17). Amounts do not include premiums and discounts on bonds payable.

[6] Data taken from the U.S. Department of Commerce, Bureau of Economic Analysis.

The government of Guam believes that presenting these two calculations of public debt per capita and public debt as a share of GDP will enhance the overall report and provide clarity as to the uniqueness of the U.S. Territories as was identified in the aforementioned previous GAO report on the District of Columbia.

Net Pension Liability Explanation

The draft GAO-19-525 Report notes that the government of Guam's Net Pension Liability (NPL) increased from $1.2 billion to $1.6 billion and references several changes having been made to the government of Guam's retirement system that took effect January 1, 2018, including increasing the contribution rate and creating a new defined benefit plan for existing employees. It appears to represent that such an increase in the NPL was due to this new retirement plan that will have took effect three months after FY 2017 ended. The government of Guam would like to provide clarity on this issue.

Pursuant to the requirements of Government Accounting Standards Board (GASB) Statement No. 73[7], such standard was implemented as of the FY 2017 Government-Wide Audited Financial Statements[8]. Although this prospectively added an Ad Hoc Cost of Living Allowances (COLA) and Supplemental Annuity Benefits for Defined Benefit Plan (DBP) Retirees and Ad Hoc COLA Plan for Defined Contribution Retirement System Retirees (DCRS), if such implementation was retroactively applied or implemented in FYs 2015 and 2016, the NPL may not have represented a material change in FY 2017. But, prospectively adding these two additional items to the NPL adjusted the NPL by approximately $163 million and $41.07 million, respectively[9], totaling $204.07 million. Additionally, the Ad Hoc COLA Plan and Supplemental Annuity Benefits for DBP Retirees and the Ad Hoc COLA Plan for DCRS Retirees do represent contractual pension commitments, rather they are an annual consideration in the budgetary process.

Additionally, the Discount Rate utilized to calculate the NPL in the FY 2015 Government-Wide Audited Financial Statements was 7.0%[10] whereas the FY 2017 Discount Rate used was 6.70%. Due to a lower Discount Rate used in FY 2017, the NPL increased as compared to FY 2015.

These two factors; (1) the implementation of GASB Statement No. 73 and (2) the use of a lower Discount Rate in FY 2017 as compared to FY 2015, explain much of the increase in the NPL from $1.2 billion in FY 2015 to $1.6 billion in FY 2017. Once again, the creation of a new DB pension plan[11] as cited in the draft GAO-19-525 Report will have an impact on the FY 2018 Government-Wide Audited Financial Statements but does not have an impact as of the period scope of the draft GAO-19-525 Report.

Pension Liabilities a Minimal Fiscal Risk: Elimination of the Unfunded Actuarial Accrued Liability by May 1, 2033

[7] GASB Statement No. 73 is Accounting and Financial Reporting for Pensions and Related Assets that are not within the Scope of GASB Statement No. 68, and Amendments to Certain Provisions of GASB Statements No. 67 and No. 68

[8] See FY 2017 Government-Wide Audited Financial Statements: Note 1(X).

[9] See FY 2017 Government-Wide Audited Financial Statements: Note 11(A).

[10] See FY 2015 Government-Wide Audited Financial Statements: Note 11(A).

[11] See Guam Public Law 33-186.

The government of Guam's Unfunded Actuarial Accrued Liability (UAAL) is required to be fully funded by May 1, 2033 in accordance with Guam law[12]. Such Guam law requires that the UAAL be amortized over a period of eighty-two (82) years following May 1, 1951 pursuant to an amendment extending such amortization period by two (2) years. The government of Guam has continued to rely upon the annual Actuarial Valuation conducted and provided by the Government of Guam Retirement Fund (GGRF) to ensure the Contribution Rate to be paid as a percent of total salaries of all members of the GGRF (all government of Guam employees) meet the actuarially determined rate.

An amortization period of fifteen (15) to twenty (20) years has been found to be the preferred range for UAAL amortization periods by the Government Finance Officers Association Best Practice, the Conference of Consulting Actuaries Public Plans Community, and the Academy of Actuaries.

Although the draft GAO-19-525 Report states "Pension liabilities present a fiscal risk" as a Key Finding, the government of Guam suggests that given an amortization period as of the end of FY 2017 of fifteen (15) years and eight (8) months and a statutorily required funded period of May 1, 2033, the draft GAO-19-525 Report could identify the pension liabilities as **not**, or minimally posing, a fiscal risk given the aforementioned preferred range for UAAL amortization periods.

It is my hope that the GAO fully considers the recommendations and explanations provided by my Fiscal Discipline Team toward further enhancing the GAO's report on U.S. Territories' Debt. Once again, thank you for the opportunity to provide an official response to the draft GAO-19-525 Report. If you have any further questions or concerns, please do not hesitate to contact my Fiscal Discipline Team.

Senseramente,

Lou Leon Guerrero

LOURDES A. LEON GUERRERO
Maga'hågan Guåhan
Governor of Guam

[12] See § 8137(b), Chapter 8, Title 4 of the Guam Code Annotated.

Appendix VII: Accessible Data

Data Tables

Accessible data for figure 1: composition of Puerto Rico's public debt, fiscal year 2016

Puerto Rico's Public Debt	In billions	Percentage
Total debt	65.2	
Primary government debt	40.8	62.6%
Component unit debt	24.3	37.4%
All other component units	2.5	3.8%
Puerto Rico Highway & Trans.	4.3	6.7%
Government Development Bank	4.0	6.1%
Puerto Rico Aqueduct & Sewer	4.5	6.8%
Puerto Rico Electricity & Power	9.1	13.9%

Accessible data for figure 2: composition of Puerto Rico's revenue, fiscal year 2016

Puerto Rico's Revenue	In billions	Percentage
Total revenue	30.0	
Program revenue	17.7	59.0%
General revenue	12.3	41.0%
Non-tax revenue	1.8	6.1%
Total taxes	10.4	34.9%
Other	0.1	0.5%
Sales and use	2.3	7.7%
Excise	3.4	11.5%
Income	4.6	15.2%

Accessible data for figure 3: actual vs. projected growth in Puerto Rico Gross National Product (GNP), 2005-2023

Fiscal Year	Actual - GAO analysis	Projected – FOMB October 2018	Projected – FOMB, May 2019	Projected - Puerto Rico Government
2005	1.94			
2006	0.51			
2007	2.92			
2008	-2.86			
2009	-3.83			
2010	-3.57			
2011	-1.68			
2012	0.54			
2013	-0.13			
2014	-1.76			
2015	-0.81			
2016	-1.60			
2017	-2.98			
2018	-4.67	-8	-4.7	-7.6
2019		7.9	4.0	4.8
2020		5.5	1.5	2.8
2021		2.9	-0.9	2.6
2022		2.5	0.2	2
2023		-0.7	0.1	0.3

Accessible data for figure 4: composition of United States Virgin Islands' public debt, fiscal year 2016

U.S. Virgin Islands' Public Debt	In dollars	Percentage
Total debt	2.6 billion	
Primary government debt	2.2 billion	85.2%
Component unit debt	386.0 million	14.8%
All other component units	6.9 million	0.3%
Port Authority.	49.3 million	1.9%
University of Virgin Islands	78.8 million	3.0%
Water and Power Authority	250.9 million	9.6%

Accessible data for figure 5: composition of United States Virgin Islands' revenue, fiscal year 2016

U.S. Virgin Islands' Revenue	In dollars	Percentage
Total revenue	2.3 billion	
Program revenue	1.0 billion	44.8%
General revenue	1.3 billion	55.2%
Non-tax revenue	390.6 million	16.7%
Total taxes	898.2 million	38.5%
Real property	54.1 million	2.3%
Other	68.3 million	2.9%
Gross receipts	160.8 million	6.9%
Excise	242.0 million	10.4%
Income	373.0 million	16.0%

Accessible data for figure 6: composition of American Samoa's public debt, fiscal year 2017

American Samoa's public debt	Percentage	In millions
Component units	26.4	32.3
Primary government debt	73.6	89.9
Total public debt		122.2

Accessible data for figure 7: composition of CNMI's public debt, fiscal year 2017

CNMI's Public Debt	In millions	Percentage
Total debt	116.3	100%
Primary government debt	76.0	65.4%
Component unit debt	40.2	34.6%
Commonwealth port authority	39.9	34.3%
Commonwealth development authority	0.3 million	0.3%

Accessible data for figure 8: composition of Guam's public debt, fiscal year 2017

Guam's Public Debt	In dollars	Percentage
Total debt	2.6 billion	100%
Primary government debt	1.2 billion	45.6%
Component unit debt	1.4 billion	54.4%
Other component units	70.9 million	2.7%
Guam airport authority	226.6 million	8.7%
Guam waterworks authority	533.9 million	20.4%
Guam Power Authority	592.4 million	22.6%

In: Key Government Reports. Vol. 33 ISBN: 978-1-53616-566-1
Editor: Ernest Clark

Chapter 5

THE NATION'S FISCAL HEALTH: ACTIONS NEEDED TO ACHIEVE LONG-TERM FISCAL SUSTAINABILITY*

Gene L. Dodaro

THE FEDERAL GOVERNMENT IS ON AN UNSUSTAINABLE LONG-TERM FISCAL PATH

Congress and the administration face serious economic, security, and social challenges that require difficult policy choices in the near term in setting national priorities and helping promote economic growth. This will influence the level of federal spending and how the government obtains needed resources.

At the same time, the federal government is highly leveraged in debt by historical norms. For example, debt held by the public as a share of

* This is an edited, reformatted and augmented version of United States Government Accountability Office; Testimony before the Committee on the Budget U.S. Senate, Publication No. GAO-19-611T, dated June 26, 2019.

GDP at the end of fiscal year 2018 was 78 percent, compared to an average of 46 percent since 1946.

Over the long term, the imbalance between spending and revenue that is built into current law and policy is projected to lead to continued growth of the federal deficit and debt held by the public as a share of GDP.

Debt held by the public was $15.8 trillion—or 78 percent of gross domestic product (GDP)—at the end of fiscal year 2018. It is projected to surpass its historical high of 106 percent within 13 to 20 years, and climb between about 250 to 500 percent by 2092, according to projections by GAO and others (see figure). Absent policy changes, the current federal fiscal path is unsustainable.

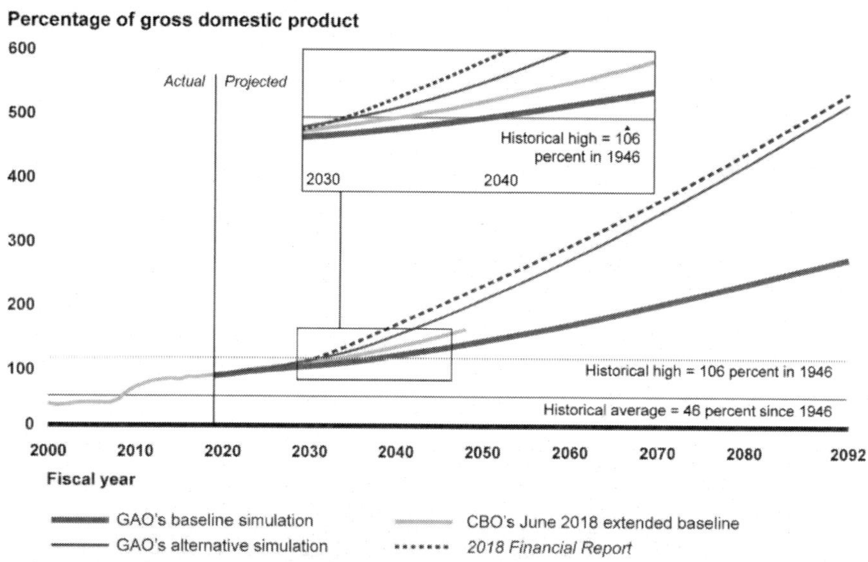

Source: GAO, Congressional Bydget Office, and 2018 Financial Report. | GAO-19-611T.

Note: GAO's simulations incorporate CBO's January 2019 baseline, which assumes lower emergency spending than CBO's June 2018 extended baseline, consistent with amounts appropriated at the time of that report.

Debt Held by the Public under Projections from GAO, the Congressional Budget Office (CBO), and the *Fiscal Year 2018 Financial Report of the United States Government (2018 Financial Report).*

In the long-term, the key drivers of growing federal spending are health care programs (due to the aging population and per beneficiary spending) and net interest. Net interest is projected to eventually become the largest category of federal spending, surpassing:

- Nondefense discretionary spending in 2024,
- Defense discretionary spending in 2025,
- Medicare spending in 2042, and
- Social Security spending in 2046.

In 2092, according to GAO's alternative simulation, net interest is projected to account for about 40 percent of federal spending, compared to 8 percent in fiscal year 2018.

IMPENDING FISCAL PRESSURES ADD TO NEED FOR TIMELY ACTION

The federal budget is further strained by fiscal pressures, including known financial challenges for key programs (as shown below), and risks like natural disasters that could lead to unknown amounts of future spending. The longer action is delayed, the more drastic the changes will have to be.

In addition, GAO has identified numerous opportunities for Congress and executive branch agencies to take steps in the near term that could improve the federal government's fiscal condition. These opportunities include addressing billions of dollars in improper payments and the over $400 billion annual tax gap, evaluating the significant amount of revenue forgone through tax expenditures, as well as implementing GAO recommendations for defense operations. These actions would improve stewardship over federal resources in the near term. However, these actions alone cannot put the federal government on a sustainable fiscal path.

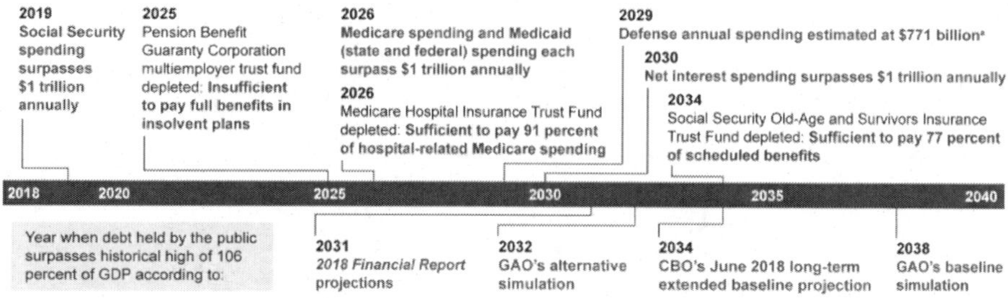

Source: Trustees for Social Security and Medicare, Congressional Budget Office (CBO), Centers for Medicare & Medicaid Services, GAO, and 2018 Financial Report. | GAO-19-611T.

[a]CBO did not report defense spending projections separately from total discretionary spending in its long-term projections after 2029.

A LONG-TERM PLAN IS NEEDED TO ACHIEVE FISCAL SUSTAINABILITY

To address the growing federal debt and put the government on a more sustainable fiscal path, policymakers will need to consider a long-term plan that addresses the entire range of federal activities including both revenue and spending.

A long-term fiscal plan could include fiscal rules and targets that promote fiscal sustainability by imposing numerical guidelines on the budget (known as targets). Types of fiscal rules include:

- Budget balance rules that constrain deficit levels,
- Debt rules that limit public debt as a percentage of GDP,
- Revenue rules that set ceilings or floors on revenues, and
- Expenditure rules that limit spending.

Fiscal rules have been used by the United States and other countries to help promote fiscal sustainability. According to the International Monetary Fund, as of 2015 more than 70 countries had combined two or more fiscal rules. For example, the European Union's stability and growth pact combines an expenditure rule, budget balance rule, and a debt rule (e.g., debt-to-GDP), which are designed to ensure that countries in the European Union pursue sound public finances and coordinate their fiscal policies.

Rules can be designed to balance flexibility and enforceability. For example:

- Fiscal rules can include clauses allowing for flexibility to help respond to fiscal risks or unexpected events like recessions or natural disasters.
- Institutions like independent fiscal councils can help formulate and implement sound fiscal policy.
- Correction mechanisms can be designed to trigger automatically to respond to past deviations from the rule.

It will be important that any future U.S. fiscal rules target the right factors, enforce budget agreements, and limit exemptions. A fiscal target that sets a common goal to control the debt, and well-designed rules that form a path to achieve that target, could form part of a long-term plan for fiscal sustainability.

Unlike fiscal rules, the current approach used to set the U.S. government debt limit is not a control on debt but rather an after-the-fact measure that restricts authority to borrow. It does not restrict Congress and the President's ability to enact spending and revenue legislation that affects the level of debt. Failure to increase or suspend the debt limit in a timely manner disrupts the market for Treasury securities and can increase borrowing costs. Congress should consider alternative approaches to the debt limit as part of a long-term fiscal plan. GAO has recommended possible alternatives such as linking action on the debt limit to the budget resolution.

Chairman Enzi, Ranking Member Sanders, and Members of the Committee:

Thank you for the opportunity to be here today to discuss our nation's fiscal health and the actions needed to chart a more sustainable long- term fiscal path. Congress and the administration face serious economic, security, and social challenges that require difficult policy choices in the near term in setting national priorities and helping promote economic growth. These choices will influence the level and composition of federal spending and how the government obtains needed resources. Policymakers also face a federal government highly leveraged in debt by historical norms and on an unsustainable long-term fiscal path caused by an imbalance between revenue and spending that is built into current law and policy.

Decisions in the near term to support economic growth and address national priorities need to be accompanied by a broader fiscal plan to put the federal government on a sustainable long-term path. Such a plan is essential to ensure that the United States remains in a strong economic position to meet its security and social needs, as well as to preserve flexibility to address unforeseen events, such as natural disasters, economic downturns, wars, and cyberattacks.

Today, I will discuss the nation's fiscal health, specifically focusing on issues such as the federal government's unsustainable fiscal outlook, growing fiscal pressures that could further strain the federal budget, and the need for actions to address the growing debt. I will also discuss opportunities for Congress and the executive branch to take steps in the near term that would help improve the government's fiscal condition.

In April 2019, we issued our third annual report on the nation's fiscal health.[1] The report illuminated the need for a long-term fiscal plan by outlining the fiscal condition of the U.S. government and its future path based on current fiscal policy. My statement is based upon our 2019 annual report on the nation's fiscal health; our work on natural disasters and climate change; GAO's 2019 High-Risk List; the 2019 fragmentation, overlap, and duplication annual report; and other related work.[2] We also reviewed relevant fiscal laws and used our long-term fiscal outlook model to simulate potential fiscal changes to achieve certain debt targets.

---

[1] GAO, *The Nation's Fiscal Health: Action Is Needed to Address the Federal Government's Fiscal Future,* GAO-19-314SP (Washington, D.C.: Apr. 10, 2019).

[2] For example, GAO, *2019 Annual Report: Additional Opportunities to Reduce Fragmentation, Overlap, and Duplication and Achieve Billions in Financial Benefits,* GAO-19-285SP (Washington, D.C.: May 21, 2019) and *High-Risk Series: Substantial Efforts Needed to Achieve Greater Progress on High-Risk Areas*, GAO-19-157SP (Washington, D.C.: Mar. 6, 2019). A list of our related products is included at the end of this statement.

These efforts are based upon work conducted in accordance with all sections of GAO's Quality Assurance Framework that are relevant to our objectives. The framework requires that we plan and perform the engagement to obtain sufficient and appropriate evidence to meet our stated objectives and to discuss any limitations in our work. We believe that the information and data obtained, and the analysis conducted, provide a reasonable basis for any findings and conclusions. More details on the scope and methodology for our reports can be found in the full reports cited throughout this statement.

THE FEDERAL GOVERNMENT IS ON AN UNSUSTAINABLE LONG- TERM FISCAL PATH

Over the long term, the imbalance between spending and revenue that is built into current law and policy is projected to lead to continued growth of the deficit and debt held by the public as a share of gross domestic product (GDP). This situation—in which debt grows faster than GDP—means the current federal fiscal path is unsustainable.

Growing Debt-to-GDP Ratio

For most of the nation's history, the debt-to-GDP ratio tended to increase during wartime and decline during peacetime. Historically, recessions have contributed to increases in this ratio, but the ratio has declined with economic recovery. This pattern is visible in Figure 1. Publicly held debt as a share of GDP peaked at 106 percent just after World War II (in 1946) and has averaged 46 percent since then. However, debt has risen in more recent years, reaching 78 percent of GDP at the end of fiscal year 2018.

Total debt is comprised of debt held by the public (the value of all federal securities sold to investors outside of the federal government) and intragovernmental debt (debt held by government accounts). As of the end of May 2019, the total federal debt was about $22 trillion, consisting of about $16.2 trillion in debt held by the public and about $5.8 trillion in intragovernmental debt.

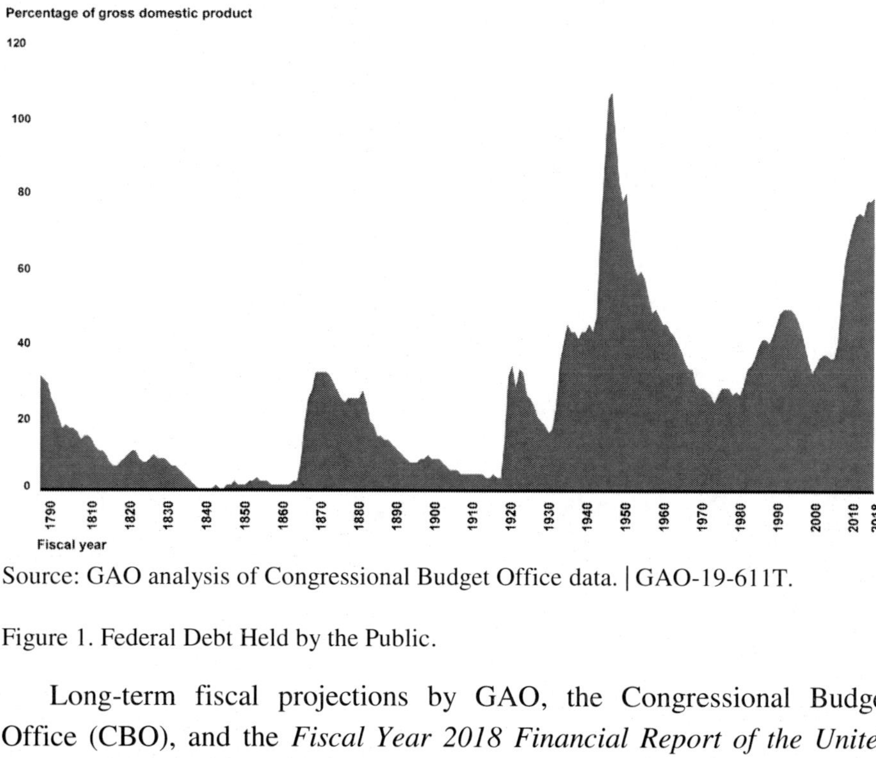

Source: GAO analysis of Congressional Budget Office data. | GAO-19-611T.

Figure 1. Federal Debt Held by the Public.

Long-term fiscal projections by GAO, the Congressional Budget Office (CBO), and the *Fiscal Year 2018 Financial Report of the United States Government (2018 Financial Report)*[3] all show that debt held by the public as a share of GDP will grow substantially in the coming years.[4] All of these projections show that, absent a change in policy, debt held by the public would grow to be greater than the size of the U.S. economy and it

[3] See GAO, *Financial Audit: Fiscal Years 2018 and 2017 Consolidated Financial Statements of the U.S. Government,* GAO-19-294R (Washington, D.C.: Mar. 28, 2019). The Financial Report of the United States Government is prepared by the Secretary of the Treasury in coordination with the Director of the Office of Management and Budget.

[4] The timing and pace of debt-to-GDP growth depend on the underlying data and assumptions made in the projections. All projections involve some degree of uncertainty. For more information on these long-term fiscal projections and their assumptions, see GAO-19-314SP.

would surpass its historical high of 106 percent of GDP within the next 13 to 20 years (see Figure 2.)

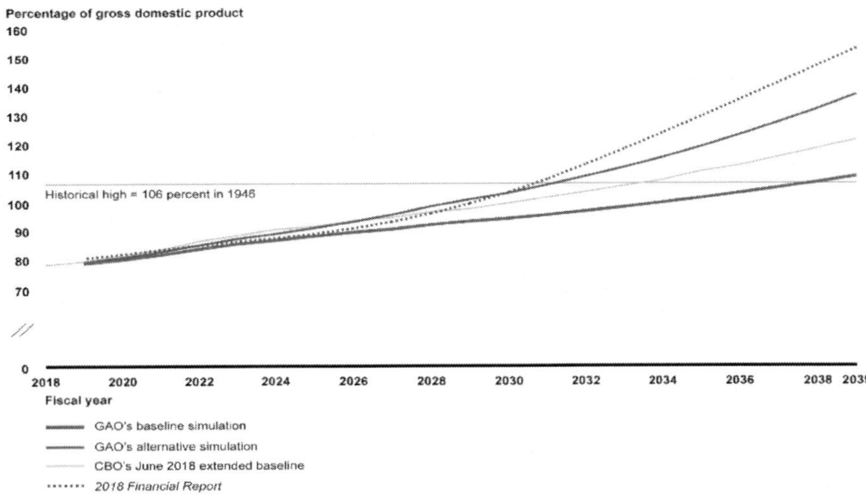

Source: GAO Congressional Budget Office, and 2018 Financial Report. | GAO-19-811T.

Note: GAO's baseline simulation generally assumes current laws continue into the future (e.g., that tax provisions expire as scheduled), while GAO's alternative simulation changes some of the assumptions to reflect historical trends, rather than current law (e.g., that tax provisions that are scheduled to expire are extended). GAO's simulations incorporate CBO's January 2019 baseline, which assumes lower emergency spending than CBO's June 2018 extended baseline, consistent with amounts appropriated at the time of that report. For more information on GAO's, CBO's, and the *2018 Financial Report's* long-term fiscal projections and their assumptions, see GAO-19-314SP.

Figure 2. Debt Held by the Public as Share of Gross Domestic Product, 2018-2039.

Further, all the projections show that debt held by the public as a share of GDP will continue to grow to unsustainable levels over the long term. Figure 3 shows that debt held by the public as a share of GDP grows substantially in all the projections we discuss in this statement. In 2092, debt held by the public is expected to be more than 250 percent of GDP under GAO's baseline simulation, and more than 500 percent of GDP under GAO's alternative simulation and the *2018 Financial Report* projections.[5]

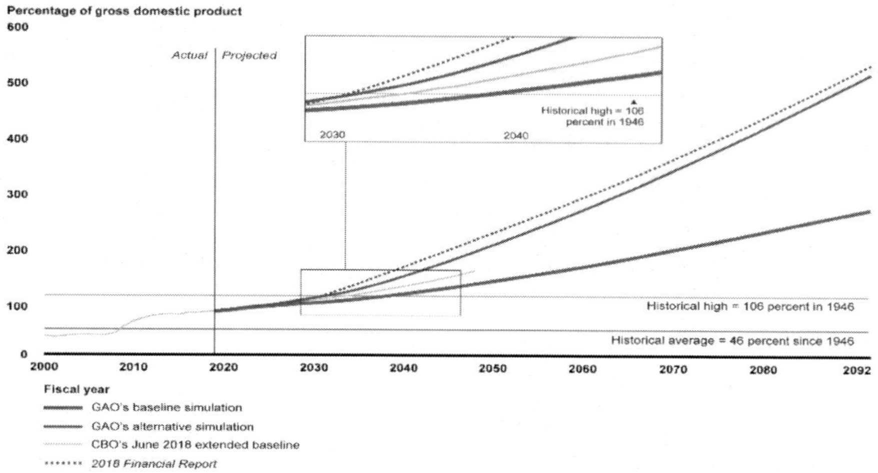

Source: GAO, Congressional Budget Office, and 2018 Financial Report. | GAO-19-611T.

Note: GAO's baseline simulation generally assumes current laws continue into the future (e.g., that tax provisions expire as scheduled), while GAO's alternative simulation changes some of the assumptions to reflect historical trends, rather than current law (e.g., that tax provisions that are scheduled to expire are extended). GAO's simulations incorporate CBO's January 2019 baseline, which assumes lower emergency spending than CBO's June 2018 extended baseline, consistent with amounts appropriated at the time of that report. For more information on GAO's, CBO's, and the *2018 Financial Report's* long-term fiscal projections and their assumptions, see GAO-19-314SP.

Figure 3. Debt Held by the Public as Share of Gross Domestic Product, 2000-2092.

Both the current fiscal condition and the long-term projections of fiscal sustainability are driven by the economy and by laws enacted by Congress and the President. In fiscal year 2018, for example, the tax reform law, commonly known as the Tax Cuts and Jobs Act, the Bipartisan Budget Act of 2018, and the Consolidated Appropriations Act, 2018, increased the

[5] CBO projects that debt held by the public will surpass 150 percent of GDP in 2048, the latest year included in its June 2018 extended baseline.

projected debt-to-GDP ratio in all of the projections discussed earlier. CBO estimated that legislation enacted from June 2017 to April 2018—primarily these three laws—would increase deficits by $2.7 trillion between 2018 and 2027.[6] According to CBO, annual federal deficits are projected to reach $1 trillion in 2022, compared to $779 billion in fiscal year 2018.

Future policy decisions about levels of federal spending, revenues, the federal role in the delivery of health care, and other areas could also change the projections. In addition, changes in projected health care costs, interest rates, spending levels, revenues, or economic growth would likely affect the debt-to-GDP ratio. For example, a recession or other economic crisis would likely increase the debt-to-GDP ratio beyond its projected levels because of a decline in GDP growth, and an increase in spending on federal social safety net programs.

Heath Care Spending and Net Interest Remain Key Drivers of Long-Term Federal Spending

Although growth in health care spending has slowed recently, total health care spending (public and private) in the United States continues to grow faster than the economy. Federal spending for major health care programs—Medicare, Medicaid, the Children's Health Insurance Program, and federal subsidies for health insurance purchased through the marketplaces established by the Patient Protection and Affordable Care Act and related spending—makes up about a quarter of the federal budget. Federal health care spending also accounts for more than a quarter of total public and private health care spending. As figure 4 shows, this spending has historically exceeded the growth of GDP and is projected to continue to do so.

[6] CBO's April 2018 projections also estimated an additional $1 trillion in reductions to projected deficits because of changes to its economic forecast. This reduction is almost entirely because of increased projections of revenues, about half of which is attributable to the macroeconomic feedback related to the Tax Cuts and Jobs Act.

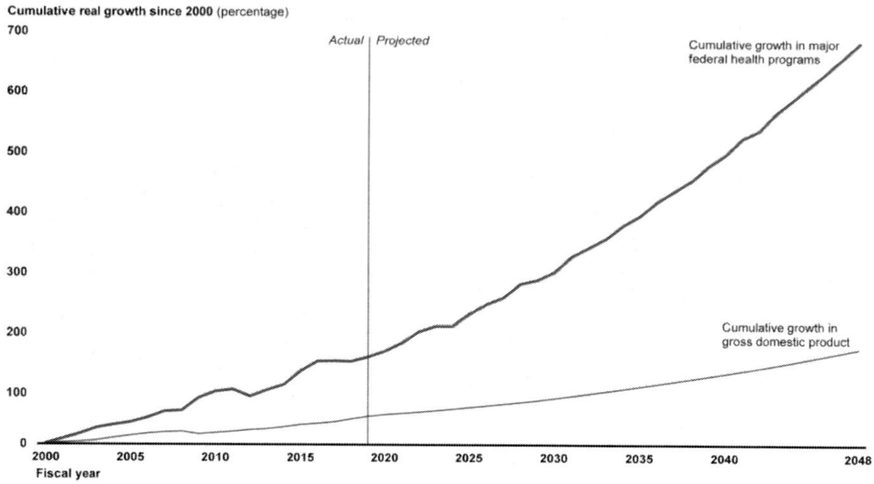

Source: GAO analysis of Congressional Budget Office and Bureau of Economic Analysis data. | GAO-19-611T.

Note: Cumulative growth in both gross domestic product (GDP) and federal spending on major health care programs has been adjusted for inflation. GDP is the value of all goods and services produced in a country in a given year. Major federal health care programs consist of Medicare, Medicaid, the Children's Health Insurance Program, and federal subsidies for health insurance purchased through the marketplaces established by the Patient Protection and Affordable Care Act and related spending.

Figure 4. Federal Spending on Major Health Care Programs Grows Faster Than Gross Domestic Product.

In the long term, growth in federal spending on health care is driven by increasing enrollment in health care programs—particularly in Medicare, stemming primarily from the aging population—and by the increase in health care spending per beneficiary.[7]

- Aging population. In its 2018 long-term budget outlook report, CBO projected that, by 2048, 22 percent of the population will be age 65 or older, compared to 16 percent in 2018. This demographic trend is largely driven by lower fertility rates and increases in life expectancy. The trend has been accelerated by the

[7] See appendix II for our recommendations to help control the costs of Medicare and Medicaid.

relatively large baby boom generation, which began turning 65 in 2011 (see figure 5). As the number of people older than 65 increases, Medicare and Medicaid enrollment is expected to increase.[8]

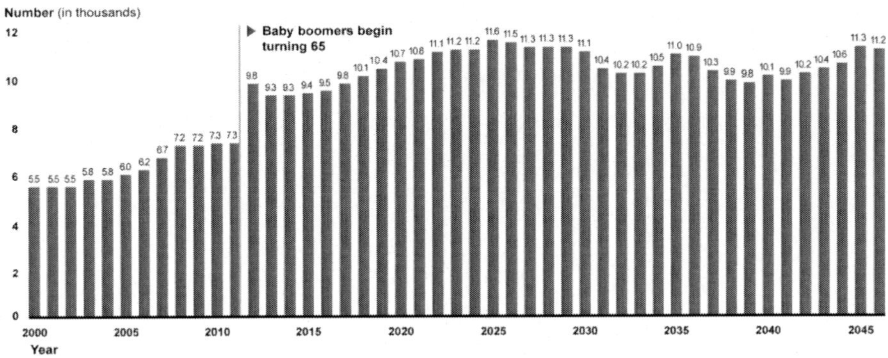

Source: GAO analysis of U.S. Census Bureau information. | GAO-19-611T.
Note: Census data estimates of population are as of July 1 in each year.

Figure 5. Daily Average Number of People Turning 65.

- Per beneficiary spending. The amount of money spent on health care per person has historically risen faster than per capita economic output and is projected to do so in the future. In its 2018 long-term budget outlook report, CBO projected that the growth in health care spending per person will account for about two-thirds of the increase in spending for the major health care programs as a share of GDP between 2018 and 2048.

Both the *2018 Financial Report's* long-term fiscal projections and GAO's simulations show spending on net interest growing such that over the long term it becomes the largest category of spending.[9]

---

[8] For more information on Medicare and Medicaid, see GAO, Medicare and Medicaid – High Risk, accessed June 5, 2019, https://www.gao.gov/key_issues/medicare_payment_management_integrity/issue_summary and https://www.gao.gov/key_issues/medicaid_financing_access_integrity/issue_summary.

[9] CBO's projections in its June 2018 long-term outlook report also show net interest growing as a percentage of total spending. However, since CBO's June 2018 extended baseline

According to CBO, spending on net interest totaled $325 billion in 2018 (8 percent of total federal spending), which is already larger than some other categories of spending, such as agriculture, transportation, veterans' benefits, and veterans' services combined. As shown in figure 6, spending on net interest is projected to continue to grow, surpassing:

- Nondefense discretionay spending in 2024,
- Defense discretionary spending in 2025,
- Medicare spending in 2042, and
- Social security spending in 2046.

In 2092, net interest is projected to account for about 40 percent of federal spending, according to GAO's alternative simulation.

Interest spending grows for two main reasons:

- Growing debt. At any given interest rate (above zero percent), interest payments increase as the debt grows. Debt held by the public will continue to increase as the federal government borrows money to finance the annual deficit (including interest costs) and for other cash needs (including government lending for student loans). The federal government is paying the interest on the debt held by the public and not paying down the total principal outstanding.
- Increases in interest rates. Increases in interest rates have a compounding effect on debt. For any given level of debt, a change in interest rates changes interest costs. In recent years, interest rates on Department of the Treasury (Treasury) securities have remained low, so interest costs have been low. However, CBO projects that the average interest rate on all debt held by the public will rise to 4.4 percent in 2048, compared to 2.4 percent in 2018 (see Figure 7). In its June 2018 long-term budget outlook report, CBO also noted that since the trend of increasing interest rates

projections only go out to 2048, spending on net interest does not quite overtake Social Security spending in the projection period.

reflects long-term economic trends, it would be likely to continue even at the current debt level.[10]

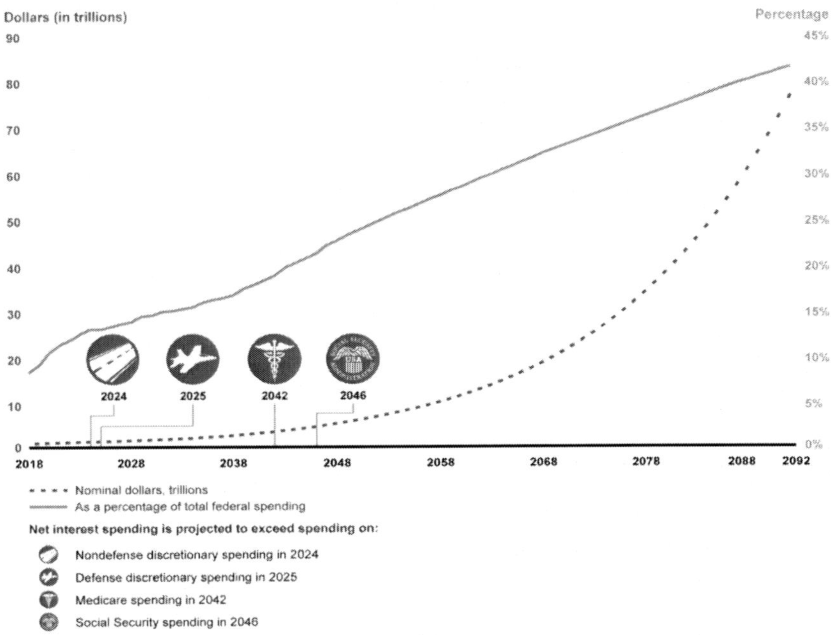

Source: GAO and GAO analysis of Congressional Budget Office data. | GAO-19-611T.

Note: Projected spending on net interest, Medicare, and Social Security is based on GAO's 2019 alternative simulation. Projected nondefense discretionary and defense discretionary spending is based on the Congressional Budget Office's January 2019 baseline budget projections.

Figure 6. Net Interest Spending in Dollars and as a Percentage of Total Federal Spending.

---

[10] CBO regularly updates its economic projections, including its projections of interest rates, as part of its reports on the 10-year budget and economic outlook.

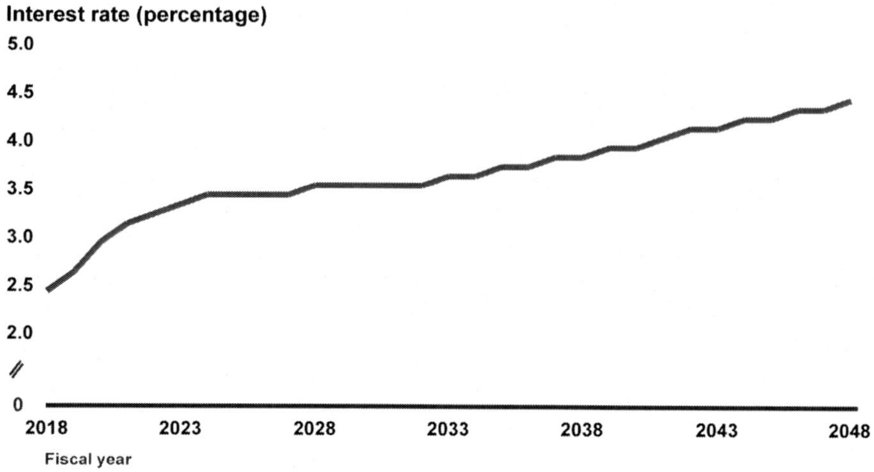

Source: GAO analysis of CBO data. | GAO-19-611T.

Figure 7. Congressional Budget Office (CBO) Projections of the Average Interest Rate on All Federal Debt Held by the Public, Fiscal Years 2018-2048.

Impending Fiscal Pressures Add to Need for Timely Action

Growing pressures further strain the federal budget and are contributing to the growing debt. These pressures include known impending financial challenges for major programs, as well as fiscal risks (such as spending on natural disasters) that could lead to unknown amounts of future spending. As shown in figure 8, annual spending for some major programs, such as Social Security and Medicare, is expected to each surpass $1 trillion. Several key program trust fund balances are projected to be depleted in coming years if no changes are made. The longer action to address these issues is delayed, the more drastic the changes will have to be.

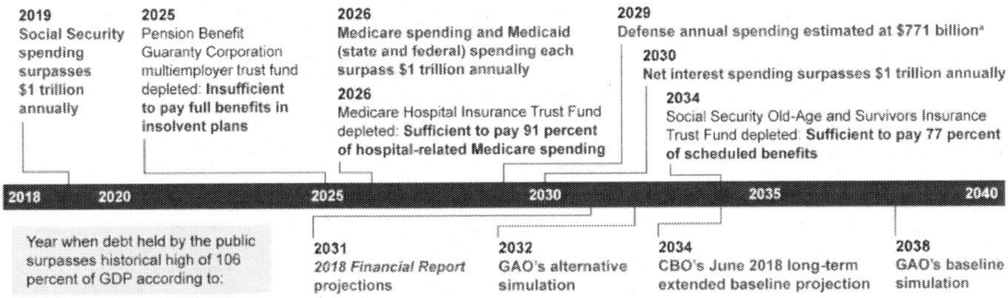

Source: Trustees for Social Security and Medicare. Congressional Budget Office (CBO), Centers for Medicare & Medicaid Services, GAO, and 2018 Financial Report. | GAO-19-6111T.

[a]CBO did not report defense spending projections separately from total discretionary spending in its long-term projections after 2029.

Figure 8. Key Dates for Major Programs and Future Debt.

Examples of Federal Fiscal Risks

- **Housing finance.** The federal government continues to provide significant support to the housing finance market, even though the market has largely recovered since the 2007 to 2009 financial crisis. Congress should consider establishing objectives for the future federal role in housing finance, and housing and regulatory agencies should take actions to help manage mortgage-related risk, among other things.
- **Surface transportation.** Repairing and upgrading our nation's surface transportation system will cost hundreds of billions of dollars, according to estimates. Congress needs to pass a long-term, sustainable solution for funding surface transportation.
- **The Pension Benefit Guaranty Corporation (PBGC).** PBGC's liabilities exceeded its assets by about $51 billion as of the end of fiscal year 2018. The financial stability of PBGC's single- and multiemployer programs faces many structural challenges that require congressional action.

Source: GAO. | GAO-19-611T.

Failure to act will lead to an increasingly constrained federal budget, limiting the federal government's flexibility to respond quickly and adequately to emerging issues and unforeseen events. Economic downturns, natural disasters, wars, cyberattacks, and health pandemics are among the events that pose fiscal risks.[11] Better understanding fiscal risks can help policymakers anticipate changes in future spending and can enhance oversight of federal resources. We have recommended ways for Congress and executive branch agencies to address several fiscal risks (see text box). For more information on these risks and our recommendations to address them, see appendix I. These risks are not fully budgeted for and could affect the government's future fiscal condition.

Natural Disasters and Climate Change Create Fiscal Exposures

An example of a fiscal exposure facing the nation is the rising number of natural disasters and increasing state, local, and tribal reliance on federal disaster assistance. Such assistance can come from federal responsibilities, programs, and activities, such as national flood insurance, that may legally commit or create the expectation for future spending. Federal agencies can become involved in responding to a disaster when effective response and recovery are beyond the capabilities of the state and affected local governments. In such cases, the Robert T. Stafford Disaster Relief and Emergency Assistance Act (Stafford Act), permits the President to declare a major disaster in response to a request by the governor of a state or territory or by the chief executive of a tribal government.[12] Overall, the number of disaster declarations has fluctuated over the years, reaching a high of 98 disasters in fiscal year 2011 (see Figure 9). There were 55 disasters declared in fiscal year 2018.

[11] Fiscal risks or fiscal exposures are responsibilities, programs, and activities that may legally commit the federal government to future spending, or create expectations for future spending based on current policy, past practices, or other factors. See our infographic on federal fiscal risks at https://www.gao.gov/assets/670/668649.pdf.

[12] 42 U.S.C. § 5170.

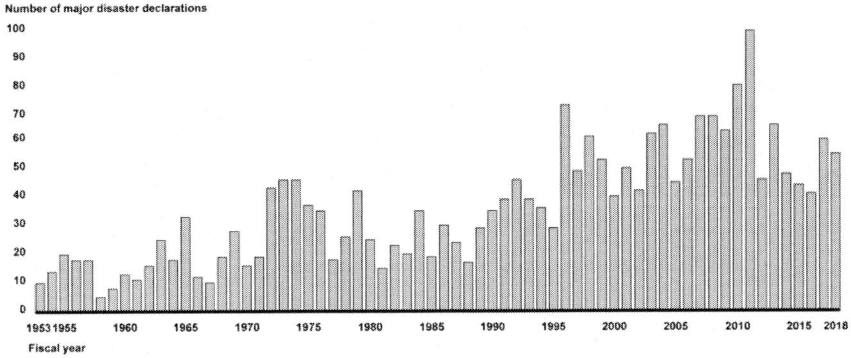

Source: GAO analysis of Federal Emergency Management Agency data. | GAO-19-611T.

Figure 9. Number of Major Disaster Declarations, Fiscal Years 1953–2018.

In addition, associated requests for disaster assistance could increase the federal government's fiscal exposure. From 2008 through 2016, the Federal Emergency Management Agency (FEMA) received 294 Individual Assistance declaration requests from states, U.S. territories, and tribes to help individuals meet their immediate needs after a disaster.[13] Of these requests, the President declared 168 and denied 126 requests.

Since 2005, federal funding for disaster assistance has totaled at least $450 billion,[14] most recently for catastrophic hurricanes, flooding, wildfires, and other losses in 2017 and 2018. The Disaster Relief Fund is the primary source of federal disaster assistance for state, local, territorial,

---

[13] We have previously reported that requests to the federal government for Individual Assistance are often granted. See GAO, *Federal Disaster Assistance: Individual Assistance Requests Often Granted, but FEMA Could Better Document Factors Considered*, GAO-18-366 (Washington, D.C.: May 31, 2018).

[14] This total includes, for fiscal years 2005 through 2014, $278 billion that GAO found that the federal government had obligated for disaster assistance. See GAO, *Federal Disaster Assistance: Federal Departments and Agencies Obligated at Least $277.6 Billion during Fiscal Years 2005 through 2014,* GAO-16-797 (Washington, D.C.: Sept. 22, 2016). It also includes, for fiscal years 2015 through 2018, $124 billion in select supplemental appropriations to federal agencies for disaster assistance and approximately $7 billion in annual appropriations to the Disaster Relief Fund (a total of $28 billion for the 4-year period). For fiscal years 2015 through 2018, it does not include other annual appropriations to federal agencies for disaster assistance. Lastly, on June 6, 2019, the Additional Supplemental Appropriations for Disaster Relief Act of 2019 was signed into law, which provides approximately $19.1 billion for disaster assistance. Pub. L. No. 116-20, 133 Stat. 871 (2019).

and tribal governments when a major disaster or emergency is declared. Although the Disaster Relief Fund receives funding through the annual appropriations process the federal government does not budget fully for the costs of disaster assistance (see Figure 10). According to the Congressional Research Service, more than 85 percent of net appropriations for disaster relief are provided through supplemental appropriations on an ad hoc basis.[15] These disaster relief supplemental appropriations generally do not count toward existing discretionary budget limits.[16]

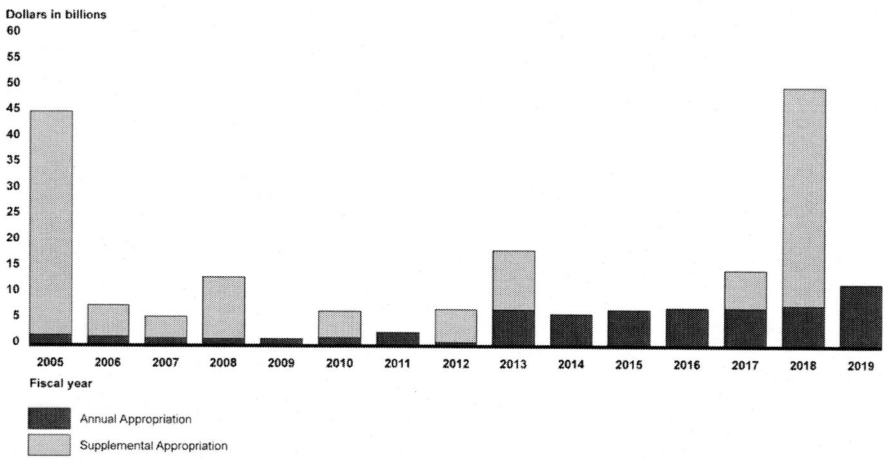

Source: GAO analysis of appropriation laws. | GAO-19-611T.

Note: The 2005 supplemental appropriation includes a rescission of $23.4 billion included in Pub. L. No. 109-148 on December 30, 2005. Without the rescission, the total supplemental appropriation to the Disaster Relief Fund in fiscal year 2005 was $66.5 billion. No other rescissions are included in the figure.

Figure 10. Appropriations to the Disaster Relief Fund, Fiscal Years 2005–2019.

Further, future federal disaster costs are projected to increase as certain extreme weather events become more frequent and intense because of climate change risks—as observed and projected by the U.S. Global

[15] Congressional Research Service, *The Disaster Relief Fund: Overview and Issues*, R45484 (Washington, D.C.: Feb. 1, 2019).

[16] The Budget Control Act of 2011 allows spending limits to be adjusted upward to accommodate appropriations for emergencies when Congress and the president designate specified accounts as emergency funding or for Overseas Contingency Operations in statute. Pub. L. No. 112-25, tit. I, § 101, 125 Stat. 240, 243 (2011).

Change Research Program and the National Academies of Sciences, Engineering, and Medicine.[17] According to the Office of Management and Budget (OMB), since 1993 budget authority for activities related to climate change has totaled about $154 billion—primarily for technologies to reduce emissions and for scientific research on climate change impacts.

However, we found that this amount does not include information on relevant federal fiscal exposures including costs for disaster assistance programs.

Managing fiscal exposure due to climate change has been on GAO's High-Risk List since 2013, in part, because of concerns about the increasing costs of disaster response and recovery efforts.[18] For instance, the National Flood Insurance Program has not collected sufficient premiums and does not have sufficient dedicated resources to cover expected costs without borrowing from Treasury.[19] As of September 2018, FEMA, which administers the National Flood Insurance Program, owed $20.5 billion to Treasury for money borrowed to pay claims and other expenses.[20] We have reported that FEMA is unlikely to collect enough in premiums in the future to repay this debt.[21] Due to its financial challenges, the National Flood Insurance Program has been on GAO's High-Risk List since 2006.[22]

In 2008, we recommended that FEMA take steps to ensure that its rate-setting methods, as a starting point for setting premium rates, accurately reflect the risk of losses from flooding. These steps should include, for example, verifying the accuracy of flood probabilities, damage estimates,

---

[17] GAO, *Climate Change: Information on Potential Economic Effects Could Help Guide Federal Efforts to Reduce Fiscal Exposure*, GAO-17-720 (Washington, D.C.: Sept. 28, 2017). See also U.S. Global Change Research Program, *Impacts, Risks, and Adaptation in the United States: Fourth National Climate Assessment, Volume II* (Washington, D.C.: 2018).

[18] See GAO-19-157SP, 110.

[19] For more information on federal insurance programs and the budget, see GAO, *Fiscal Exposures: Federal Insurance and Other Activities that Transfer Risk or Losses to the Government*, GAO-19-353 (Washington, D.C.: Mar. 27, 2019).

[20] The amount owed is net of $16 billion of debt that was canceled in October 2017. Additional Supplemental Appropriations for Disaster Relief Requirements Act, 2017, Pub. L. No. 115-72, § 308, 131 Stat. 1224, 1228-29 (Oct. 26, 2017).

[21] GAO, *Flood Insurance: Comprehensive Reform Could Improve Solvency and Enhance Resilience*, GAO-17-425 (Washington, D.C.: Apr. 27, 2017).

[22] See GAO-19-157SP, 272.

and flood maps; ensuring that the effects of long-term planned and ongoing development, as well as climate change, are reflected in the flood probabilities used; and reevaluating the practice of aggregating risks across zones.[23]

Further, we have an open matter for Congress to consider from our April 2017 report that examined actions Congress and FEMA could take to reduce federal fiscal exposure and improve resilience to floods. We stated that Congress should consider comprehensive reform, which could include actions in six areas: (1) addressing the current debt, (2) removing existing legislative barriers to FEMA's ability to revise premium rates to reflect the full risk of loss, (3) addressing affordability, (4) increasing consumer participation, (5) removing barriers to private-sector involvement, and (6) protecting National Flood Insurance Program flood resilience efforts.[24]

More complete information on programs for which costs are likely to increase due to climate change, such as disaster assistance, could help policymakers better understand the long-term effects of decisions and the trade-offs between spending with long-term benefits, such as resilience investments, and short-term benefits, such as post-disaster repairs. This information could also help the federal government develop a government-wide strategy for addressing climate change that focuses on reducing federal fiscal exposure.

We have identified a number of ways to reduce the federal fiscal risk related to natural disasters. For example:

- Updating the methodology for major disaster declarations. In 2012, we recommended that FEMA develop and implement an updated methodology that provides a more comprehensive assessment of a jurisdiction's capacity to respond to and recover from a disaster without federal assistance.[25] Our analysis showed that FEMA

---

[23] GAO, *Flood Insurance: FEMA's Rate-Setting Process Warrants Attention*, GAO-09-12, (Washington, D.C.: Oct. 31, 2008).

[24] GAO-17-425.

[25] GAO, *Federal Disaster Assistance: Improved Criteria Needed to Assess a Jurisdiction's Capability to Respond and Recover on Its Own*, GAO-12-838 (Washington, D.C.: Sept. 12, 2012).

primarily relied on a single criterion, the per capita damage indicator, to determine whether to recommend to the President that a jurisdiction receive Public Assistance funding.[26] However, FEMA's per capita indicator, set at $1 in 1986, has not been adjusted for the rise in (1) per capita personal income since it was created in 1986 or (2) inflation from 1986 to 1999 (though the indicator has been adjusted for inflation each year from 2000 through the present).

The per capita indicator as of 2019 is $1.50. However, based on our past analysis, the indicator would have been $2.07 in 2012 had it been adjusted for inflation from 1986 to 1999, illustrating that the indicator is artificially low. Further, we found that, had FEMA updated its methodology based on per capita personal income, as many as 44 percent of federal disaster declarations from fiscal years 2004 through 2011 (totaling $3.59 billion) would not have met the eligibility criteria that FEMA primarily used to determine whether federal assistance should be provided, which would have likely resulted in fewer disaster declarations.

FEMA has not implemented our recommendation, but the Disaster Recovery Reform Act of 2018 (DRRA) requires FEMA to initiate rulemaking to (1) update the factors considered when evaluating requests for major disaster declarations, including reviewing how FEMA estimates the cost of major disaster assistance, and (2) consider other impacts on the capacity of a jurisdiction to respond to disasters, by October 2020.[27] Until FEMA implements a new methodology, the agency will not have an accurate assessment of a jurisdiction's capabilities and runs the risk of recommending that the President award Public Assistance to jurisdictions that have the capacity to respond and recover on their own.

---

[26] The Public Assistance program provides for debris removal; emergency protective measures; and the repair, replacement, or restoration of disaster-damaged, publicly owned facilities and the facilities of certain private nonprofit organizations that provide services otherwise performed by a government agency.

[27] Pub. L. No. 115-254, § 1239, 132 Stat. 3186, 3466 (2018).

- Strengthening resilience efforts. In July 2015, we recommended that FEMA and its partners establish a comprehensive investment strategy to identify, prioritize, and implement federal disaster resilience investments.[28] FEMA and its partners have developed a draft National Mitigation Investment Strategy that may address this recommendation, but it is too early to assess its responsiveness because it has not been finalized. FEMA plans to issue the strategy publicly in July 2019. Further, as we have reported, enhancing resilience can reduce fiscal exposure by reducing or eliminating long-term risk to people and property from natural hazards. For example, a 2018 interim report by the National Institute of Building Sciences estimated approximate benefits to society in excess of costs for several types of resilience projects. While precise benefits are uncertain, the report estimated that for every dollar invested in designing new buildings to particular design standards, society could accrue benefits amounting to about $11 on average.[29]
- Pre-disaster hazard mitigation. We also found that the bulk of federal disaster resilience funding provided to states and localities comes after they have experienced a disaster, particularly a large or catastrophic disaster.[30] The DRRA allows the President to set aside, with respect to each major disaster, a percentage of certain grants to use for pre-disaster hazard mitigation.[31] In May 2019, FEMA announced that it is seeking public comments on the new program. FEMA anticipates issuing the first Notice of Funding Opportunity for this new program before the end of 2020. This new grant program will provide additional funding to make resilience investments before disaster strikes and could potentially help to reduce future risk.

---

[28] GAO, *Hurricane Sandy: An Investment Strategy Could Help the Federal Government Enhance National Resilience for Future Disasters*, GAO-15-515 (Washington, D.C.: July 30, 2015).

[29] GAO, *Climate Change: Opportunities to Reduce Federal Fiscal Exposure*, GAO-19-625T (Washington, D.C.: June 11, 2019).

[30] GAO-15-515.

[31] Pub. L. No. 115-254, § 1234, 132 Stat. at 3461.

Additional Opportunities to Contribute Toward Fiscal Health

In addition, we have identified numerous opportunities for Congress and executive branch agencies to take steps in the near term that could improve the federal government's fiscal condition. These opportunities include addressing billions of dollars in improper payments and the over $400 billion annual tax gap, and evaluating the significant amount of revenue forgone through tax expenditures. There are also opportunities for the Department of Defense, which has the largest share of discretionary spending, to exercise careful stewardship over its resources in light of its high risk challenges. Collectively, these actions would improve stewardship over federal resources in the near term. However, these actions alone cannot put the federal government on a sustainable fiscal path and do not eliminate the need for a long-term fiscal plan. More information on the actions needed in these areas is included in appendix II.

A Long-Term Plan Is Needed to Achieve Fiscal Sustainability

A long-term fiscal plan is needed to address the growing federal debt and put the federal government on a more sustainable long-term fiscal path. To formulate such a plan, policymakers will need to consider policy changes to the entire range of federal activities and address both revenue and spending.

Fiscal Rules Can Guide Fiscal Policy Decisions to Control Debt

Other Countries Have Used Fiscal Rules to Control Debt

As part of a long-term plan, fiscal rules can support efforts to achieve fiscal sustainability by imposing numerical limits on the budget (known as targets) to guide fiscal policy. They have been used at both the national government level in the United States and other countries, as well as at the supranational level, such as the European Union (EU), to help promote fiscal responsibility and sustainability.

According to experts at the International Monetary Fund (IMF) and the Organization for Economic Co-operation and Development (OECD), several types or combinations of fiscal rules have the potential to contribute to fiscal sustainability:

- Budget balance rules, which constrain deficit levels and specify that the debt-to-GDP ratio converges to a defined finite level;
- Debt rules, which set an explicit limit or target for public debt as a percentage of GDP;
- Revenue rules, which set ceilings or floors on revenues and aim to increase revenue collection or prevent excessive tax burdens; and
- Expenditure rules, which limit spending, typically in absolute terms or growth rates and occasionally as a percent of GDP.

As part of our ongoing work on fiscal rules requested by the Chairman, we are examining in the design, implementation, and enforcement of these types of rules in other countries.

Governments can use a combination of different fiscal rules to address shortcomings of any one individual rule. According to the IMF, as of 2015, more than 70 countries had combined two or more fiscal rules, and most countries that use fiscal rules today have more than one in place. For example, at the supranational level, the EU's stability and growth pact combines an expenditure rule, budget balance rule, and a debt rule (e.g., debt-to-GDP), which are designed to ensure that countries in the EU pursue sound public finances and coordinate their fiscal policies. The pact permits sanctions against member states that fail to comply with these fiscal rules. In recent years, however, several EU nations have struggled to meet the targets set forth in the agreement.

Economic literature notes that governments can design mechanisms to help fiscal rules strike a balance between flexibility and enforceability. For example:

- Many fiscal rules include clauses which allow for a level of flexibility in responding to fiscal risks or unexpected events like recessions or natural disasters.
- Other fiscal rules include features such as independent fiscal councils, which are institutions that can help formulate and implement sound fiscal policy, and constitutional mandates, which enshrine the rule in a country's constitution with the intent of making it more difficult to reverse or abandon.
- Some countries choose to use automatic correction mechanisms, which are designed to trigger automatically to respond to past deviations from a rule.

International economic organizations, such as the IMF and OECD, have found that fiscal rules are associated with successful efforts to stabilize debt. However, empirical evidence suggests that while fiscal rules may improve balance sheets, the correlation is weaker between fiscal rules and reductions in the debt-to-GDP ratio. In general, observers and budget experts have noted that success depends on effective enforcement of fiscal rules and sustained commitment by both policymakers and the public. Some experts believe that if governments try to subvert fiscal rules through creative accounting it could undermine credibility or transparency.

The Federal Government Has Previously Enacted Fiscal Rules

The U.S. federal government has previously enacted fiscal rules in the form of laws that constrain and enforce fiscal policy decisions (see Table 1). These experiences illustrate the challenge in designing rules that are both achievable and effective in addressing the key drivers of the nation's growing debt.

Generally, if spending exceeds a target specified by these laws, the President is required to issue an automatic, across-the-board cancellation of budgetary resources, known as sequestration. This order would reduce budget authority by a uniform percentage in the amount necessary to reach the target. Sequestration procedures were established under BBEDCA and continue under subsequent fiscal laws.[32]

Table 1. Previously-enacted federal fiscal rules

Law	Fiscal years in effect	Requirements	Limitations
Balanced Budget and Emergency Deficit Control Act of 1985 (BBEDCA) Pub. L. No. 99-177, 99 Stat. 1037 (1985).	1986–1993[a]	Created deficit limits to establish a balanced budget.	Some factors that affected the deficit were not within Congress's control, such as economic or demographic changes.
Budget Enforcement Act of 1990 (BEA) Pub. L. No. 101-508, 104 Stat 1388-1 (1990).	1991–2002	• Limited annual discretionary spending. • Implemented a pay-as- you-go (PAYGO) rule for new direct spending and revenue legislation,[b] under which the net effect of new laws could not increase the deficit in any given year.	Controls on discretionary spending and new legislation did not control the growth in spending that results from previously-enacted laws, such as Medicare.
Statutory Pay-As-You-Go Act of 2010 (Statutory PAYGO Act) Pub. L. No. 111-139, 124 Stat. 8 (2010).	2010–present (no expiration date)	Requires that the net effect of new direct spending and revenue laws cannot increase the deficit.	Like the BEA, the Statutory PAYGO Act does not control the growth in spending that results from previously enacted laws. The act also does not control discretionary spending.
Budget Control Act of 2011 (BCA) Pub. L. No. 112-25, 125 Stat. 240 (2011).	2012–2021 for discretionary spending 2012–2027 for direct (or mandatory) spending	• Limits annual discretionary spending. • Required Congress and the President to reach agreement on further deficit reduction. Absent such an agreement, discretionary spending was further reduced and reductions in direct	• Spending for emergencies and overseas contingency operations do not count towards discretionary spending limits.[d] • Subsequent laws changed the discretionary spending limits or enforcement procedures, which increased annual deficits.[e]

[32] For more information on sequestration see GAO, *2014 Sequestration: Opportunities Exist to Improve Transparency of Progress Toward Deficit Reduction Goals,* GAO-16-263 (Washington, D.C.: Apr. 14, 2016) and *2013 Sequestration: Agencies Reduced Some Services and Investments, While Taking Certain Actions to Mitigate Effects,* GAO-14-244 (Washington, D.C.: Mar. 6, 2014).

Law	Fiscal years in effect	Requirements	Limitations
		• spending took effect.[c]	• The law did not specify reductions to direct spending; rather, it provided for automatic, across-the- board reductions in direct spending if Congress and the President did not reach a deficit reduction agreement. • Congress and the President did not reach agreement on further deficit reduction as required.

Source: GAO analysis of applicable laws. | GAO-19-611T.

[a]As enacted, BBEDCA contained a provision requiring the Comptroller General to report to the President whether revenues and outlays for the coming fiscal year would result in a deficit exceeding the maximum amount allowed under BBEDCA for that fiscal year and the budget reductions necessary to reach the prescribed deficit level. Pub. L. No. 99-177, § 251(b), 99 Stat. 1037, 1068-1069 (1985). The President was then required to order reductions in spending consistent with the Comptroller General's report. Pub. L. No. 99-177, § 252(a)(3). In 1986 the Supreme Court held this provision unconstitutional because it assigned executive powers to the Comptroller General in violation of the doctrine of separation of powers. Bowsher v. Synar, 478 U.S. 714 (1986). Subsequently, BBEDCA was amended by the Balanced Budget Emergency Deficit Control Reaffirmation Act of 1987. Pub. L. No. 100-119, 101 Stat. 754 (1987). Among other things, the 1987 law extended the time frame for balancing the budget to fiscal year 1993.

[b]Direct spending, often referred to as mandatory spending, consists of budgetary resources provided by entitlement authority and laws other than appropriations acts.

[c]The BCA established the Joint Select Committee on Deficit Reduction (Joint Committee), which was tasked with proposing legislation to reduce the deficit by $1.2 trillion or more through fiscal year 2021. The Joint Committee was to report its proposal by December 2, 2011, and Congress and the President were to enact legislation by January 15, 2012. The Joint Committee did not report a proposal and such legislation was not enacted. This failure triggered (1) sequestration of discretionary spending in fiscal year 2013, (2) reductions to annual discretionary spending limits through fiscal year 2021, and (3) automatic, across-the-board reductions to direct spending.

[d]The BCA allows its spending limits to be adjusted for certain categories such as emergency appropriations and appropriations for overseas contingency operations.

[e]These include the American Taxpayer Relief Act of 2012 (Pub. L. No. 112-240), the Bipartisan Budget Act of 2013 (Pub. L. No. 113-67), the Bipartisan Budget Act of 2015 (Pub. L. No. 114-74), and the Bipartisan Budget Act of 2018 (Pub. L. No. 115-123).

Certain programs are exempt from sequestration, while special rules apply to others. For example, Social Security, Medicaid, and veterans' compensation are exempt, while Medicare reductions are limited to 2 percent.

As a result, programs without special status bear a greater reduction than they would if cuts were applied evenly to all programs. In addition, the sequestration process does not distinguish between programs that have already been reduced through legislation and those that have not.

The federal government's experience with these fiscal rules provides insights that can inform fiscal policy deliberations:

- Targeting the right factors. To effectively reduce the deficit and debt, policymakers will need to examine the factors that have the greatest impact on the government's fiscal condition and structure any fiscal rules and targets to reflect these factors. For example, in the long-term, federal spending is being driven by federal health care programs and interest on debt held by the public, which results from previously-enacted laws. It is important for future fiscal rules to target all spending (entitlement programs, other mandatory spending, and discretionary spending) as well as revenues.
- Enforcing budget agreements. As we have previously reported, enforcing a budgetary agreement is more successful than forcing an agreement where none exists.[33] The experience of the BCA, for example, underscores this principle as the threat of sequestration did not lead to a deficit reduction agreement.
- Limiting exemptions. Since the BCA has been in effect, hundreds of billions of dollars in discretionary budget authority has been provided in areas that do not count towards its spending limits. Specifically, the BCA allows its spending limits to be adjusted for certain categories such as emergency appropriations and appropriations for overseas contingency operations.[34] While the government needs flexibility to address unforeseen events, it is

---

[33] See GAO, *Budget Process: Enforcing Fiscal Choices,* GAO-11-626T (Washington, D.C.: May 4, 2011).

[34] For more information on overseas contingency operations spending, see GAO, *Overseas Contingency Operations: Alternatives Identified to the Approach to Fund War- Related Activities,* GAO-19-211 (Washington, D.C.: Jan. 28, 2019).

important to design fiscal rules that can be adhered to absent a genuine crisis.

No process can force choices that the President and Congress are unwilling to make. However, having an agreed-upon goal can justify and frame the choices that must be made. With that in mind, a fiscal target that establishes a common goal for controlling the size of the federal debt relative to the economy, as well as well-designed rules that put the federal government on a path to achieve that target, could form part of a long-term plan to put the government on a sustainable fiscal path. In our ongoing work, we are examining key considerations for designing and implementing fiscal rules and targets for the U.S. government.

Achieving a Debt-to-GDP Target Would Require Spending and Revenue Changes

One way to quantify the magnitude of policy changes needed to achieve fiscal sustainability is by calculating the fiscal gap. The fiscal gap represents the difference between revenue and program spending (i.e., spending other than interest payments) that would need to be closed immediately and permanently to hold debt as a share of GDP at the end of a given period to the same level as the beginning of the period. To close the gap, policymakers would need to reduce program spending, increase revenue, or, more likely, do both. The longer action is delayed, the greater and more drastic the changes will have to be, placing an additional burden on future generations.

To illustrate this point, Table 2 shows the immediate changes that would be needed for the federal government to reach various debt targets at the end of a 75-year projection period. These targets represent a range of illustrative examples; we do not endorse any particular target. Adopting a fiscal target is a matter for policymakers to consider as they weigh the consequences of spending and revenue decisions and their effect on the federal debt.

Table 2. Illustrative examples of spending or revenue changes needed to achieve debt targets

Debt target, percent of gross domestic product (end of 75 years)	Immediate and permanent reduction in the annual projected primary deficit required to achieve debt target (percent of gross domestic product)[a]	Immediate and permanent reduction in annual projected program spending alone to achieve debt target	Immediate and permanent increase in annual projected revenue alone to achieve debt target
Percent	Percent	Percent	Percent
100	6	25	35
78 (actual level as of fiscal year 2018)	6	27	37
60 (European Union target)	7	28	38
0 (pay off the debt)	8	31	43

Source: GAO's 2019 alternative simulation. | GAO-19-611T.

Note: This analysis was produced using GAO's 2019 long-term fiscal outlook model, the alternative simulation. GAO most recently updated the data used in this model for its 2019 report on the nation's fiscal health (GAO-19-314SP). The model does not account for potential macroeconomic effects of fiscal policy changes over time.

[a]These figures represent reductions in the primary deficit, which is the difference between revenues and program spending. Interest payments are excluded.

The table shows the magnitude of actions needed to achieve certain levels of debt held by the public as a percentage of gross domestic product over a 75-year period by reducing spending alone or increasing revenue alone. More likely, both spending and revenue changes will be needed to achieve fiscal sustainability.

Debt Limit Is Not a Control on Debt: Alternative Approach Is Needed

Treasury is taking extraordinary actions to continue funding federal government activities. Treasury began taking these actions shortly after the debt limit suspension period ended on March 1, 2019.[35] Treasury will continue taking these actions until the debt limit is raised or suspended. With these extraordinary actions in place, CBO estimates that Treasury will have sufficient cash to make its usual payments until late into fiscal year 2019.

One cannot overstate the importance of preserving investors' confidence that debt backed by the full faith and credit of the U.S. government will be honored. Failure to increase (or suspend) the debt limit in a timely manner (before the extraordinary actions run out) could have serious negative consequences for the Treasury market and borrowing costs.

Our work has shown that uncertainty in the past around whether the debt limit would be raised or suspended has distorted the secondary market and led to increases in borrowing costs for Treasury.[36] During the 2013 debt limit impasse, investors reported that they took the unprecedented action of systematically avoiding certain Treasury securities—those that matured around the dates when Treasury projected it would exhaust the extraordinary actions. For these securities, interest rates increased dramatically and liquidity declined in the secondary market, where securities are traded among investors.

Rates in the secondary market ultimately affect Treasury's borrowing costs, as investors generally demand similar rates at auction to those in the secondary market. The significant increases in interest rates on these Treasury securities reflected a new level of investor uncertainty about Treasury's ability to pay its bills and avoid a delayed payment or a default. We estimated that total borrowing costs incurred through September 30, 2014, on Treasury securities issued during the 2013 debt limit impasse increased by roughly $38 million to more than $70 million, depending on the specifications used.

---

[35] Extraordinary actions are actions that Treasury takes as it nears the debt limit to avoid exceeding the limit. The Bipartisan Budget Act of 2018 temporarily suspended the debt limit from February 9, 2018, through March 1, 2019. Bipartisan Budget Act of 2018, Pub. L. No. 115-123, div. C, tit. III, § 30301, 132 Stat. 64, 132 (2018).

[36] GAO, *Debt Limit: Market Response to Recent Impasses Underscores Need to Consider Alternative Approaches,* GAO-15-476 (Washington, D.C.: July 9, 2015).

As part of a long-term fiscal plan, Congress should consider alternative approaches to the debt limit. As currently structured, the debt limit—a legal limit on the total amount of federal debt that can be outstanding at one time[37]—does not restrict Congress and the President's ability to enact spending and revenue legislation that affects the level of debt; nor does it otherwise constrain fiscal policy.[38] The debt limit is an after-the- fact measure; the spending and tax laws that result in debt have already been enacted. It restricts Treasury's authority to borrow to finance decisions already made. If the level of publicly held debt or its share of GDP is to be used as a fiscal management tool to change the long-term fiscal path, it needs to be considered as part of overall budget decisions at the time those decisions are being made.

In 2015, we held a forum with experts and identified three options for Congress to delegate its borrowing authority, while maintaining control and oversight, and better align decisions about the level of debt with decisions on spending and revenue, and minimize disruption to the market.

- Option 1: Link action on the debt limit to the budget resolution.
- Option 2: Provide the administration with the authority to propose a change in the debt limit that would take effect absent enactment of a joint resolution of disapproval within a specified time frame.
- Option 3: Delegate broad authority to the administration to borrow as necessary to fund enacted laws.[39]

The government must act soon to change the long-term fiscal path or risk significant disruption to individuals and the economy. Congress will need to discuss the entire range of federal activities and spending—

[37] The debt limit is codified at 31 U.S.C. § 3101(b), as amended, and applies to federal debt issued pursuant to the authority of 31 U.S.C. chapter 31. A very small amount of total federal debt is not subject to the debt limit. This amount primarily comprises unamortized discounts on Treasury bills and Zero Coupon Treasury bonds; debt securities issued by agencies other than Treasury, such as the Tennessee Valley Authority; and debt securities issued by the Federal Financing Bank.

[38] GAO, *Debt Limit: Delays Create Debt Management Challenges and Increase Uncertainty in the Treasury Market*, GAO-11-203 (Washington, D.C.: Feb. 22, 2011).

[39] More detail about these options and a discussion of the advantages and challenges to each can be found in GAO-15-476.

entitlement programs, other mandatory spending, discretionary spending, and revenue. Moving forward, the federal government will need to make tough choices in setting priorities and ensuring that spending leads to positive results. Having a long-term fiscal plan that includes fiscal rules and targets, and decisions about how to better manage borrowing authority, would help with these tough decisions.

Thank you, Chairman Enzi, Ranking Member Sanders, and Members of the Committee, this concludes my prepared statement. I would be pleased to answer any questions.

APPENDIX I: OPPORTUNITIES TO ADDRESS FEDERAL FISCAL RISKS

In addition to the fiscal risks related to natural disasters and climate change as discussed in the body of this statement, better understanding fiscal risks like housing finance, surface transportation, and the Pension Benefit Guaranty Corporation, can help policymakers anticipate changes in future spending and can enhance oversight of federal resources. We have recommended ways for Congress and executive branch agencies to address these fiscal risks.

Housing Finance Reform

The federal government continues to provide significant support to the housing finance market, even though the market has largely recovered since the 2007 to 2009 financial crisis. In 2008, the federal government placed the Federal National Mortgage Association (Fannie Mae) and the Federal Home Loan Mortgage Corporation (Freddie Mac) under conservatorship and entered into preferred stock purchase agreements with these government-sponsored enterprises (GSE) to help ensure their financial stability. At the end of fiscal year 2018, the federal government reported about $113 billion of investments in the GSEs, which is net of about $91 billion in valuation losses.

The ultimate role of the GSEs could affect the financial condition of other federal entities, including the Federal Housing Administration (FHA), which in the past expanded its lending role in distressed housing and mortgage markets. At the end of fiscal year 2018, FHA's portfolio of federally-insured mortgages exceeded $1.2 trillion. The Government National Mortgage Association (Ginnie Mae) guarantees the performance of almost $2 trillion in securities backed by federally insured mortgages—the majority insured by FHA. We have reported on the need for Congress to consider legislation for making changes to the future federal role in housing finance that addresses the structure of the GSEs; establishes clear, specific, and prioritized goals; and considers all relevant federal entities, such as FHA and Ginnie Mae.[40]

In addition, the share of nonbank mortgage originators and servicers grew since the 2007-2009 financial crisis. According to data from Inside Mortgage Finance, nonbanks originated roughly half of all mortgages sold to the GSEs in 2017 and the first three quarters of 2018. Nonbank servicers of loans backing mortgage-backed securities issued by the GSEs have grown from 25 percent in 2014 to 38 percent as of the third quarter of 2018. For FHA-insured mortgages, nonbank originations represented 74 percent in 2003, declined to 56 percent in 2010, and then increased to 86 percent in fiscal year 2017. While Federal Housing Finance Agency (FHFA) and Department of Housing and Urban Development officials told us nonbanks have helped provide access to mortgage credit, several stakeholders and experts identified the increased presence of nonbank lenders can present additional liquidity risk in the housing finance system. We recommended that Congress consider granting FHFA the authority to examine third parties like nonbank lenders that do business with Fannie

---

[40] GAO, *Housing Finance: Prolonged Conservatorships of Fannie Mae and Freddie Mac Prompt Need for Reform*, GAO-19-239 (Washington, D.C.: Jan. 18, 2019). For more information on resolving the federal role in housing finance, see GAO-19-157SP, 95.

Mae and Freddie Mac, in order to identify and address deficiencies that could affect them.[41]

The Nation's Surface Transportation System

The nation's surface transportation system—including highways, transit, maritime ports, and rail systems—is critical to the economy and affects the daily lives of most Americans. However, according to estimates, it will cost hundreds of billions of dollars to repair and upgrade it to meet current and future demands. Meanwhile, traditional funding sources are eroding and the federal government lacks a long-term sustainable strategy for funding it. The major source of federal funding, the Highway Trust Fund, is increasingly unable to maintain current spending levels for highway and transit programs.[42] Spending is projected to exceed revenues after 2021.

In its January 2019 budget outlook, CBO estimated that $159 billion in additional funding would be required to maintain current spending levels plus inflation from 2022 through 2029.[43] Congress needs to pass a long-term, sustainable solution for funding surface transportation. Such a solution would balance revenues to and spending from the Highway Trust Fund.

The Pension Benefit Guaranty Corporation

The Pension Benefit Guaranty Corporation's (PBGC) financial future is uncertain because of long-term challenges related to its funding and governance structure. PBGC's liabilities exceeded its assets by about $51

---

[41] GAO, *Nonbank Mortgage Servicers: Existing Regulatory Oversight Could Be Strengthened [Reissued on April 14, 2016]*, GAO-16-278 (Washington, D.C.: Mar. 10, 2016).

[42] For more information on funding the nation's surface transportation system, see GAO-19-157SP, 86.

[43] As part of its baseline projection, CBO assumes that this payment will be made after the Highway Trust Fund is exhausted in 2021.

billion as of the end of fiscal year 2018—an increase of about $16 billion from the end of fiscal year 2013 (see Figure 11).[44]

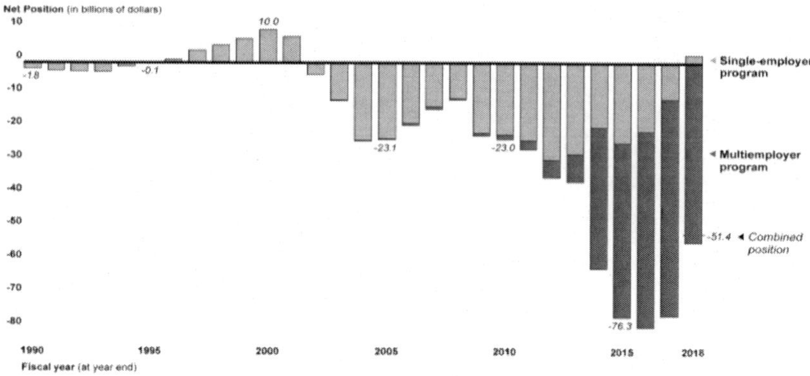

Source: Pension Benefit Guaranty Corporation (PBGC). | GAO-19-611T.

Figure 11. Pension Benefit Guaranty Corporation's Net Financial Position of the Single-Employer and Multiemployer Programs Combined, Fiscal Years 1990-2018.

PBGC estimated that its exposure to potential additional future losses for underfunded plans in both the single and multiemployer programs was nearly $185 billion; the single-employer program accounts for $175 billion of this amount. PBGC projected that there is more than a 90 percent likelihood that the multiemployer program will be insolvent by the year 2025 and a 99 percent likelihood by 2026. Although the single-employer program is currently in surplus, past experience shows that large claims can cause its condition to change quickly.

We have suggested a number of matters for congressional consideration to strengthen PBGC, including (1) authorizing a redesign of PBGC's single employer program premium structure to better align premium rates with risk, (2) adopting additional changes to PBGC's governance structure, (3) strengthening funding requirements for plan sponsors as appropriate given national economic conditions, (4) working with PBGC to develop a strategy for funding PBGC claims over the long term as the defined benefit pension system continues to decline, and (5) enacting additional structural reforms to reinforce and stabilize the

[44] For more information on PBGC insurance programs, see GAO-19-157SP, 267.

multiemployer system, and balance the needs and potential sacrifices of contributing employers, participants, and the federal government.

APPENDIX II: NEAR-TERM OPPORTUNITIES TO CONTRIBUTE TOWARD FISCAL HEALTH

Changes in spending and revenue to ensure long-term fiscal sustainability will require legislative actions to alter fiscal policies. Meanwhile, Congress and executive branch agencies have opportunities in the near term to improve the government's fiscal condition and act as stewards of federal resources. Although these opportunities alone cannot put the federal government on a sustainable fiscal path, they would improve both the fiscal situation and the federal government's operations.

Continue to Address Fragmentation, Overlap, and Duplication

Since 2011, we have reported annually on federal programs, agencies, offices, and initiatives that have duplicative goals or activities as well as opportunities to achieve greater efficiency and effectiveness that result in cost savings or enhanced revenue collection. Congress and executive branch agencies have partially or fully addressed 621 of the 805 actions (77 percent) we identified from 2011 to 2018, resulting in about $262 billion in financial benefits. In our May 2019 report, we presented 98 new actions for Congress or executive branch agencies.[45] We estimate tens of billions more dollars could be saved by fully implementing our open actions.[46] See table 3 for examples of areas with open actions with potential financial benefits of $1 billion or more.

---

[45] GAO-19-285SP. See GAO's Duplication and Cost Savings webpage for links to the 2011 to 2019 annual reports: http://www.gao.gov/duplication/overview.

[46] In calculating our total estimated realized and potential financial benefits, we relied on individual estimates from a variety of sources, which considered different time periods and utilized different data sources, assumptions, and methodologies. These totals represent a rough estimate of financial benefits. Realized benefits have been rounded down to the

Table 3. Examples of areas with open actions with potential financial benefits of $1 billion or more

Area name and description	Mission	Potential financial benefits[a] (source)
*DOE's Treatment of Hanford's Low-Activity Waste: The Department of Energy (DOE) may be able to reduce certain risks by adopting alternative approaches to treating a portion of its low-activity radioactive waste. (GAO-17-306)	Energy	Tens of billions (GAO)
Defense Headquarters: The Department of Defense could review and identify further opportunities for consolidating or reducing the size of headquarters organizations. (GAO-12-345, GAO-13-293, GAO-14-439, GAO-15-10)	Defense	$9.4 billion (National Defense Authorization Act)
*Advanced Technology Vehicles Manufacturing Loan Program: Unless DOE can demonstrate demand for new Advanced Technology Vehicles Manufacturing loans and viable applications, Congress may wish to consider rescinding all or part of the remaining credit subsidy appropriations. (GAO-14-343SP)	Energy	Up to $4.3 billion (DOE)
*Disability and Unemployment Benefits: Congress should consider passing legislation to prevent individuals from collecting both full Disability Insurance benefits and Unemployment Insurance benefits that cover the same period. (GAO-12-764)	Income security	$2.5 billion over 10 years (Office of Management and Budget)
*Social Security Offsets: The Social Security Administration (SSA) needs data on pensions from noncovered earnings to better enforce offsets and ensure benefit fairness, which could result in cost savings if enforced both retrospectively and prospectively, according to the Congressional Budget Office (CBO) and SSA. Congress could consider giving the Internal Revenue Service the authority to collect the necessary information. Estimated savings would be less if SSA only enforced the offsets prospectively as it would not reduce benefits already received. (GAO-05-786T)	Income security	$2.4 to $7.9 billion over 10 years (CBO and SSA)
*Crop Insurance: Congress could consider limiting the subsidy for premiums that an individual farmer can receive each year from the Federal Crop Insurance program, reducing the subsidy, or some combination of limiting and reducing these subsidies and making changes to the program to reduce its delivery costs. (GAO-17-501, GAO-12-256)	Agriculture	Up to $1.4 billion annually (GAO)

nearest $1 billion. Estimated potential benefits are subject to increased uncertainty, depending on whether, how, and when they are addressed, and are presented using a notional statement of magnitude.

Area name and description	Mission	Potential financial benefits[a] (source)
Medicare Clinical Laboratory Payments: The Centers for Medicare & Medicaid Services should take steps to avoid paying more than necessary for clinical laboratory tests. (GAO-19-67)	Health	Over $1 billion, or billions (GAO)
Department of Energy Environmental Liability: DOE could develop a program-wide strategy to improve decision-making on cleaning up radioactive and hazardous waste. (GAO-19-28)	Energy	Billions (GAO)
*Identity Theft Refund Fraud: The Internal Revenue Service and Congress could improve the agency's efforts to prevent refund fraud associated with identity theft. (GAO-18-418, GAO-16-508)	General government	Billions (GAO)

Legend: * = Legislation is likely to be necessary to fully address all actions in this area.

Source: GAO. | GAO-19-611T.

Note: All estimates of potential financial benefits are dependent on various factors, such as whether action is taken and how it is taken. Actual benefits may be less, depending on costs associated with implementing the action, unintended consequences, and the impact of other factors that could and should be controlled for. The individual estimates in this table should be compared with caution, as they come from a variety of sources, which consider different time periods and utilize different data sources, assumptions, and methodologies.

[a]We developed the notional estimates, which are intended to provide a sense of potential magnitude of financial benefits. Notional estimates have been developed using broad assumptions about potential benefits which are rooted in previously identified losses, the overall size of the program, previous experience with similar reforms, and similar rough indicators of potential benefits. We generally determine the notional label ("millions" vs. "tens of millions" vs. "hundreds of millions") using a risk-based approach that takes into account such factors as the possible minimum and maximum values of the financial benefits estimate (where available), the quality of the data underlying those values, the certainty of those values, and/or the rigor of the estimation method used.

Actions Needed to Address Improper and Other Payments

Improper payments—payments that should not have been made or that were made in an incorrect amount—have consistently been a government-wide issue and if addressed could yield significant savings.[47]

---

[47] Improper Payments Information Act of 2002, Pub. L. No. 107-300, 116 Stat. 2350 (2002), *codified as amended at* 31 U.S.C. § 3321 note. An improper payment is statutorily defined as any payment that should not have been made or that was made in an incorrect amount (including overpayments and underpayments) under statutory, contractual, administrative,

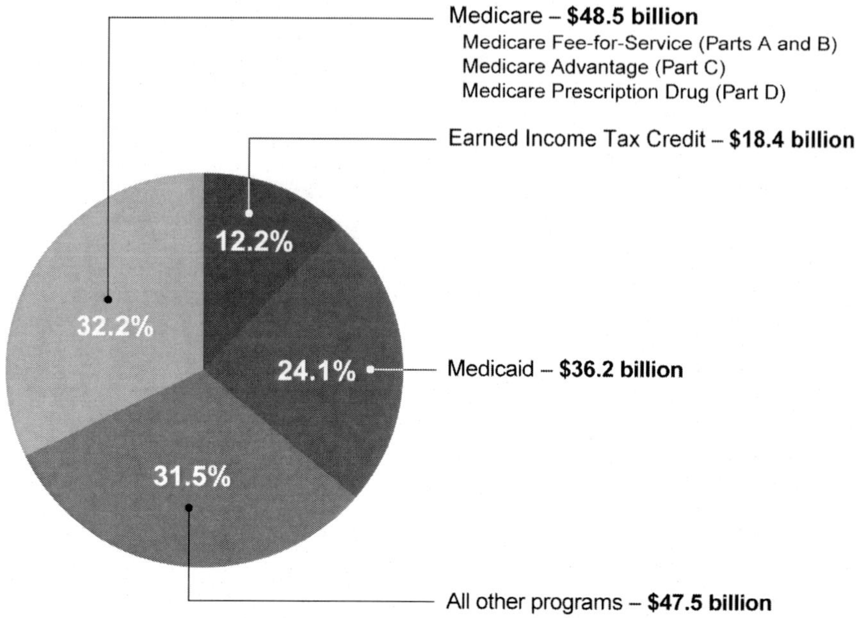

Source: GAO analysis of agencie's fiscal year 2018 data. | GAO-19-611T.

Figure 12. Improper Payment Estimates Were Concentrated in Three Areas in Fiscal Year 2018.

For fiscal year 2018, agencies reported total improper payment estimates of about $151 billion. Since fiscal year 2003, cumulative improper payment estimates government-wide have totaled about $1.5 trillion.[48]

Medicare programs, Medicaid, and the Earned Income Tax Credit account for about 69 percent of the total improper payment estimates reported by agencies for fiscal year 2018 (see Figure 12).[49]

---

or other legally applicable requirements. It includes any payment to an ineligible recipient, any payment for an ineligible good or service, any duplicate payment, any payment for a good or service not received (except for such payments where authorized by law), and any payment that does not account for credit for applicable discounts. OMB guidance also provides that when an agency's review is unable to discern whether a payment was proper as a result of insufficient or lack of documentation, this payment must also be considered an improper payment.

[48] Prior-year improper payment estimates have not been adjusted for inflation.

[49] Certain federal programs and activities determined to be at risk for improper payments did not report estimates of improper payments for fiscal year 2018, including the Premium Tax Credit and Temporary Assistance for Needy Families, among others.

Because health care is one of the major drivers of the long-term fiscal outlook, it is especially critical to take appropriate measures to reduce improper payments in Medicare and Medicaid.[50]

It is important for agencies to identify the root causes of improper payments and then implement internal controls aimed at both prevention and detection. However, the government's ability to understand the full extent to which improper payments occur is hindered by (1) incomplete, unreliable, or understated estimates; (2) risk assessments that may not accurately assess the risk of improper payment; and (3) noncompliance with criteria listed in federal law.

Our work has identified a number of strategies and specific actions agencies can take to reduce improper payments, which could yield significant savings and help ensure that taxpayer funds are adequately safeguarded. For example,

- Improvements to agency estimates. In May 2018 we recommended OMB develop guidance to help ensure agencies' estimating processes for identifying improper payments reflect key risks, for example whether a payee is ineligible for a payment.[51] As of April 2019, OMB has not implemented this recommendation.
- Amendments to the Social Security Act. We have suggested that Congress consider amending the Social Security Act to explicitly allow the Social Security Administration to share its full death data with Treasury's Do Not Pay working system for data matching.[52] As of June 2019, no relevant legislation has been enacted.

---

[50] For more information on our work on Medicare and Medicaid including improper payments for these programs, see GAO-19-157SP, 241 and 250.

[51] GAO, *Improper Payments: Actions and Guidance Could Help Address Issues and Inconsistencies in Estimation Processes*, GAO-18-377 (Washington, D.C.: May 31, 2018).

[52] GAO, *Improper Payments: Strategy and Additional Actions Needed to Help Ensure Agencies Use the Do Not Pay Working System as Intended*, GAO-17-15 (Washington, D.C.: Oct. 14, 2016).

Actions Needed to Address Medicare and Medicaid Payments and Control Health Care Spending

Spending for the Medicare and Medicaid programs—both projected to exceed $1 trillion annually in fiscal year 2026—is a key driver of long-term federal spending. We have identified a number of actions for Congress and agencies to implement related to Medicare and Medicaid payments that could result in billions of dollars in savings, including the following:

- Medicare—Payments by place of service. In 2015, we recommended that Congress consider directing the Department of Health and Human Services (HHS) to equalize Medicare payment rates between settings for evaluation and management office visits and other services, and return associated savings to the Medicare program.[53] Several organizations have estimated that equalizing payment rates would save Medicare billions of dollars, with some estimates predicting savings of nearly $1 billion to $2 billion a year. Both Congress and the Centers for Medicare and Medicaid Services (CMS) have taken some actions to address this issue; however, these actions do not fully address the issue.
- Medicare—Prior authorization. CMS has used prior authorization, which generally requires health care providers and suppliers to demonstrate compliance with Medicare coverage and payment rules before certain items or services are provided to patients. In April 2018, we found that estimated savings from CMS's prior

[53] GAO, *Medicare: Increasing Hospital-Physician Consolidation Highlights Need for Payment Reform*, GAO-16-189 (Washington, D.C.: Dec. 18, 2015). Medicare often pays providers at a higher rate when the same service is performed in a hospital outpatient department rather than in a physician office. On November 21, 2018, CMS issued a final rule that reduced payment rates for certain services furnished by the off-campus hospital outpatient departments—those that are not located on a hospital campus— that existed or were under construction in 2015. On December 4, 2018, the American Hospital Association and 4 other plaintiffs filed suit in the U.S. District Court for the District of Columbia arguing that CMS lacks the authority to change the payment rate for these hospital outpatient departments. *American Hospital Association v. Azar,* No. 18-cv-02841 (D.D.C. filed Dec. 4, 2018.

authorization demonstrations could be about $1.1 to $1.9 billion, but, at the time of our review, the demonstrations were paused, ended, or scheduled to end.[54] We recommended that CMS take steps to continue prior authorization, which could save an additional tens of millions of dollars.

CMS has taken steps to resume a paused demonstration, extend the end date of a demonstration, and add items to the permanent program. We will continue to monitor agency guidance on the resumed and extended demonstrations and the results of independent evaluations of ended demonstrations. We also will evaluate additional steps CMS takes to continue prior authorization in Medicare, such as identifying new opportunities for prior authorization.

- Medicare—Payments to cancer hospitals. In 2015 we estimated that certain cancer hospitals received, on average, about 42 percent more in Medicare inpatient payments per discharge than what Medicare would have paid a local teaching hospital under the prospective payment system (PPS) to treat cancer beneficiaries with the same level of complexity.[55] We recommended that Congress consider requiring Medicare to pay these cancer hospitals as it pays these teaching hospitals, or provide HHS with the authority to otherwise modify how Medicare pays cancer hospitals. These actions could save hundreds of millions of dollars each year.
- Medicare—Medicare Advantage. CMS pays plans in Medicare Advantage—private health plans that offer health care coverage to Medicare beneficiaries—a predetermined amount per beneficiary adjusted for health status based on a risk score. In 2013 we found

---

[54] GAO, *Medicare: CMS Should Take Actions to Continue Prior Authorization Efforts to Reduce Spending*, GAO-18-341 (Washington, D.C.: Apr. 20, 2018).

[55] GAO, *Medicare: Payment Methods for Certain Cancer Hospitals Should Be Revised to Promote Efficiency*, GAO-15-199 (Washington, D.C.: Feb. 20, 2015). To control costs and reward efficiency, Medicare pays the majority of hospitals under the prospective payment system which is based on the clinical classification of each service; however, certain cancer hospitals are largely paid on the basis of reported costs.

that CMS's adjustment to risk scores for 2010 through 2012 to account for diagnostic coding differences was too low, resulting in estimated excess payments of at least $3.2 billion to Medicare Advantage plans.[56]

Congress has taken steps to increase the minimum adjustment made for differences in diagnostic coding patterns between these two groups, which are expected to result in savings of approximately $2.5 billion from fiscal years 2013 through 2022. CMS could still take steps to better account for beneficiary characteristics such as sex and residential location, and use more current and refined data in determining Medicare Advantage payments. CMS could achieve billions of dollars in additional savings by better adjusting for differences between Medicare Advantage plans and traditional Medicare providers in the reporting of beneficiary diagnoses.

- Medicaid—Supplemental payments. Supplemental payments—those made to providers in addition to regular claims-based payments—totaled more than $48 billion in fiscal year 2016. Based on problems we identified with the supplemental payments in multiple reports, we recommended that Congress consider requiring CMS to (1) improve state reporting of certain supplemental payments, including requiring annual reporting of payments made to individual facilities and other information that the agency determines is necessary, and (2) clarify permissible methods of calculating these payments.[57]

  We have also made several recommendations to CMS to improve the agency's oversight of these payments. In November 2018, CMS announced that it was planning a proposed rule that may improve oversight of Medicaid supplemental payments, which, if

[56] GAO, *Medicare Advantage: Substantial Excess Payments Underscore Need for CMS to Improve Accuracy of Risk Score Adjustments*, GAO-13-206 (Washington, D.C.: Jan. 31, 2013).

[57] GAO, *Medicaid: CMS Oversight of Provider Payments Is Hampered by Limited Data and Unclear Policy*, GAO-15-322 (Washington, D.C.: April 10, 2015) and *Medicaid: More Transparency of and Accountability for Supplemental Payments Are Needed*, GAO-13-48 (Washington, D.C.: Nov. 26, 2012).

effectively implemented, could save hundreds of millions or billions of dollars.

- Medicaid—Demonstration waivers. In 2013 we found that HHS did not adequately ensure that four states' Medicaid demonstration projects would be budget neutral to the federal government before approving them, as required by HHS policy.[58] We recommended that Congress could consider requiring HHS to improve the Medicaid demonstration review process. In recent years HHS issued guidance changing the methods it uses to determine whether demonstrations are budget neutral. As of July 2018, CMS estimated that the federal share for the 10 demonstrations that have been renewed under one new method has been reduced by more than $121 billion over a 7- year period. Continuing to apply this guidance to other demonstrations, along with taking additional actions to ensure budget neutrality, could further reduce demonstration spending limits by billions of dollars.
- Medicaid—Spending oversight. In multiple reports in 2018, we found that CMS was not sufficiently identifying and targeting risk in its Medicaid spending oversight activities, which can result in potential overpayments and unallowable expenditures.[59] For example, we found that CMS devotes similar levels of staff resources to review expenditures despite differing levels of risk across states. Specifically, the number of staff reviewing California's expenditures—which represent 15 percent of federal Medicaid spending—was similar to the number reviewing Arkansas' expenditures, which represents 1 percent of federal Medicaid spending. We made five recommendations to the agency to improve how it identifies and targets risk areas in its oversight

[58] GAO, *Medicaid Demonstration Waivers: Approval Process Raises Cost Concerns and Lacks Transparency*, GAO-13-384 (Washington, D.C.: Jun. 25, 2013).

[59] GAO, *Medicaid: CMS Needs to Better Target Risks to Improve Oversight of Expenditures*, GAO-18-564 (Washington, D.C.: Aug. 6, 2018); *Medicaid Managed Care: Improvements Needed to Better Oversee Payment Risks*, GAO-18-528 (Washington, D.C.: Jul. 26, 2018); and *Medicaid: CMS Should Take Steps to Mitigate Program Risks in Managed Care*, GAO-18-291 (Washington, D.C.: May 7, 2018).

of expenditures, which, if implemented, could save hundreds of millions of dollars. CMS agreed with the recommendations, but has not provided a timeframe for implementation.

Multiple Strategies Needed to Address Persistent Tax Gap

The tax gap is the difference between tax amounts that taxpayers should pay and what they actually pay voluntarily and on time. The average annual net tax gap was $406 billion for tax years 2008 through 2010, according to Internal Revenue Service (IRS) estimates (see figure 13).[60]

Given the size of the tax gap, even modest reductions would yield significant financial benefits and help improve the government's fiscal condition. Since any long-term fiscal plan will require consideration of revenue increases, it is important to collect more of what is already owed.

The tax gap arises when taxpayers, whether intentionally or inadvertently, fail to (1) accurately report tax liabilities on tax returns (underreporting), (2) pay taxes due from filed returns (underpayment), or (3) file a required tax return altogether or on time (nonfiling). Underreporting accounted for 84 percent of the tax gap estimate across tax years 2008 to 2010, as shown in Figure 14.

Reducing the tax gap will be a challenging task requiring action on multiple fronts.[61] Our work has identified a number of strategies and specific actions IRS and Congress can take to reduce the tax gap.

- Enhanced electronic filing. Requiring additional taxpayers, such as corporations, to electronically file tax and information returns could help IRS improve compliance in a resource-efficient way.[62]

---

[60] The average annual net tax gap equals the average annual gross tax gap ($458 billion) minus the amount IRS expects to recover through enforcement actions and late payments ($52 billion).

[61] For more information on the tax gap, see GAO, *Tax Gap: Multiple Strategies Are Needed to Reduce Noncompliance,* GAO-19-558T (Washington, D.C.: May 9, 2019).

- Additional third-party information reporting. Expanding the information reported to IRS by third parties could increase voluntary tax compliance. For example, reporting could be required for certain payments that rental real estate owners make to service providers, such as contractors who perform repairs on their rental properties.[63]

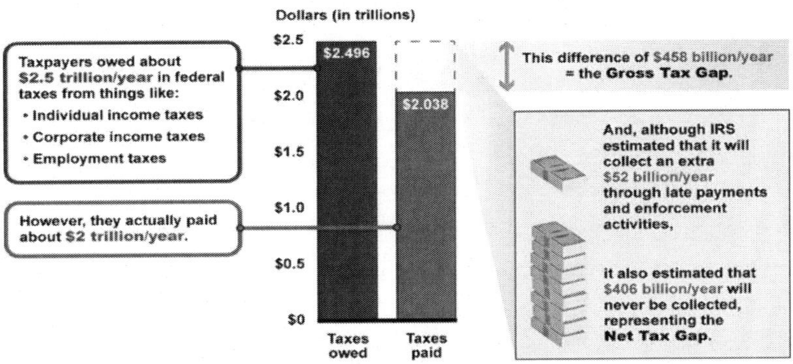

Source: Internal Revenue Service (IRS). | GAO-19-611T.

Note: IRS released its most recent tax gap estimate in April 2016 for tax years 2008 to 2010.

Figure 13. IRS's Annual Average Tax Gap Estimate for Tax Years 2008–2010.

- Math error authority. Providing IRS with authority—with appropriate safeguards—to correct math errors and to correct errors in cases where information provided by a taxpayer does not match information in government databases, among other things, could help IRS correct errors and avoid burdensome audits and taxpayer penalties.[64]

---

[62] GAO, *Partnerships and S Corporations: IRS Needs to Improve Information to Address Tax Noncompliance*, GAO-14-453 (Washington, D.C.: May 14, 2014).

[63] GAO, *Tax Gap: IRS Could Do More to Promote Compliance by Third Parties with Miscellaneous Income Reporting Requirements*, GAO-09-238 (Washington, D.C.: Jan. 28, 2009) and *Tax Gap: Actions That Could Improve Rental Real Estate Reporting Compliance*, GAO-08-956 (Washington, D.C.: Aug. 28, 2008).

[64] GAO, *Recovery Act: IRS Quickly Implemented Tax Provisions, but Reporting and Enforcement Improvements Are Needed,* GAO-10-349 (Washington, D.C.: Feb. 10, 2010).

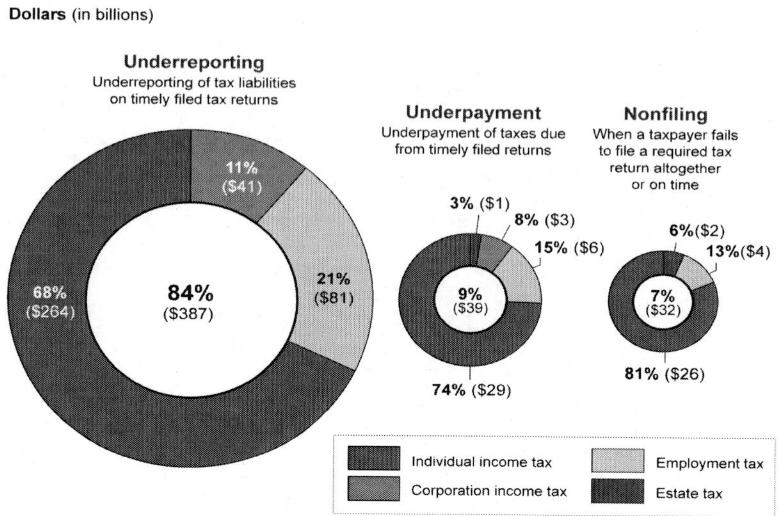

Source: GAO analysis of Internal Revenue Service (IRS) information. | GAO-19-611T.

Note: Data may not sum to totals because of rounding. Individual income tax includes individual business income tax. Estate tax underreporting noncompliance is not shown in this graphic because it represents less than 0.5 percent of total underreporting noncompliance. Excise tax is not shown in this graphic because the IRS does not have excise tax underreporting noncompliance or nonfiling noncompliance estimates, and its estimate for excise tax underpayment noncompliance represents less than 0.5 percent of total underpayment noncompliance. In addition, IRS does not have a corporation income tax estimate for nonfiling noncompliance.

Figure 14. Estimated Average Annual Gross Tax Gap by Type of Noncompliance and Tax, Tax Years 2008-2010.

- Paid preparer regulation. Providing IRS with the authority to regulate paid tax return preparers could improve the accuracy of the tax returns they prepare.[65]
- Leveraging the Return Review Program. Evaluating the costs and benefits of expanding IRS's Return Review Program—a tool to

---

[65] GAO, *Paid Tax Return Preparers: In a Limited Study, Preparers Made Significant Errors,* GAO-14-467T (Washington, D.C.: April 8, 2014). A previous study found similar results: see *Paid Tax Return Preparers: In a Limited Study, Chain Preparers Made Serious Errors,* GAO-06-563T (Washington, D.C.: Apr. 4, 2006).

detect potentially fraudulent returns—could streamline the detection and treatment of other types of noncompliance.[66]

- Compliance research strategy. IRS should develop and document a strategy that outlines how IRS will use National Research Program data to update compliance efforts. Such a strategy would help IRS determine resource trade-offs in its compliance research, while providing Congress with a better understanding of the merits of the research.[67]
- Improving IRS strategic workforce planning. Addressing IRS's fragmented human capital activities—through fully implementing its workforce planning initiative—would help the agency better meet challenges to achieving its mission.[68]

Increased Attention to the Results from Tax Expenditures

Evaluating the significant amount of revenue forgone through tax expenditures could help aid fiscal decision-making. In fiscal year 2018, tax expenditures reduced income tax revenues by approximately $1.38 trillion based on Treasury estimates.[69] Tax expenditures (e.g., tax credits, exemptions) are provisions of the tax code that reduce taxpayers' tax liability and therefore the amount of tax revenue paid to the government.

---

[66] GAO, *Tax Fraud and Noncompliance: IRS Could Further Leverage the Return Review Program to Strengthen Tax Enforcement*, GAO-18-544 (Washington, D.C.: Jul. 24, 2018).

[67] GAO, *Tax Gap: IRS Needs Specific Goals and Strategies for Improving Compliance,* GAO-18-39 (Washington, D.C.: Oct. 31, 2017).

[68] GAO, *Internal Revenue Service: Strategic Human Capital Management is Needed to Address Serious Risks to IRS's Mission*, GAO-19-176 (Washington, D.C.: Mar. 26, 2019).

[69] We calculated the total amount based on Treasury's estimates of each tax expenditure. The sum of the tax expenditure estimates is useful for gauging the general magnitude of revenue forgone through provisions of the tax code, but aggregate tax expenditure estimates must be interpreted carefully. Summing revenue loss estimates does not take into account possible interactions between individual provisions or potential behavioral responses to changes in these provisions on the part of taxpayers. Additionally, Treasury's tax expenditure estimates include the effect of certain tax credits on receipts only and not the effect of the credits on outlays, which Treasury reports separately, but does not take into account interactions between individual provisions.

They are sometimes used to provide economic relief to selected groups of taxpayers, to encourage certain behavior, or to accomplish other goals.

Although they are routinely used as a policy tool, tax expenditures are not regularly reviewed and their outcomes are not measured as closely as spending programs' outcomes. We have made recommendations in this area that remain open.

- Evaluation of tax expenditures. In September 2005, we recommended that OMB take actions to develop a framework for evaluating tax expenditure performance, and to regularly review tax expenditures in executive branch budget and performance review processes.[70] However, OMB has not developed this framework and has not reported progress in evaluating tax expenditures since the President's fiscal year 2012 budget.
- Identify contributions to agency goals. In July 2016, we recommended that OMB work with agencies to identify which tax expenditures contribute to agency goals. OMB generally agreed with the recommendation but had not taken action as of March 2019.[71]

  Absent such analysis, policymakers have little way of knowing whether these tax provisions support achieving the intended federal outcomes. Policymakers also lack information to compare their costs and efficacy with other policy tools.

Improving Stewardship over Defense-Related Resources

The Department of Defense (DOD) accounts for about half of all discretionary spending. In addition, DOD is responsible for more than 70 percent of the government's Property, Plant, and Equipment. It is therefore

[70] GAO, *Government Performance and Accountability: Tax Expenditures Represent a Substantial Federal Commitment and Need to Be Reexamined*, GAO-05-690 (Washington, D.C.: Sept. 23, 2005).

[71] GAO, *Tax Expenditures: Opportunities Exist to Use Budgeting and Agency Performance Processes to Increase Oversight*, GAO-16-622 (Washington, D.C.: July 7, 2016).

important for DOD to exercise careful stewardship over its resources and manage these resources efficiently and effectively. DOD has six areas on our High-Risk List representing some of the fundamental functions of the agency.[72] Several government-wide high-risk areas also have direct implications for DOD and its operations, including (1) the government-wide personnel security clearance process, (2) ensuring the cybersecurity of the nation, (3) improving management of IT acquisitions and operations, (4) strategic human capital management, and (5) managing federal real property. We have made recommendations to help DOD make progress addressing these challenges.

DOD's six high-risk areas are:

- DOD Weapon Systems Acquisition. DOD can get better returns on its over one trillion dollar weapon system investments by following knowledge-based practices and developing an action plan for performance measures.
- DOD Approach to Business Transformation. DOD should accurately track efficiencies gained and costs reduced as it transforms its business functions through a transition to shared services and other efficiency initiatives.
- DOD Business Systems Modernization. DOD needs to improve management of its business system acquisitions, improve management of its portfolio of business system investments, and leverage its federated business enterprise architecture to identify and address potential duplication and overlap across systems.
- DOD Contract Management. DOD faces challenges in how it defines, strategically manages, and budgets for its contracted services, which typically account for about half of the department's $300 billion in annual contract obligations.
- DOD Support Infrastructure Management. DOD needs to better align its infrastructure capacity with its force structure needs and achieve efficiencies by reducing both excess infrastructure and

---

[72] GAO-19-157SP.

base support costs, and maximizing the use of its underutilized facilities.

- DOD Financial Management. DOD needs to assure that leaders across the department continue to improve their efforts to address long-standing financial management problems.

Added to GAO's High-Risk List in 1995, DOD's financial management continues to face long-standing issues, such as ineffective processes, systems, and controls. DOD remains one of the few federal entities that cannot accurately account for, and report on, its spending or assets. In a positive development, DOD underwent the first agency-wide financial statement audit for its fiscal year 2018 financial statements. However, the auditors were unable to express an opinion due to insufficient evidence.

DOD has acknowledged that achieving a clean audit opinion will take time. DOD established a process to remediate any audit findings and ultimately to improve the quality of financial information that is most valuable in managing the department's day-to-day operations. It stated that over the next several years, the resolution of audit findings will serve as an objective measure of progress toward that goal. DOD will need to develop and effectively monitor corrective action plans to appropriately address audit findings in a timely manner.

In addition, our work has identified a number of actions DOD can take to help improve the federal government's fiscal condition:

- Defense distribution centers. In June 2017, we found that, while DOD had taken steps to increase the use of the Defense Logistics Agency's U.S. distribution centers, the department also has other opportunities to use its entire network of U.S. centers more efficiently such as by minimizing unnecessary overlap and duplication.[73] We recommended that DOD assess and direct the implementation of actions, as appropriate, that can be taken using

[73] GAO, *Supply Chain Management: DOD Could More Efficiently Use Its Distribution Centers,* GAO-17-449 (Washington, D.C.: June 21, 2017).

existing authorities to close, realign, or dispose of existing infrastructure to more efficiently use the department's network of U.S. distribution centers. DOD concurred with this recommendation and in July 2017 began to assess options to close, realign, or dispose of existing infrastructure to more efficiently use its network of U.S. distribution centers. DOD estimated by taking such actions, it could potentially save approximately $527 million over 5 years.

- Department of Defense special and incentive pays. The Department of Defense obligates billions of dollars annually on special and incentive pay programs to compensate and incentivize servicemembers for occupations that are dangerous, less desirable, or require special skills. In February 2017, we found that DOD needed to take actions to fully ensure the effectiveness of these programs.[74]

  These actions include incorporating key principles of effective human capital management in its special and incentive pay programs to ensure that the programs are effectively designed and that resources are optimized for the greatest return on investment. For example, using non-monetary incentives to increase retention could lead to program savings totaling tens of millions of dollars annually.
- Foreign military sales administrative account. The U.S. government sells defense equipment and services worth tens of billions of dollars each year to its foreign partners through the Foreign Military Sales (FMS) program. To cover the program's operating costs, DOD collects an administrative fee from purchasers and places it into the administrative account of the FMS trust fund. Since 1989, a portion of FMS program operating expenses, for military pay and unfunded civilian retirement and other benefits, have been paid instead from other appropriated funds.

---

[74] GAO, *Military Compensation: Additional Actions Are Needed to Better Manage Special and Incentive Pay Programs,* GAO-17-39 (Washington, D.C.: Feb. 3, 2017).

In 2018, we found that the FMS administrative account had grown to contain over $4 billion and that it likely would continue to have sufficient funds to pay for program expenses through at least fiscal year 2024 even if the account were to cover more annual expenses than expected.[75] Congress could enhance federal revenue by at least tens of millions of dollars annually through expanding the definition of allowable expenses authorized to be covered by the FMS administrative account, thereby likely reducing the need to cover these expenses with other appropriated funds.

[75] GAO, *Foreign Military Sales: Controls Should Be Strengthened to Address Substantial Growth in Overhead Account Balances,* GAO-18-401 (Washington, D.C.: May 10, 2018).

In: Key Government Reports. Vol. 33
Editor: Ernest Clark
ISBN: 978-1-53616-566-1

Chapter 6

FEDERAL HOUSING ADMINISTRATION: IMPROVED PROCEDURES AND ASSESSMENT COULD INCREASE EFFICIENCY OF FORECLOSED PROPERTY CONVEYANCES*

United States Government Accountability Office

ABBREVIATIONS

asset disposition system	P260 Asset Disposition and Management System
CWCOT	Claims without Conveyance of Title program
enterprises	government-sponsored enterprises
FAQ	frequently asked questions
FHA	Federal Housing Administration

* This is an edited, reformatted and augmented version of United States Government Accountability Office; Report to Congressional Committees, Publication No. GAO-19-517, dated June 2019.

HOA	homeowners association
HOC	homeownership center
HUD	Department of Housing and Urban Development
REO	real estate-owned
servicers	mortgage servicers

Why GAO Did This Study

FHA insures hundreds of thousands of single-family home mortgages annually. When an FHA borrower defaults, the mortgage servicer in many cases forecloses, obtains title to the property, and conveys ownership to FHA. FHA inspects the property, acquires it if it complies with condition standards and title requirements, and lists the property for sale. FHA may reconvey noncompliant properties to servicers. During conveyance, homes may sit vacant for months and can deteriorate, contributing to neighborhood blight.

Senate Report 114-243 included a provision for GAO to review FHA's effectiveness and efficiency in reaching determinations of conveyable condition. This chapter discusses (1) timelines for FHA property conveyances in 2010–2017 and whether servicers and FHA met time requirements, and (2) changes FHA has made to the conveyance process in recent years and any ongoing process challenges. GAO analyzed FHA data on properties conveyed in 2010–2017, reviewed FHA's policies and procedures, and interviewed 20 randomly selected mortgage servicers accounting for more than one-third of active FHA mortgages.

What GAO Recommends

GAO recommends that FHA (1) enhance the content and communication of policies and procedures on conveyance condition, (2) provide written direction on alternatives to reconveyance, and (3) develop a plan to assess a pilot program. FHA agreed with the second and third recommendations and did not agree or disagree with the first.

WHAT GAO FOUND

From July 2010 through December 2017, the process for conveying foreclosed properties to the Federal Housing Administration (FHA) took a median of 70 days. The conveyance process—which GAO measured from a mortgage servicer's obtaining title to and possession of the property to FHA's marketing of the property—involves servicers making repairs, transferring ownership, and filing a mortgage insurance claim, and FHA inspecting the property. FHA attributes the length of time to complete the process partly to foreclosure processing delays that left properties vulnerable to damage and vandalism, which can increase the time servicers need to bring properties into conveyance condition. Property damage also may increase the likelihood that FHA will reconvey a property (transfer it to the servicer) for not complying with condition standards, further extending the conveyance process. For about 55 percent of properties conveyed in July 2010–December 2017, servicers exceeded the required time to obtain title and possession of a foreclosed property and convey it to FHA. For 2017 alone, the corresponding figure was 72 percent. As a result, servicers were not eligible to be reimbursed for all repairs and interest expenses for those properties when filing insurance claims with FHA.

In recent years, FHA changed aspects of its conveyance process to help address some of the execution challenges the agency and servicers have faced. For example, in 2016, FHA enhanced its data system for conveyed properties to reduce manual administrative processing. FHA also began a pilot program in 2017 to decrease the number of properties FHA reconveys by inspecting properties before conveyance. However, GAO found shortcomings in FHA policies, procedures, and assessment efforts that are inconsistent with federal evaluation criteria and internal control standards, as follows:

- FHA's policies and procedures lack detail that could help servicers and contractors determine if a property is in compliance, and the agency has not examined alternative methods of communicating this information. Fifteen of the 20 servicers GAO interviewed said existing policies, procedures, and communications often were not clear or specific enough to address property conditions or repair decisions they encountered. FHA also relies on brief written policies to explain standards and makes limited or no use of other methods, such as photographs or industry-wide calls.
- FHA has not provided written direction on when to use alternatives to reconveyance—such as agreements under which servicers make repairs or repay FHA for any repair costs after conveyance—for properties not meeting condition standards. In the absence of such direction, FHA may not be addressing these properties in the most consistent or effective manner.
- FHA has not developed a plan to assess the outcome of its inspection pilot. Without rigorous assessment, FHA risks making decisions about the future of the pilot based on inaccurate or incomplete information.

Addressing these shortcomings could help improve the efficiency and effectiveness of FHA's property conveyance process.

June 20, 2019

The Honorable Susan M. Collins
Chairwoman

The Honorable Jack Reed
Ranking Member
Subcommittee on Transportation, Housing
and Urban Development, and Related Agencies
Committee on Appropriations
United States Senate

The Honorable David E. Price
Chairman

The Honorable Mario Diaz-Balart
Ranking Member
Subcommittee on Transportation, and Housing
and Urban Development, and Related Agencies
Committee on Appropriations
House of Representatives

The Federal Housing Administration (FHA) within the Department of Housing and Urban Development (HUD) facilitates homeownership by insuring lenders against losses on mortgages that finance purchases of properties or refinance existing FHA mortgages. In fiscal year 2018, FHA insured about one million single-family mortgages, providing about $209 billion in mortgage insurance. Each year, mortgage servicers (servicers) foreclose on a portion of the FHA-insured mortgages that go into default and file insurance claims with FHA.[1] One method of disposing of foreclosed properties involves a servicer conveying a property's title (transferring ownership) to FHA, which then markets and sells the home. Servicers conveyed about 31,700 foreclosed properties to FHA in calendar year 2017, the most recent year for which data were available when we conducted our analysis. In general, the properties are vacant for some or all of the period between foreclosure and FHA's sale of the home.[2] We and others previously reported that vacant properties can deteriorate if not maintained and can contribute to crime, blight, and declining property values in surrounding neighborhoods.[3]

---

[1] Mortgage servicers are bank or nonbank entities that perform activities such as accepting loan payments, initiating collection actions for delinquent payments, modifying loan terms, and foreclosing if necessary. Mortgages may be serviced by the originator of the loan or another entity.

[2] HUD regulations allow occupied properties to be conveyed to FHA in certain cases, such as when state or local law prohibits the eviction of a tenant who is making regular monthly payments. According to FHA, this happens in less than 1 percent of conveyances.

[3] For example, see GAO, *Vacant Properties: Growing Number Increases Communities' Costs and Challenges*, GAO-12-34 (Washington, D.C.: Nov. 4, 2011); and *Mortgage*

To convey a foreclosed property to FHA, a servicer must complete several steps that include, but are not limited to, obtaining good and marketable title, ensuring the property is vacant and secured, and removing exterior and interior debris.[4] Once the servicer conveys the title to FHA, FHA inspects the property to determine whether it meets conveyance requirements before selling the property out of its real estate- owned (REO) inventory.[5] In this chapter, we define the conveyance process as beginning when the servicer obtains good and marketable title and takes possession of the property and ending when FHA markets the property.

Timely execution of the conveyance process can help minimize the time properties sit vacant and get foreclosed properties on the market sooner.

Senate Report 114-243, accompanying the Transportation and Housing and Urban Development, and Related Agencies Appropriations Bill, 2017, includes a provision for us to review FHA's effectiveness and efficiency in reaching determinations of conveyable condition on foreclosed properties.[6] This chapter examines (1) time lines for FHA foreclosed property conveyances from July 2010 through December 2017 and the extent to which servicers and FHA met time requirements, and (2) changes FHA has

---

Foreclosures: Additional Mortgage Servicer Actions Could Help Reduce the Frequency and Impact of Abandoned Foreclosures, GAO-11-93 (Washington, D.C.: Nov. 15, 2010).

[4] According to HUD regulations, good and marketable title means the title is free from all liens, including any unpaid ground rents, taxes, or special assessments. See 24 C.F.R. § 203.386.

[5] In two prior reports on FHA's REO process, we found that FHA's divided approach to custody of foreclosed properties (between servicers and FHA) could delay the start of steps needed to sell properties and may have contributed to FHA taking substantially longer to market properties than other mortgage entities. As a result, in an April 2002 report, we recommended that HUD determine and implement the optimal method of establishing unified property custody, seeking additional statutory authority if needed. Although HUD generally agreed with the recommendation, it said it would need to research the feasibility of implementation. HUD ultimately determined it would not be advisable to establish unified property custody and did not implement our recommendation. In a June 2013 report, we made 10 recommendations to increase the potential for higher returns on disposed REO properties and improve oversight of the REO disposition program, all of which HUD implemented. See GAO, *Single-Family Housing: Opportunities to Improve Federal Foreclosure and Property Sale Processes*, GAO-02-305 (Washington, D.C.: Apr. 17, 2002); and *Federal Housing Administration: Improving Disposition and Oversight Practices May Increase Returns on Foreclosed Property Sales*, GAO-13-542 (Washington, D.C.: June 20, 2013).

[6] S. Rep. No. 114-243, at 125 (2016).

made to the conveyance process in recent years and any ongoing process challenges.[7]

To examine time lines for property conveyances and the extent to which servicers and FHA met time requirements, we reviewed FHA regulations and policies about the time frames FHA, its contractors, and mortgage servicers must meet for conveyed properties. We also analyzed property foreclosure and conveyance data from two FHA data systems for properties conveyed to FHA in 2010–2017 (2017 was the most recent year for which data were available when we conducted our analysis). Our time line analyses begin in July 2010 because FHA changed how it managed the conveyance process in June 2010. To assess the reliability of FHA's data, we reviewed FHA documentation and conducted electronic testing, including checks for outliers, missing data fields, and erroneous values. We determined these data were sufficiently reliable for purposes of characterizing the length of the conveyance process and servicer and FHA timeliness.

To determine recent changes FHA made to the conveyance process and any ongoing process challenges, we reviewed updates to FHA regulations, policies, and procedures for conveyances since 2010 and interviewed FHA officials on reasons for the changes. We also interviewed FHA headquarters and field office officials and FHA contractors with responsibilities for property inspections and approving servicer property preservation costs about any challenges they experience executing the conveyance process. We conducted semistructured interviews with a nongeneralizable random sample of 20 large- and medium-sized servicers of FHA-insured mortgages about any challenges they have had with conveyance policies and procedures, including time lines and property preservation allowances. These servicers accounted for more than one-third of active FHA-insured mortgages as of December 31, 2017. We also visited eight recently conveyed or reconveyed properties in the Baltimore, Maryland, and Atlanta, Georgia, areas to observe property conditions and understand any challenges in documenting and addressing condition issues.

[7] Unless otherwise noted, all years in this report are calendar years.

Appendix I describes our scope and methodology in greater detail.

We conducted this performance audit from September 2017 to June 2019 in accordance with generally accepted government auditing standards.

Those standards require that we plan and perform the audit to obtain sufficient, appropriate evidence to provide a reasonable basis for our findings and conclusions based on our audit objectives. We believe that the evidence obtained provides a reasonable basis for our findings and conclusions based on our audit objectives.

BACKGROUND

Established by the National Housing Act, FHA's single-family mortgage insurance program helps home buyers obtain financing by providing insurance on single-family mortgage loans. The mortgage insurance allows FHA-approved private lenders to provide qualified borrowers with mortgages on properties with one to four housing units and generally compensates lenders for nearly all the losses incurred on such loans. To support the program, FHA imposes up-front and annual mortgage insurance premiums on FHA borrowers.[8] The agency has played a particularly large role among first-time, minority, and low-income home buyers. For example, in fiscal year 2017, about 82 percent of FHA- insured home purchase loans went to first-time home buyers and more than 33 percent went to minority home buyers.

Foreclosure Mitigation and Property Disposition Methods

FHA requires servicers to undertake certain home retention and foreclosure mitigation actions to help delinquent homeowners catch up on

[8] The Mutual Mortgage Insurance Fund, which supports this program, is statutorily required to maintain at least a 2 percent capital ratio, defined as the fund's economic net worth divided by the remaining principal balance on all insured loans in the fund.

late mortgage payments. Before initiating foreclosure actions, FHA requires servicers to contact the borrower, collect information on the borrower's finances, and attempt informal methods of resolving the delinquency. If informal steps are not appropriate for a borrower's circumstances, the servicer evaluates the borrower for a series of home retention actions, which include a formal forbearance and repayment plan and a loan modification. Under certain circumstances, the servicer may consider a foreclosure mitigation option, such as a preforeclosure (short) sale or a deed-in-lieu of foreclosure.[9] If the home retention and foreclosure mitigation actions are unsuccessful, the servicer or mortgage note holder is generally entitled to pursue foreclosure to obtain title to the property. The foreclosure process is governed by state laws, but foreclosed properties are typically auctioned at a foreclosure sale. Most foreclosed properties are disposed of in one of two ways.

- Claims without Conveyance of Title (CWCOT). Through FHA's CWCOT program, the servicer attempts to secure a third-party purchase of an eligible property for an adjusted fair market value that is less than the amount of the servicer's projected claim.[10]
- Conveyance. If the foreclosure process is completed and no third party purchases the home at the foreclosure sale, the home usually becomes the property of the servicer. Servicers convey these properties to FHA, which sells them out of its REO inventory.

During the default and foreclosure process, servicers must meet two FHA time requirements.[11] The first requires servicers to initiate a foreclosure (first legal action) or utilize a loss mitigation option within 6 months of borrower default. The second requirement, for the "reasonable

---

[9] In a preforeclosure sale, the servicer agrees to accept the proceeds from the sale of the property to a third party, although the sale price is less than the sum of the principal, accrued interest, and other expenses owed. In a deed-in-lieu, a delinquent borrower avoids foreclosure by agreeing to transfer the property title to the lender.

[10] In 2014, FHA began utilizing its revised CWCOT program, which requires servicers to offer all eligible properties for sale through CWCOT before using the conveyance process.

[11] According to FHA servicing guidance, a loan goes into default 30 days after the borrower has missed a full payment.

diligence" period, requires servicers to obtain good and marketable title and possession of a property within a specified time frame that varies by state. The servicer secures the property and obtains possession once the property is vacant. Servicers are subject to financial penalties for missing these deadlines. In both cases, servicers must curtail the debenture interest that they otherwise would be entitled to collect from the date of the missed time frame.[12]

Servicers are responsible for maintaining vacant foreclosed properties in accordance with FHA requirements, which specify allowable reimbursable amounts to preserve and protect the property. A servicer needing additional funds to complete the required maintenance must submit an "overallowable" request to FHA.

Property Conveyance Process

When a servicer forecloses on a property with an FHA-insured mortgage and the property is not sold to a third party through CWCOT, the property is held in the servicer's name until the servicer conveys the title to FHA. As seen in figure 1, these properties span a range of home types and ages. FHA requires servicers to preserve and protect the property and ensure it meets FHA's conveyance condition standards before conveying title. FHA's preservation and protection requirements include a number of specific steps for securing, maintaining, and repairing properties and documenting property conditions.[13] FHA reimburses the servicer for up to $5,000 per property for required work, and the servicer may request overallowable funds if needed. FHA's conveyance condition standards are

[12] Servicers typically use borrowed funds to finance the payment of outstanding debt on mortgages in the process of foreclosure. When servicers bid on properties at foreclosure sales, they continue to use borrowed funds to finance the recovered properties. Servicers pay interest on these borrowings, which is referred to as the cost of funds, until they file claims with FHA when properties are conveyed. FHA compensates servicers for their interest expenses at what is known as the debenture interest rate. The rate is set by statute at the monthly average yield on U. S. Treasury securities for the month in which the default on the mortgage occurred, adjusted to a constant maturity of 10 years. See 12 U.S.C. § 1715o.

[13] Servicers generally hire vendors to complete property preservation and protection work and any work needed to get the property into conveyance condition.

broader requirements, including that a property be undamaged by natural disaster and in "broom swept" condition, have all damage covered by hazard insurance repaired, and be undamaged by the servicer's failure to properly secure or maintain the property.[14]

Source: GAO. | GAO-19-517.

Figure 1. Examples of Properties Conveyed to the Federal Housing Administration in 2018.

HUD regulations state that the servicer must obtain good and marketable title and convey the property to HUD within 30 days of the date on which the servicer filed the foreclosure deed for record or certain other key dates, whichever is later.[15] If a servicer does not believe it will be

---

[14] Servicers generally are not required to fix damage caused by the borrower.

[15] For mortgages insured on or after November 19, 1992, servicers must obtain good and marketable title and transfer the property to FHA within 30 days of the later of the filing of the foreclosure deed for record; recording date of the deed-in-lieu of foreclosure; acquiring possession of the property; expiration of the redemption period; or the date of any extension provided by FHA. See 24 C.F.R. § 203.359(b).

able to convey the property by this time, it may request an extension from FHA. The servicer files an insurance claim with FHA when it conveys the title. If a servicer does not convey the property within the required time frame and has not received an approved extension, the servicer must curtail the debenture interest and property preservation and protection expenses it claims as of the date of the missed deadline.[16]

Shortly after conveyance, FHA pays the Part A claim to the servicer, which includes the unpaid principal balance and debenture interest on the insured mortgage. At this time, FHA becomes responsible for maintaining the property until it is sold. FHA pays the part of the claim that covers eligible property preservation and protection expenses incurred by the servicer once the servicer submits title evidence and documentation of expenses (in Part B of the claim form). FHA inspects the property and reviews title evidence before selling the property out of its REO inventory. In some cases, FHA reconveys the title to the servicer if it finds the servicer did not comply with requirements related to property condition or title. When a property is reconveyed, FHA reassigns the title to the servicer and requests repayment of the claim amount. The servicer then must correct any title or property condition issues before it may convey the property and submit a claim to FHA again.

Throughout this process, FHA and servicers use the P260 Asset Disposition and Management System (asset disposition system) to communicate and upload documentation about the properties. FHA articulates its property preservation and protection requirements and conveyance condition standards in a mortgagee letter and policy handbook that we refer to collectively as FHA's conveyance condition policies and procedures.[17]

From 2010 through 2017, servicers conveyed about 610,000 properties to FHA. The number of properties conveyed annually peaked in 2012 at

---

[16] If the servicer missed one of the earlier deadlines—the first legal action or reasonable diligence time frames—it already should have curtailed debenture interest from that point.

[17] See Department of Housing and Urban Development Mortgagee Letter 2016-02 (Washington, D.C.: Feb. 5, 2016); and Handbook 4000.1, Single Family Housing Policy Handbook (Washington, D.C.: Dec. 30, 2016). Mortgagee letters are written instructions that FHA periodically issues to its approved lenders and servicers.

about 111,000 (see Figure 2). In 2017, servicers conveyed fewer than 32,000 properties to FHA. The decline in recent years is consistent with improvements in the housing market since the 2007–2011 housing crisis.[18]

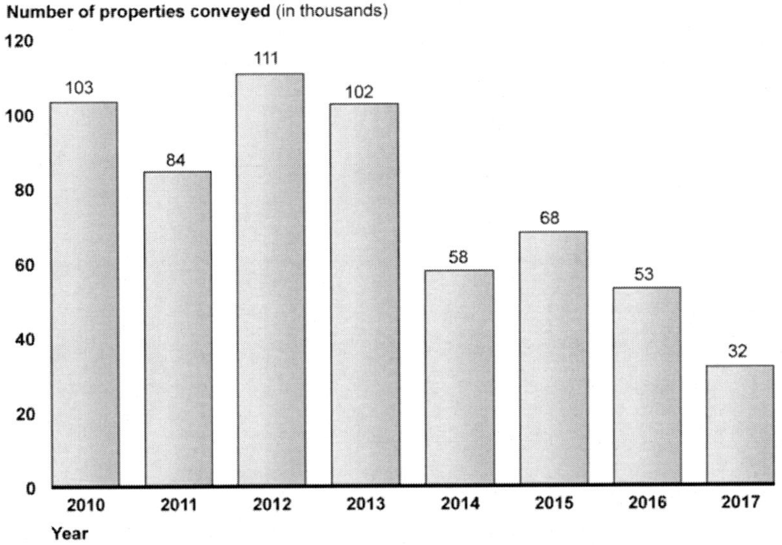

Source: GAO analysis of FHA data. | GAO-19-517.

Figure 2. Number of Properties Conveyed to the Federal Housing Administration (FHA), 2010–2017.

Roles and Responsibilities in the Conveyance Process

In this chapter, we define FHA's property conveyance process as beginning when the servicer both obtains good and marketable title and takes possession of a property and ending when FHA assigns a marketing contractor to sell the property out of its REO inventory (see Figure 3).

[18] According to the S&P/Case Shiller National Home Price Index, average home prices fell each year in 2007–2011, for a total decline of almost 27 percent.

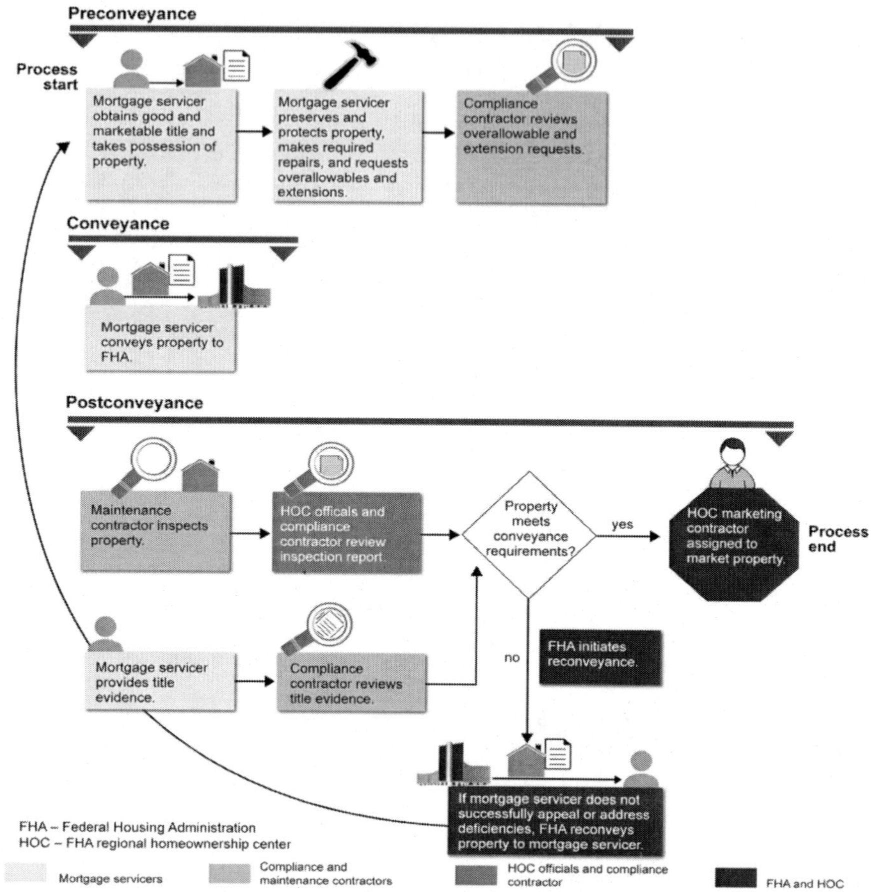

Source: GAO. | GAO-19-517.

Figure 3. Federal Housing Administration's Property Conveyance Process.

Several FHA contractors and offices play key roles in the conveyance process.

- Compliance contractor. A nationwide compliance contractor called the mortgagee compliance manager is responsible for protecting FHA's interests in properties conveyed to FHA and communicates directly with servicers about the properties. The compliance contractor reviews property inspections to ensure properties meet conveyance condition standards, reviews requests from servicers for extensions of conveyance times or for overallowable expenses, reviews servicer claims for compliance with requirements, and responds to servicer inquiries about pre- and postconveyance responsibilities. The compliance contractor is located in Oklahoma City, Oklahoma, and is overseen by FHA's National Servicing Center.

- Maintenance contractor. Maintenance contractors, called field service managers, are responsible for inspecting properties recently conveyed to FHA and preserving properties in FHA's REO inventory. FHA has multiple maintenance contractors; they are responsible for properties in different regions. Upon conveyance, the maintenance contractor conducts a comprehensive property inspection to determine if the property meets conveyance condition standards and completes the HUD Property Inspection Report. The maintenance contractor also conducts other inspections at a property before conveyance, as warranted, including a preconveyance inspection at the request of the servicer and an overallowable inspection if requested by the compliance contractor. While these contractors conduct general maintenance on the property, they typically do not make major repairs, because FHA generally sells conveyed properties in as-is condition.
- Marketing contractor. Marketing contractors, called asset managers, are responsible for marketing and selling the homes in FHA's REO inventory.
- FHA homeownership centers. FHA carries out its mortgage insurance and REO disposition programs through four regional offices called homeownership centers (HOC). The centers are located in Atlanta, Georgia; Denver, Colorado; Philadelphia, Pennsylvania; and Santa Ana, California.[19] Officials in each HOC

[19] The Atlanta HOC serves Alabama, the Caribbean, Florida, Georgia, Illinois, Indiana, Kentucky, Mississippi, North Carolina, South Carolina, and Tennessee. The Denver HOC serves Arkansas, Colorado, Iowa, Kansas, Louisiana, Minnesota, Missouri, Montana, New Mexico, Nebraska, North Dakota, Oklahoma, South Dakota, Texas, Utah, Wisconsin, and Wyoming. The Philadelphia HOC serves Connecticut, Delaware, District of Columbia, Maine, Maryland, Massachusetts, Michigan, New Hampshire, New Jersey, New York,

are responsible for overseeing the maintenance and marketing contractors for their region and reviewing HUD Property Inspection Reports to determine if conveyed properties should be reconveyed to the servicer due to condition issues. This determination is then forwarded to the compliance contractor for an additional review.

- HUD's Office of Finance and Budget. Staff from this office are responsible for reviewing servicer mortgage insurance claims for compliance with FHA requirements. The office selects a sample of claims from the past 3 years to review whether the property preservation and protection expenses were within allowable limits and whether the servicer curtailed debenture interest and property preservation and protection expenses accurately, among other things.

Other Participants in the Mortgage Market

A number of other federal and federally sponsored entities participate in the mortgage market. Along with FHA, the Department of Veterans Affairs and the Department of Agriculture operate programs that guarantee single-family mortgages made by private lenders.[20] Additionally, two government-sponsored enterprises—Fannie Mae and Freddie Mac (enterprises)—purchase and securitize single-family mortgages.[21]

Ohio, Pennsylvania, Rhode Island, Vermont, Virginia, and West Virginia. The Santa Ana HOC serves Alaska, Arizona, California, Hawaii, Idaho, Nevada, Oregon, and Washington.

[20] The Department of Veterans Affairs Loan Guaranty program is an entitlement for veterans, certain members of the National Guard or Reservists who are currently serving, and spouses of certain veterans. The Department of Agriculture's Single Family Housing Guaranteed Loan Program guarantees mortgages for low- and moderate-income households in eligible rural areas.

[21] Congress established the enterprises as for-profit, shareholder-owned corporations. The enterprises purchase conventional mortgages that meet their underwriting standards.
They package the mortgages they purchase into mortgage-backed securities, which are sold to investors in the secondary mortgage market. In exchange for a fee, the enterprises guarantee the timely payment of interest and principal on the securities they issue. In 2008, the Federal Housing Finance Agency placed the enterprises into conservatorships out of

However, the property disposition programs for these entities are not directly analogous to FHA's. In contrast to FHA, the Department of Veterans Affairs and the enterprises take custody of and are responsible for properties closer to the time of the foreclosure sale.[22] The enterprises require servicers to convey properties to them within 24 hours of foreclosure sale or deed-in-lieu of foreclosure, while the Department of Veterans Affairs requires servicers to provide notice of their intent to convey properties within 15 days of foreclosure sale. Also in contrast to FHA, the Department of Agriculture does not take possession of foreclosed properties with guaranteed loans, but rather oversees their disposition by lenders.

In FHA's case, properties are often held in the lender's or servicer's name for an extended period after the foreclosure sale. Following the foreclosure sale, FHA requires servicers to oversee properties during redemption periods, to evict residents if properties not in redemption periods are occupied, and to continue property preservation and protection activities.[23] In addition, before conveyance, servicers must identify and pay any homeowners association (HOA) fees and utility bills that are due. As described in Figure 3, servicers also must make any required repairs, meet other conveyance requirements, and pass an FHA property inspection, or face the prospect of having the property reconveyed. FHA officials said this approach reduces FHA's holding time and costs and that the agency does not have the infrastructure to manage and fund property repairs itself.

---

concern that their deteriorating financial condition threatened the stability of financial markets.

[22] However, all the entities have property preservation requirements that servicers must follow for vacant properties securing delinquent loans.

[23] Certain states provide the previous owners of foreclosed properties with a right of redemption that allows them to pay amounts owed to the lender and reclaim ownership. During redemption periods, the previous owner or current occupant is allowed to remain in the residence and the REO property owner or servicer generally is not permitted to pursue activities such as evicting property residents or securing properties.

FHA'S PROPERTY CONVEYANCE PROCESS OFTEN TAKES A LONG TIME, AND SERVICERS AND CONTRACTORS PERFORMANCE AGAINST TIME REQUIREMENTS VARIED

Conveyance Times Increased after 2011, Partly due to Greater Use of Other Disposition Methods and Extended Default and Foreclosure Periods

Data on Time Frames for Conveyance and Reconveyance

From July 2010 through December 2017, the property conveyance process took a median of 70 days, but this figure varied widely by year.[24] Our analysis of FHA data found that, from 2011 through 2015, the median number of days to complete the conveyance process increased four-fold (from 41 to 161 days) and varied more widely around the median each successive year (see Figure 4).[25] Conveyance time frames declined substantially in 2016 and 2017 (to a median of 137 days and 112 days, respectively) while continuing to vary considerably around the median. In comparison, FHA officials said the conveyance process generally should take about 37 days to complete—30 days for servicers to make necessary repairs and convey title to FHA and 7 days for FHA to inspect the property, communicate any condition issues identified during the inspection, and assign a marketing contractor to promote and sell it.[26]

---

[24] We collected data on FHA property conveyances from January 2010 through December 2017, but excluded properties conveyed before July 2010 from our analysis because FHA changed the way it managed property conveyances in June 2010. Specifically, at that time FHA launched the third generation of its Management and Marketing contractor program. Under prior arrangements, FHA's contractors were responsible for both the maintenance and marketing of FHA's REO properties. Under the current structure, separate contractors perform these functions. FHA also began a new compliance management contract in June 2010.

[25] From July 2010 through December 2010, the median length of the conveyance process was 82 days. FHA officials told us the length of the conveyance process that year was affected by program changes, including the introduction of a new Management and Marketing contractor program.

[26] These time frames are consistent with regulatory and contract performance requirements discussed later in this report.

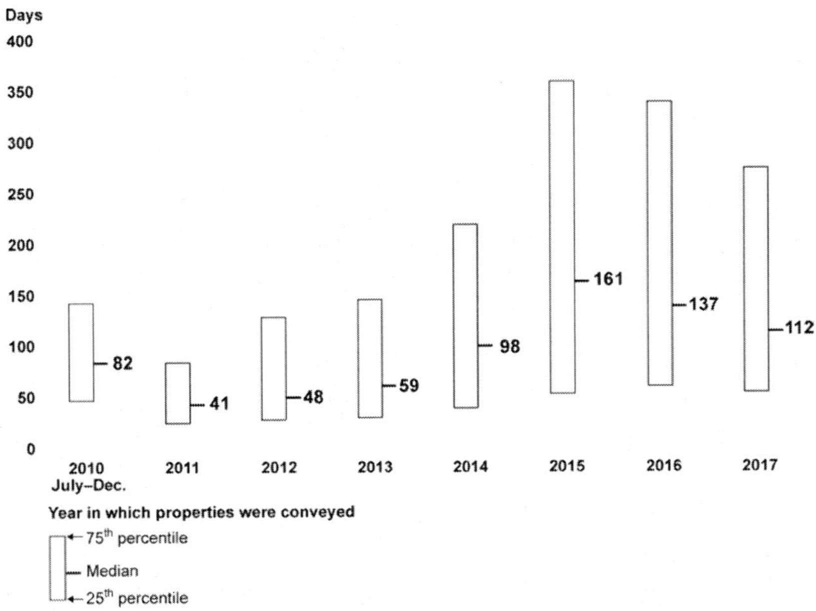

Source: GAO analysis of FHA data. | GAO-19-517.

Note: We excluded properties conveyed from January through June 2010 from our analysis because FHA changed how it managed the conveyance process in June 2010.

Figure 4. Length of the Federal Housing Administration's (FHA) Property Conveyance Process, July 2010–December 2017.

We also found that the time it took properties to complete the conveyance process varied by HOC region. For the entire July 2010–December 2017 period, the Philadelphia HOC had the highest median time frame (91 days) and the Atlanta HOC the lowest (56 days). The Santa Ana and Denver HOCs had medians of 78 and 67 days, respectively. A number of factors may have contributed to differences among the HOCs, such as the number of properties conveyed in each region (which can affect servicer and HOC capacity) and the age of the housing stock (which can affect the time needed to make repairs).

Mold and ceiling damage in kitchen

Mold damage in basement

A door that was broken into

Ceiling damage from a roof leak

Source: GAO. | GAO-19-517.

Figure 5. Damage at Properties in the Atlanta and Baltimore Areas That the Federal Housing Administration Designated for Reconveyance.

The time to complete the conveyance process includes, when applicable, the time needed for FHA to reconvey a property—that is, transfer ownership to the servicer due to condition or title issues—and for the servicer to convey it to FHA a second time.[27] FHA officials said they try to avoid reconveyances because they prolong the conveyance process and result in FHA incurring additional preservation and protection costs.

---

[27] Our analysis of available FHA data on reconveyance reasons indicates that about 69 percent of properties were reconveyed from October 31, 2016, through December 2017 because of condition issues and about 28 percent due to title issues, such as liens on the property. Less than 2 percent of properties were reconveyed because they had both condition and title issues.

Figure 5 shows examples of condition issues at properties we visited in the Baltimore, Maryland, and Atlanta, Georgia, metropolitan areas that were in the reconveyance process.[28]

Our analysis of FHA data found that reconveyances were not common enough to significantly affect median conveyance time frames, but substantially lengthened the conveyance process when they did occur. As shown in Table 1, servicers conveyed 406,863 properties to FHA from 2012 through 2017—the period within our scope for which FHA had reliable reconveyance data. In comparison, FHA reconveyed 8,874 properties to servicers during that time frame.[29] The annual number of reconveyances rose from 1,019 in 2012 to 1,935 in 2015, before declining to 1,099 in 2017.

Table 1. Number of properties conveyed and reconveyed annually, 2012–2017

Year	Number of properties conveyed to FHA	Number of properties reconveyed to servicers
2012	108,852	1,019
2013	100,434	1,752
2014	55,287	1,595
2015	65,170	1,935
2016	49,101	1,474
2017	28,019	1,099
Total	406,863	8,874

Legend: FHA = Federal Housing Administration.

Source: GAO analysis of FHA data. | GAO-19-517.

Note: Reconveyances may have not occurred in the same year as the original conveyance.

We also found that the median time to complete FHA's conveyance process in 2012–2017 was more than 614 days longer for reconveyed properties than the median for properties not reconveyed. However, the difference between the medians declined over time, dropping from 777 days in 2012 to 267 days in 2017 (see Figure 6).

[28] To reconvey a property, FHA first issues the servicer a preliminary notice of intent to reconvey that lists the reasons for the reconveyance. Servicers may appeal the notices.

[29] According to FHA officials, data on reconveyances in the asset disposition system were not reliable before calendar year 2012.

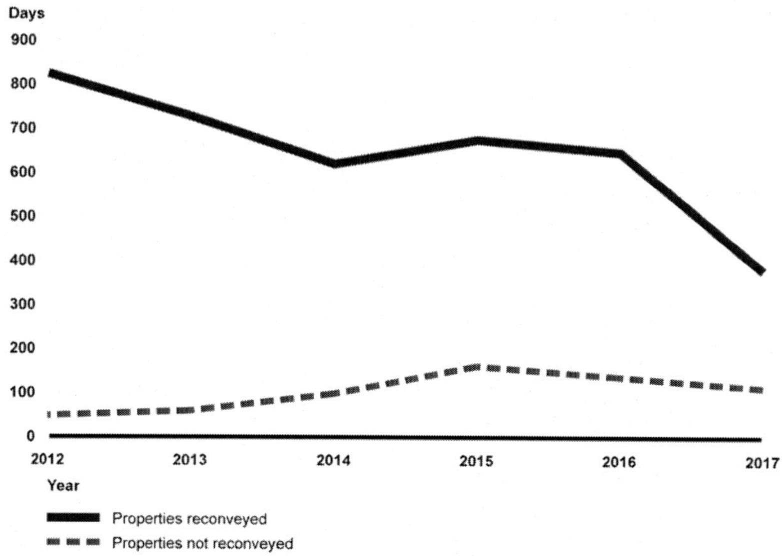

Source: GAO analysis of FHA data. | GAO-19-517.

Figure 6. Median Length of Conveyance Process for Properties That Were and Were Not Reconveyed to Servicers by the Federal Housing Administration (FHA), 2012–2017.

Servicers and FHA must take several steps to complete the conveyance process for reconveyed properties, which may account for some of the length of the time frames. Once the compliance contractor has notified the servicer that a property has condition issues that must be resolved to avoid reconveyance, the servicer may appeal. FHA officials said appeals can add up to 120 days to the conveyance process. If the servicer is unable to resolve the issues and the appeals are denied, FHA reconveys the property and the servicer must reimburse FHA for the original claim amount. The servicer then must complete any required repairs, resolve any title issues, prepare a new evidence package for FHA showing that condition and title issues were addressed, and submit a request to FHA's compliance contractor to convey the property again. FHA's compliance contractor then has 10 business days to review the evidence package and notify the servicer of its decision. Once conveyance is approved, the servicer may resubmit a new mortgage insurance claim form and evidence that the property deed has been filed in FHA's name.

Factors Likely Contributing to Increased Length of Conveyance Process

Two factors that likely contributed to the increase in the time to complete FHA's conveyance process are increased use of other disposition methods and property damage stemming from extended default and foreclosure periods.

Increased Use of Third-Party Sales

FHA data indicate that from 2010 through 2017 servicers increasingly disposed of properties through third- party sales using the CWCOT program. As previously noted, in 2014 FHA began requiring servicers to offer all eligible properties for sale through CWCOT before using the conveyance process. According to our analysis of FHA property disposition data, in fiscal years 2010–2017, the share of properties disposed of through CWCOT rose from about 1.4 percent to almost 44 percent, while the share of conveyance and REO sales dropped from about 84 percent to 42 percent (see Figure 7).[30] The remaining properties were disposed of through notes sales or preforeclosure sales.[31]

Increased use of CWCOT may have extended property conveyance time frames for two reasons. First, servicers must attempt to sell all eligible properties through CWCOT while simultaneously preparing them for conveyance, which may add additional time to the conveyance process according to FHA officials. Second, properties conveyed to FHA because they are not eligible for or sold through the CWCOT program are generally in poorer condition and require more repairs, according to servicer representatives.[32] This may contribute to extended conveyance time

[30] Data on FHA property dispositions are published annually in HUD reports to Congress on the Mutual Mortgage Insurance Fund. See Department of Housing and Urban Development, *Annual Report to Congress Regarding the Financial Status of the FHA Mutual Mortgage Insurance Fund, Fiscal Year 2018* (Washington, D.C.: Nov. 15, 2018).

[31] FHA conducts note sales by auctioning pools of defaulted FHA-insured loans through its Distressed Asset Stabilization Program. The loan pools are generally sold at a price below the outstanding principal balance.

[32] Properties that are not eligible for the CWCOT program include those for which the FHA-insured mortgage is subject to indemnification and those for which the servicer's projected conveyance claim amount is less than the FHA Commissioner's adjusted fair market value for the property. Properties with surchargeable damage are also not eligible. Surchargeable

frames. For example, a representative from one mortgage industry group told us that properties ineligible for CWCOT and conveyed to FHA generally require more than the $5,000 in preservation and protection costs that FHA allows. In these cases, servicers may request additional funds from the compliance contractor, but processing the requests may prolong the conveyance process, as discussed later in this chapter.

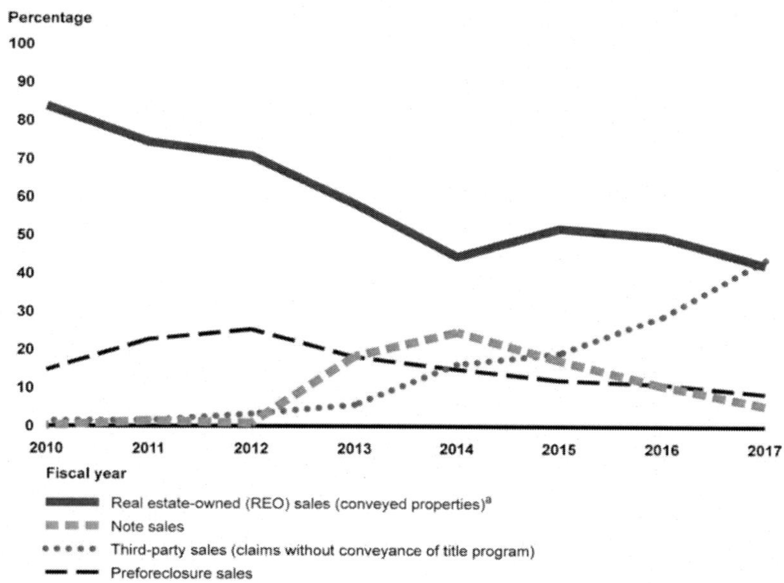

Source: GAO analysis of FHA data. | GAO-19-517.

[a]Data represent the number of properties sold from FHA's REO inventory, which includes properties conveyed to FHA in prior years.

Figure 7. Use of Federal Housing Administration (FHA) Property Disposition Methods, Fiscal Years 2010–2017.

Representatives from one servicer and two mortgage industry groups stated they prefer the CWCOT program because it reduces the need to convey properties. They said the conveyance process is costly and comes with the risk of reconveyance. FHA data show that REO sales generally had higher loss severity rates (the financial loss on a defaulted loan as a

damage is caused by fire, flood, earthquake, tornado, boiler explosion (for condominiums only), or mortgagee (servicer) neglect.

percentage of the unpaid principal balance) than properties disposed of through alternative methods, including the CWCOT program. For example, for the last quarter of fiscal year 2017, FHA reported that the loss severity rate for properties sold through REO was 54.8 percent, while the combined loss severity rate for properties disposed of through alternative methods was 43.8 percent. However, some of this difference may be attributable to the poorer condition of conveyed properties, as discussed previously.

Extended Default and Foreclosure Periods

According to FHA officials, properties with long default and foreclosure periods may be in poor condition because they deteriorate if servicers delay property maintenance and repairs.[33] FHA officials said this was common for properties conveyed to FHA after the 2012 National Mortgage Settlement because some servicers delayed foreclosure proceedings to limit their exposure to litigation in 2010 and 2011 (see sidebar).

National Mortgage Settlement

In February 2012, the Department of Justice and 49 states settled with the five largest mortgage servicers— Ally Financial, Inc. (formerly GMAC), Bank of America Corporation, Citigroup Inc., J.P. Morgan Chase & Co., and Wells Fargo & Company — to address mortgage servicing, foreclosure, and bankruptcy abuses. The agreement settled state and federal investigations finding that these servicers routinely signed foreclosure-related documents without verifying their validity and without the presence of a notary public—a practice known as "robosigning."

Source: GAO and U.S. Department of Justice | GAO-19-517.

---

[33] The length of a property's default and foreclosure period is affected by the reasonable diligence requirements in the state in which the property is located. For example, some states have a legally required redemption period. Many states also require servicers to foreclose on the borrower through court proceedings (judicial foreclosure), which may be lengthy.

FHA officials said that after the Department of Justice issued the National Mortgage Settlement in February 2012, servicers who had been delaying default and foreclosure started conveying large numbers of properties.[34] According to FHA and servicer representatives, damaged properties can take longer to convey because they require extensive repairs to meet FHA's conveyance condition standards.

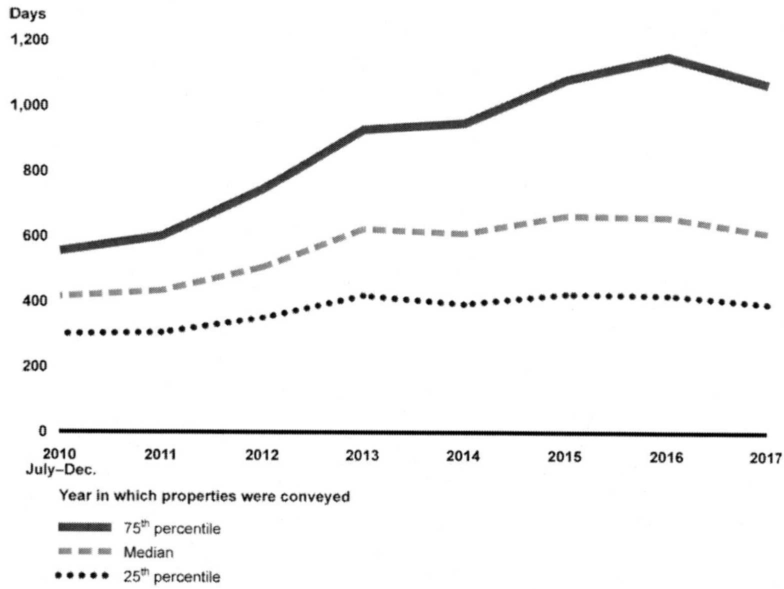

Source: GAO analysis of FHA data. | GAO-19-517.

Note: The default and foreclosure period is the time between the borrower defaulting on the mortgage and the servicer obtaining title to and possession of the property. We excluded properties conveyed from January through June 2010 from our analysis because FHA changed how it managed the conveyance process in June 2010.

Figure 8. Length of Default and Foreclosure Period for Properties Conveyed to the Federal Housing Administration (FHA), July 2010–December 2017.

[34] In 2015, FHA proposed a change to federal regulations that would have established a maximum amount of time for a servicer to file a claim with FHA and convey the property without the insurance contract being terminated. According to the proposed regulation, this change was meant to address the practice of servicers waiting to file FHA insurance claims for multiple properties at one time. HUD withdrew the proposed change in response to comments expressing concerns about the reasonableness of the proposed limit.

The results of our analysis of FHA data are broadly consistent with these observations. The number of properties conveyed to FHA increased by 31 percent (from 84,363 to 110,567) between 2011 and 2012, the year of the settlement. Additionally, the default and foreclosure period for conveyed properties (the time between the borrower defaulting on the mortgage and the servicer obtaining title to and possession of the property) increased over most of the July 2010–December 2017 time frame. As shown in figure 8, the median default and foreclosure period was 416 days for properties conveyed in July–December 2010, peaked at 664 days (about 60 percent higher) for properties conveyed in 2015, and fell to 612 days for 2017 conveyances. The overall upward trend was even more pronounced for properties with default and foreclosure periods at the 75th percentile. The 75th percentile was 555 days for properties conveyed from July through December 2010, peaked at 1,152 days (about 108 percent higher) for properties conveyed in 2016, and declined to 1,068 days for 2017 conveyances.

Certain regulatory and policy changes also may have increased the default and foreclosure periods since 2013. HUD issued a mortgagee letter in 2013 that increased the reasonable diligence time frames and allowed servicers additional time to complete foreclosures in certain states.[35] For example, the reasonable diligence time frame for properties in New York increased from 13 to19 months. Also, in 2014 mortgage servicing rules issued by the Consumer Financial Protection Bureau went into effect that restricted servicers' ability to initiate a foreclosure and gave borrowers additional time to pursue loss mitigation options. Specifically, servicers may not initiate foreclosure proceedings if a borrowers' application is pending for a loan modification or other alternatives to foreclosure.[36]

In addition, we found that properties with longer default and foreclosure periods generally took longer to complete the conveyance

---

[35] Department of Housing and Urban Development, Mortgagee Letter 2013-38 (Washington D.C.: Oct. 28, 2013).

[36] Mortgage Servicing Rules Under the Real Estate Settlement Procedures Act (Regulation X), 78 Fed. Reg. 10696 (Feb. 14, 2013); and Mortgage Servicing Rules Under the Truth in Lending Act (Regulation Z), 78 Fed. Reg. 10902 (Feb. 14, 2013).

process than properties with shorter default and foreclosure periods (see Figure 9).

Specifically, from July 2010 through December 2017 properties with the longest default and foreclosure periods—those in the highest quartile—took 93 days at the median to complete the conveyance process and 238 days at the 75th percentile. In comparison, properties with the shortest default and foreclosure periods—those in the lowest quartile—took 57 days at the median to complete the conveyance process and 136 days at the 75th percentile for that same period. As previously stated, FHA officials told us that properties with long default and foreclosure periods may have deteriorated if servicers were not maintaining them. These properties may have required additional repairs to bring them into conveyance condition.

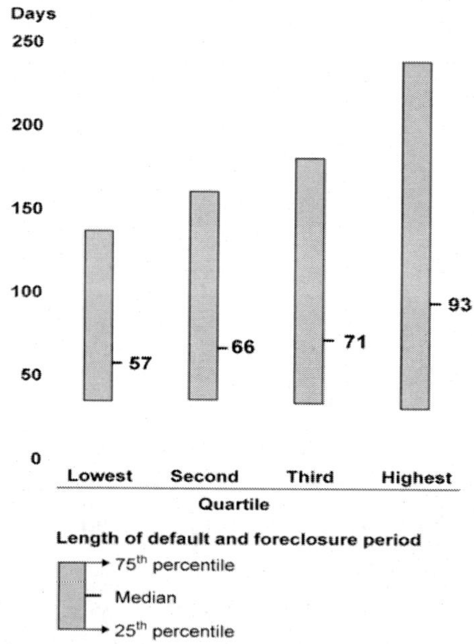

Source: GAO analysis of FHA data. | GAO-19-517.

Note: We excluded properties conveyed from January through June 2010 from our analysis because FHA changed how it managed the conveyance process in June 2010.

Figure 9. Length of the Federal Housing Administration's (FHA) Conveyance Process from July 2010 through December 2017, by Default and Foreclosure Period Quartile.

As previously noted, overall conveyance time frames declined in 2016 and 2017 from their peak in 2015. FHA officials attributed this improvement largely to the decreasing number of conveyances affected by the National Mortgage Settlement. As discussed earlier, the settlement contributed to a wave of properties that took a long time to convey, potentially due to damage sustained during extended default and foreclosure periods. FHA officials also indicated that the improved housing market in recent years has resulted in fewer foreclosures and, therefore, fewer property conveyances to FHA. Consequently, servicers and contractors may be better able to manage the workload associated with property conveyances and complete the process more quickly.

Servicers Often Did Not Convey Properties within the Required Time Frame, but Usually Provided Title Evidence on Time

From July 2010 through December 2017, servicers generally did not convey properties to FHA within the regulatory 30-day time frame (preconveyance period).[37] During the preconveyance period, servicers must ensure the property has good and marketable title, conduct routine inspections and maintenance on the property, and ensure the property meets conveyance condition standards. If servicers do not believe they will be able to convey a property within 30 days, they may request an extension. The median number of days servicers took to complete the preconveyance period increased from 31 in July–December 2010 to 140 in 2015 (see Figure 10).[38] This figure declined after 2015, dropping to 101

[37] As previously discussed, servicers must obtain good and marketable title and transfer the property to HUD within 30 days of the later of the filing of the foreclosure deed for record; recording date of deed-in-lieu of foreclosure; acquiring possession of the property; expiration of the redemption period; or date of any extension provided by FHA. While FHA does not collect some of the individual dates listed in the regulation, FHA officials said servicers submit a date on their claim forms—the date of possession and acquisition of marketable title—that represents the later of all of the dates except for the extension date. We used this date as the start date for measuring the length of the preconveyance period.

[38] As previously noted, we excluded properties conveyed to FHA before July 2010 from our analysis because they were managed using different systems and contractors than currently used.

days in 2017. Variation around the median was considerable, especially in more recent years. For example, in 2017 the time to complete the preconveyance period was 43 days at the 25th percentile, compared with 268 days at the 75th percentile.

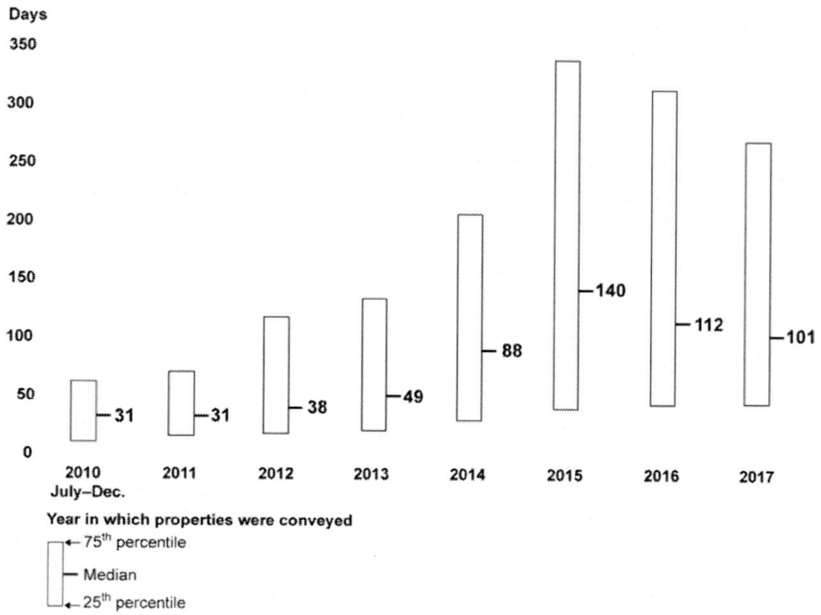

Source: GAO analysis of FHA data. | GAO-19-517.

Note: We excluded properties conveyed from January through June 2010 from our analysis because FHA changed how it managed the conveyance process in June 2010.

Figure 10. Number of Days for Servicers to Complete the Federal Housing Administration (FHA) Preconveyance Period for Properties Conveyed during July 2010–December 2017.

The percentage of properties for which servicers did not convey in 30 days plus any approved extension grew from about 31 percent in July–December 2010 to about 72 percent in 2017. For the entire period from July 2010 through December 2017, the corresponding percentage was 55 percent. Representatives of 13 of the 20 servicers we interviewed said that meeting the 30-day timeline was one of their top challenges with the conveyance process.

Representatives of servicers and mortgage industry groups cited several reasons for servicers needing additional time to convey. For example, representatives of 11 servicers cited the heavily damaged condition of the properties they acquired as one of the primary reasons for not conveying properties within 30 days. Servicer representatives also noted other reasons, including four who cited waiting for responses on hazard insurance claims and five who cited difficulty in obtaining HOA bills to pay. In addition, representatives of two mortgage industry groups and three servicers told us that meeting all the conveyance and title requirements simultaneously is a major challenge. For example, representatives of one mortgage industry group said a servicer may have completed required property repairs and paid HOA fees and utility bills, but if the property were subsequently vandalized, the servicer would have to delay conveyance to complete repairs. By that point, the servicer might no longer be current on HOA and utility payments. Servicers have the option to request an extension to the preconveyance time frame if they think they will be unable to convey a property in 30 days. Servicers requested a conveyance extension for about 40 percent of the properties conveyed from July 2010 through December 2017. FHA approved the extensions in about 40 percent of these cases.[39]

In addition, representatives from six of the 20 servicers we interviewed said FHA's process for reviewing servicers' overallowable requests (additional funds needed to complete work) negatively affected their ability to convey properties in 30 days. Once a servicer makes an overallowable request, FHA's compliance contractor has 5 business days to review it and either reject the request or approve all or some of the requested amount. (We discuss the compliance contractor's ability to meet this and other time requirements in the following section.) Servicers may appeal any rejections, in which case the compliance contractor has 3 business days to make a final determination. Six servicer representatives said that the time it takes the compliance contractor to make overallowable

---

[39] FHA officials told us that most conveyance extension requests are submitted so the servicer can file a hazard insurance claim, but they also receive such requests when the servicer believes preservation and protection work at a property will take longer than 30 days to complete.

decisions may cause them to exceed the 30-day time frame, especially when they submit multiple requests for the same property. For context, our analysis of FHA data found that in 2017, the median number of servicer overallowable requests per property was 13, and the median number of appeals per property was six.

In contrast to the preconveyance requirement, servicers usually met the time requirement for giving title evidence to FHA. Title evidence includes documentation that FHA is the legal owner of the property, including a copy of the mortgage documentation, a legal description of the property, and a copy of the recorded deed in FHA's name. Servicers may provide title evidence to FHA at any point during the conveyance process up to 45 days after filing the deed. If servicers believe they will be unable to provide title evidence within 45 days, they may submit an extension request to the compliance contractor. According to FHA data, servicers were able to provide title evidence within 45 days plus any approved extension for 84 percent of properties conveyed from July 2010 through December 2017.[40]

FHA Contractors Involved in Property Conveyances Largely Met Time Requirements

FHA's compliance and maintenance contractors generally met the required time frames for key conveyance tasks for properties conveyed from 2011 through 2017.[41] However, when the contractors did not meet

---

[40] According to FHA regulations, if the servicer is unable to provide title evidence, it is considered out of compliance with conveyance requirements and FHA may reconvey the property, cancel the servicer's claim for insurance benefits, and request reimbursement for any expenses incurred for acquisition, holding, and reconveyance from the date the claim is filed. If the title documentation the servicer provides is insufficient, the servicer may provide additional evidence in 10 days. If FHA identifies a title defect, the servicer has 60 days to correct it.

[41] We excluded July–December 2010 from this analysis because, as previously noted, FHA revised its Management and Marketing contractor program in June 2010. The revisions involved changing the requirements and scope of the contracts and hiring new contractors. According to FHA, the transition to the revised Management and Marketing program may have led to work backlogs that caused conveyance tasks to take longer to complete than in

their required time frames, the delays may have lengthened the time to complete the conveyance process for some properties.

Compliance Contractor

FHA established a time frame of 5 business days for the compliance contractor to conduct various reviews in the pre- and postconveyance periods. In the preconveyance period, the compliance contractor reviews requests for overallowables, conveyance extensions, and conveyance of a property with surchargeable damage. The contractor also reviews title evidence and extension requests for title evidence, which are generally submitted after conveyance. Table 2 shows the percentage of properties conveyed from 2011 through 2017 for which the compliance contractor met the 5 business day requirement, according to our analysis of FHA data.

Table 2. Percentage of compliance contractor reviews that met Federal Housing Administration's (FHA) time requirements, properties conveyed, 2011–2017

	Preconveyance Reviews		Postconveyance Reviews	
Overallowable requests	Conveyance extensions	Surchargeable damage	Title evidence extensions	Title evidence
90.8%	93.3%	94.2%	94.5%	86.7%

Source: GAO analysis of FHA data. | GAO-19-517.

Note: FHA has a time frame of 5 business days for the compliance contractor to conduct these reviews.

Although the contractor mostly met the required time frames, when it did not, the delay may have lengthened the time to complete the conveyance process. Our analysis of FHA data indicates that when the compliance contractor missed the deadlines, it missed them by a median of 4–10 days, depending on the requirement.[42] The compliance contractor's

prior periods. We excluded data from this atypical period to avoid skewing the results our compliance analysis.

[42] For perspective, the median length of the conveyance process for properties conveyed from July 2010–December 2017 was 70 days. Our analysis of FHA data indicates that for properties conveyed in 2011–2017, when the compliance contractor missed the 5 business day deadline, at the median it missed the deadline to review title evidence by 4 days,

review of overallowable requests, conveyance extension requests, and surchargeable damage requests generally occurs during the preconveyance period when servicers have 30 days to convey the property to FHA. As noted earlier, some servicer representatives we interviewed said that waiting for the compliance contractor to approve or deny overallowable requests hindered their ability to convey the property in 30 days.

The compliance contractor must complete at least 95 percent of the reviews within the 5-day time frame to meet FHA's standard for minimum acceptable performance. FHA uses monthly scorecards when reviewing the contractor's performance against this standard.[43] FHA officials told us they had not issued any deficiency notices to the current compliance contractor, but that discussions with the contractor can occur when it does not meet the 95 percent standard in particular months. FHA officials also noted that some of the contractor's reviews may take longer than 5 days if resolving them requires obtaining additional documentation or substantial back-and-forth communications with the servicer.

Maintenance Contractors

After conveyance, FHA's maintenance contractors have 2 calendar days from the date they are assigned a property to conduct the comprehensive property inspection and upload the results into a HUD Property Inspection Report in FHA's asset disposition system.[44] They then have 5 calendar days to complete a Property Condition Report, which details the functionality of the property's systems, the existence of any transferable warranties, and any legal actions, such as code violations or pending demolition orders. FHA starts measuring compliance with these time requirements 24 hours after the properties are assigned to the compliance contractor (to account for holidays and late afternoon assignments).

---

overallowable requests by 7 days, conveyance extension requests by 8 days, and surchargeable damage and title extension requests by 10 days.

[43] Although a detailed assessment of FHA's contractor oversight was outside the scope of our review, we requested and reviewed examples of these scorecards to determine how FHA monitored contractor performance.

[44] According to FHA officials, the asset disposition system automatically assigns a conveyed property to the maintenance contractor when the servicer files the conveyance claim.

According to our analysis of FHA data, the maintenance contractors completed property inspections and uploaded the results within 3 days (the 2-day requirement plus 24 hours) for about 90 percent of properties conveyed from 2011 through 2017. The contractors met the 5-day requirement to complete the Property Condition Report about 77 percent of the time. When the maintenance contractors missed these time frames, they missed them by a median of 1 and 2 days, respectively. The longer a property remains uninspected after the servicer has conveyed it, the greater the chance that it will be damaged or vandalized before inspection. If a property is damaged during this period, disputes may arise between FHA and the servicer about which entity is responsible for the damage. FHA is responsible for maintaining the property once the servicer complies with all HUD regulatory requirements leading to conveyance, including filing the deed (in FHA's name) for record and filing the conveyance claim. However, FHA may hold the servicer responsible for the damage if the claim was suspended due to the need for review or correction resulting from certain types of noncompliance with HUD requirements or if the servicer could not prove the damage occurred after FHA became responsible for maintaining the property. Disagreement over this issue can add time to the conveyance process.

FHA measures each maintenance contractor's performance monthly using a formula that considers both the contractor's timeliness in completing property inspections and uploading the results (2-day requirement plus 24 hours) and in completing the Property Condition Report (7-day requirement plus 24 hours) for each property. If the contractor misses either deadline, it is not considered timely for that property. FHA considers timeliness for 95 percent of properties each month as satisfactory. According to FHA officials, FHA has taken actions when the performance of maintenance contractors was not satisfactory. A HOC official said that the actions may include issuing a defective performance letter, which requires the contractor to provide a remedy plan, and issuing a cure notice in coordination with HUD's contracting office.

FHA CHANGED ASPECTS OF THE CONVEYANCE PROCESS, BUT POLICIES AND A PILOT PROGRAM STILL HAVE LIMITATIONS

FHA's Updates to Property Preservation Allowances and Data Systems Partly Addressed Certain Servicer Challenges

FHA updated aspects of the conveyance process in recent years to help address some of the challenges experienced by servicers and the agency. For example, FHA increased property preservation and protection allowances in 2016 to help address servicer feedback and to better align allowances with other mortgage industry participants, according to FHA officials. In February 2016, FHA issued Mortgagee Letter 2016-02, which increased allowance amounts that servicers may claim for specific types of property preservation and protection work. It also increased the total maximum amount servicers may claim for a property without submitting an overallowable request from $2,500 to $5,000. However, the mortgagee letter eliminated all exclusions from the maximum amount, which previously included one-time major repairs, such as a roof replacement. FHA officials said the agency increased the allowance amounts to account for the standard increases in property preservation costs over time, and to align allowances with those of the enterprises and the Department of Veterans Affairs.[45]

Seventeen of the 20 servicers we interviewed said that FHA's current property preservation and protection allowances are not sufficient to complete the work needed to convey properties. While representatives of eight of the 20 servicers told us the changes FHA made to allowances in 2016 helped them complete work within allowance amounts, representatives of the remaining 12 servicers said the changes did not help or helped in some ways but presented more challenges in other ways.

---

[45] While property disposition processes at the enterprises and the Department of Veterans Affairs differ from FHA's, those entities have preservation allowances for maintenance servicers must complete on vacant properties that may be compared to FHA's.

Representatives of an association of mortgage lenders and servicers said that they preferred the previous system, because some work was excluded from the maximum allowance. For example, representatives of one servicer said that due to the 2016 changes, they now must submit an overallowable request for standard maintenance items, such as grass cuts, once they have exceeded the maximum allowance amount.

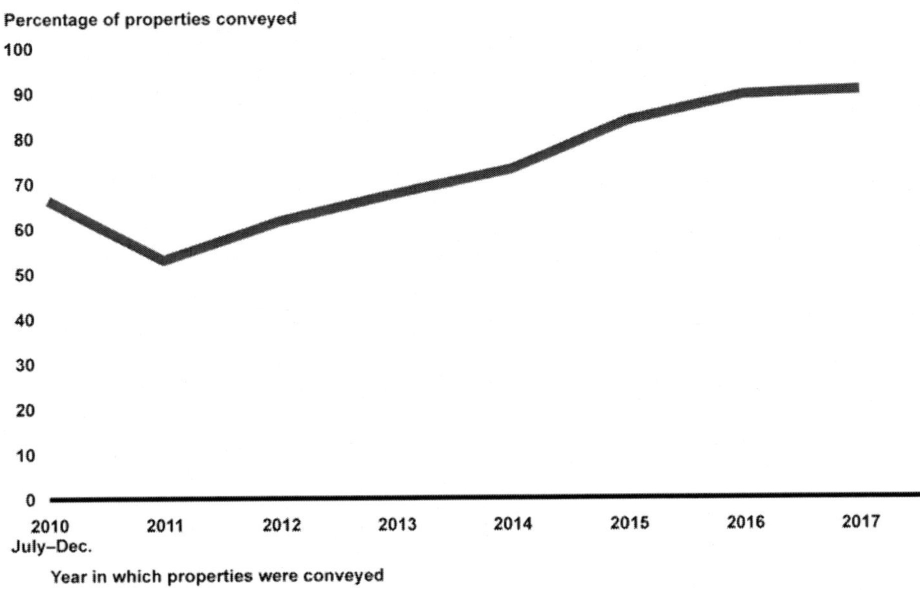

Source: GAO analysis of FHA data. | GAO-19-517.

Note: We excluded properties conveyed from January through June 2010 from our analysis because FHA changed how it managed the conveyance process in June 2010.

Figure 11. Percentage of Properties Conveyed to the Federal Housing Administration (FHA) with at Least One Overallowable Request, July 2010– December 2017.

Our analysis of FHA data found that the percentage of properties with at least one overallowable request increased steadily from 2011 through 2017—from about 53 percent to about 90 percent—despite the 2016 changes (see Figure 11).[46] For properties with at least one overallowable

[46] Sixty-six percent of the properties conveyed from July through December 2010 had at least one overallowable request.

request, the median number of requests before the 2016 changes (from July 1, 2010, through February 4, 2016) was seven, compared with eight after the changes (from February 5, 2016, through the end of 2017).[47] In 2017 alone, the median number of overallowable requests per conveyed property was 13. However, it may be too early to tell what effect the 2016 mortgagee letter will have on servicer's ability to conduct work within the allowances. FHA officials said that although the change in the allowance amounts was partly intended to reduce overallowable requests, the poor condition of many properties with extended default and foreclosure periods may have increased such requests. The officials stated that some of these properties were still being conveyed to FHA in 2017.

FHA enhanced the information system servicers and contractors use to manage conveyed properties, but officials noted the need to update another system FHA uses to process and pay claims. In March 2018, FHA incorporated its preconveyance inspection pilot, discussed in more detail later in this chapter, into the asset disposition system, the information system servicers use to convey properties to FHA.[48] FHA officials and contractors also use the system to track properties from conveyance through REO sale. With the update, servicers may request a preconveyance inspection and see the results of the inspection in the system, according to FHA officials. Before FHA added the pilot to the asset disposition system, servicers and FHA used email to communicate about properties in the pilot.

In October 2016, FHA added a feature to the asset disposition system that enables FHA officials, contractors, and servicers to electronically monitor the status of reconveyed properties. According to FHA officials, all communication between FHA and servicers on reconveyed properties previously was by email, including the servicer's notification to FHA that it was ready to convey a property again, and the photographs required to document property condition. However, according to FHA officials,

---

[47] FHA instituted the previous allowance schedule on July 13, 2010, in Mortgagee Letter 2010-18.

[48] In the preconveyance inspection pilot, FHA conducts physical inspections of certain properties prior to conveyance and provides the servicer the opportunity to fix any issues before conveying the property.

FHA's claims system is not equipped to process more than one claim per property, so claims for properties FHA reconveys and which the servicer then conveys to FHA a second time must be processed manually.

Officials from FHA's Office of Financial Services said that manual processing delays claim payments to servicers—sometimes by more than a year. Seven of the 20 servicers we interviewed identified delayed claim payments for reacquired properties as a challenge. FHA officials said that they have made an internal business case for funding to modernize the system, but have not succeeded in securing the funding in prior years.

FHA Updated Its Policies and Procedures on Conveyance Condition, but Limitations Remain

FHA updated its written direction to servicers on conveyance condition in 2016, but limitations in the contents and methods of communicating these policies and procedures have contributed to compliance challenges for some servicers. In its February 2016 mortgagee letter, FHA re-emphasized its existing directions to servicers about property conveyance, provided additional details on how to calculate claim amounts and document property preservation and protection work, and clarified descriptions of some preservation and protection requirements. Additionally, in December 2016, FHA issued an updated single-family housing policy handbook that consolidated all policies and procedures for servicers into one document, including those on maintaining and conveying foreclosed properties. However, servicers and other industry stakeholders with whom we spoke and our review of FHA's policies and procedures on conveyance condition identified several limitations, as follows.

Lack of Clarity or Specificity

Representatives from 15 of the 20 servicers we interviewed said they found FHA's policies and procedures on conveyance condition to be unclear or subjective, and 13 cited specific parts of the conveyance condition standards they found to be unclear or missing. For example, one servicer was unsure about the extent of repairs required when a property had water seepage in the basement. We found that FHA's policies and procedures include information on how to treat a basement that is flooded or a property with moisture damage, but does not address basement leaks, cracks, or seepage. Representatives of four servicers said that FHA's policies and procedures do not sufficiently address how servicers should handle properties with potential structural or foundation damage. Consistent with this viewpoint, we found that FHA's handbook and mortgagee letter do not explain what a servicer should do if it believes a property has damage affecting its structural integrity. In addition, representatives of three servicers said FHA's expectations of them are unclear when a roof is damaged but does not currently have a leak. According to FHA's policies and procedures, servicers must ensure all roofs "are free of active leaks or other sources of water intrusion." However, FHA does not specify what servicers should do if there is roof damage but no active leak. Two of the servicers said they were uncertain whether they should replace the damaged roof that is not leaking, or convey the property and risk reconveyance if it rains before FHA inspects the property and the roof leaks.

Perceived Inconsistency in Interpretation

Representatives from 10 of the 20 servicers we interviewed said FHA is somewhat or not at all consistent in determining whether properties meet FHA's conveyance requirements. Among the remaining 10, one stated that FHA is completely consistent and nine said that FHA is mostly consistent. In addition, two of the 20 servicers said the answers they receive from FHA to the same question differ depending on whom they ask. HOC officials also noted cases in which their interpretation of policies and procedures differed from the compliance contractor's. For example, officials from three HOCs told us that the compliance contractor sometimes disagrees with their determination that a property is not in conveyance condition when the contractor reviews the HOC's reconveyance decision.[49]

Limited Communication Methods

In addition to formal written policies and procedures on conveyance condition, FHA fields servicer questions, primarily through its compliance contractor, by phone. The compliance contractor also issues an annual newsletter on topics such as common reconveyance triggers and best practices for submitting successful overallowable and extension requests. However, some servicers we interviewed suggested other possible ways to communicate policies and procedures that they said they would find helpful, including the following:

- Representatives of five servicers said they would like FHA to publish an authoritative set of frequently asked questions (FAQ) on conveyance condition. FHA has an FAQ web page that includes information on conveyance condition, but, as of April 2019, did not include FAQs about the specific property preservation and protection issues discussed above (water seepage, structural integrity, and roof damage with no active leaks). In addition, a link in the web page labeled "foreclosure/conveyance" led to a few FAQs on conveyance condition and property preservation requirements, but the answers consisted solely of language from FHA's existing policies and procedures.
- One servicer's representatives suggested that FHA could issue policies and procedures in a format similar to Fannie Mae's Property Preservation Matrix and Reference Guide. This guide has features that FHA's policies and procedures do not have, as discussed below, including photographic examples, detailed requirements for photographic documentation, and "if-then"

---

[49] According to FHA's Director of the National Servicing Center, although the compliance contractor may point out issues, the HOCs have the final say in determining if a property gets reconveyed.

statements detailing what servicers should do if they encounter certain challenges at a property.

- Representatives of two servicers suggested that FHA host regular industry calls. While the compliance contractor told us that it takes ad hoc calls and holds regular teleconference calls with a number of individual servicers, an FHA official told us the contractor is only authorized to respond to servicer questions by providing relevant parts of FHA's written policies and procedures and is not supposed to respond with interpretations (clarifications, or explanations) of existing policies and procedures. Representatives from one servicer said industrywide calls with FHA staff would give servicers a way to obtain fuller explanations of FHA's expectations.
- One servicer suggested that FHA provide training to servicers about the conveyance process. The servicer noted that while FHA provides training on other aspects of its program, including loss mitigation, it does not do so for the conveyance process or submitting claims.

Limited Direction on Photographic Evidence

FHA's policies and procedures provide instructions for servicers and contractors on how to document property conditions, but contain limited direction on photographic evidence. Servicers must thoroughly document the condition of the property when they first obtain possession so that FHA does not hold them responsible for damage caused by the borrower.

Servicers also must take before and after pictures of any work they do on the property. FHA's policies and procedures on photographic documentation say only that the servicer must use digital photography, ensure a date-stamp is printed within each photograph, and ensure that each photograph is labeled to describe the contents of the photograph. FHA has not communicated in writing any requirements for photograph dimensions, color, distance, framing, or content or suggestions for documenting conditions that may be difficult to see.

Servicers and FHA officials stated that they face challenges in documenting property conditions in a way that most accurately informs the compliance contractor about the property. The compliance contractor reviews documentation, including photographs, uploaded into the asset disposition system by servicers to make decisions on overallowable and extension requests. The compliance contractor also reviews documentation from maintenance contractors on inspection results and reconveyance recommendations by HOC officials. An FHA maintenance contractor told us that the compliance contractor sometimes responds that the condition described is not apparent from the photographs in the asset disposition system. According to members of an industry group representing servicers, in some cases this may result in FHA requiring servicers to repair damage caused by the borrower, because the servicers' photographs did not prove the damage was present when they first gained possession of the property.

To illustrate how photographs can effectively or ineffectively capture property condition problems, figure 12 provides two examples of flooring issues at properties conveyed to FHA. In one photograph, the buckling of the floor is apparent, but in the other, the waterlogged and warped condition of floor is harder to discern. An experienced FHA maintenance contractor told us there are creative ways to document some conditions that are difficult to photograph. For example, to document a damp floor, one can photograph a piece of paper (which darkens when wet) before and after placing it on the floor. This method is not included in FHA's handbook or mortgagee letter.

Limitations in the content and delivery of FHA's policies and procedures on conveyance condition suggest room for improvement and are inconsistent with the federal internal control standard for communicating externally. This standard calls for management to externally communicate the necessary quality information to achieve an entity's objectives.[50] Federal agencies can help ensure compliance by communicating with and obtaining information from external parties and by periodically evaluating and selecting appropriate methods of

---

[50] GAO, *Standards for Internal Control in the Federal Government*, GAO-14-704G (Washington, D.C.: Sept. 10, 2014).

communication, taking into account factors such as the audience, the purpose and type of information being given, and legal or regulatory requirements.

Buckled flooring over a wet subfloor at a property in the Atlanta area.

Waterlogged and warped flooring from a roof leak at a property in the Baltimore area. The damage is not visible in the photo—a challenge servicers may face in documenting property condition.

Source: GAO. | GAO-19-517.

Figure 12. Examples of Flooring Damage at Properties Conveyed to the Federal Housing Administration in 2018.

However, FHA has not identified where the conveyance condition policies and procedures could be improved because it has not assessed information from servicers—for example, the frequency or content of their questions to the compliance contractor. FHA also has not thoroughly evaluated its methods for communicating its policies and procedures. As a result, FHA has limited assurance that servicers understand FHA's expectations for conveyed properties and that contractor decisions are made consistently. Weaknesses in these areas can contribute to inefficiencies such as delays in executing conveyances and reconveyance of properties to servicers.

FHA Has Not Provided Direction on Alternatives to Reconveyance for Properties That Do Not Meet Conveyance Condition Standards

FHA has not provided written direction to HOC officials on choosing among alternatives to address conveyed properties that do not meet FHA's condition standards.[51] According to officials from FHA headquarters and the National Servicing Center, HOC officials can (1) reconvey the property's title to the servicer, (2) issue a demand letter establishing a debt to FHA for the cost of the work needed, or (3) enter into a reconveyance bypass agreement with the servicer that requires the servicer to complete repairs within a certain number of days. The latter two options avoid reconveyance and therefore may expedite resale of the property. These three options are mentioned in different parts of FHA's policies and procedures, but the agency has not outlined the circumstances that would warrant use of each method.

FHA has not provided direction to the HOCs, partly because HOC officials have the authority to choose a method based on the expected financial return on the property. However, HOC officials with whom we spoke differed in the factors that they considered when deciding how to address properties that do not meet FHA's conveyance condition standards.

Officials from three HOCs cited criteria that any property with more than $5,000 in damage due to servicer neglect should be considered for reconveyance, while a bypass agreement or demand letter may be issued if the amount of servicer neglect is less than $5,000. However, FHA officials were not able to tell us where this criterion is written. An official from the fourth HOC said the decision to reconvey partly depends on the strength of the housing market. If the HOC believes it can sell the property in its current condition—even if the condition does not meet FHA's conveyance standards—the HOC will be more likely to issue the servicer a demand letter than reconvey the property. In contrast, an official from one of the other HOCs told us the state of the housing market did not factor into decisions on reconveyance. Furthermore, according to FHA officials, HOCs may also reconvey a property with only small amounts of damage if the servicer frequently conveys properties not in conveyance condition, in order to impress on the servicer the importance of complying with FHA requirements.

---

[51] FHA may allow properties to be conveyed damaged in certain prescribed situations with prior approval.

The HOC officials generally agreed that bypass agreements offer a way for small repairs to be fixed quickly. However, an official from one HOC said the HOC did not issue bypass agreements often because servicers' property preservation and protection vendors may take longer than the time specified in the agreement to complete repairs and, since the title is in FHA's name, FHA has no recourse with the servicer. An official from another HOC also said that he did not like issuing bypass agreements because servicers do not always complete repairs quickly.

FHA does not produce reports on the HOCs' use of reconveyance, demand letters, and bypass agreements, so the frequency with which the HOCs employ these methods is unknown. Some servicer representatives with whom we spoke noted apparent inconsistency among the HOCs. For example, representatives of three servicers said that some HOCs do not issue bypass agreements at all. Similarly, representatives of one servicer told us they have infrequently, if ever, received a demand letter for small condition issues at properties; rather, FHA reconveys the properties for minor condition issues.

FHA's lack of written direction on alternatives to reconveyance is inconsistent with federal internal control standards, which call for designing control activities, including policies, to achieve objectives.[52] Granting HOC officials discretion in dealing with properties that do not meet condition standards gives them flexibility to respond to specific circumstances. However, without written direction on factors to consider when determining whether they should reconvey a property, issue a demand letter, or enter into a bypass agreement with the servicer, FHA lacks reasonable assurance that HOCs make determinations consistently and in line with the agency's regulatory goals for the REO program—to dispose of properties in a manner that expands home ownership, strengthens neighborhoods and communities, and ensures a maximum return to the mortgage insurance fund.[53] Balancing these goals may require using different methods to address properties that do not meet conveyance standards. For example, in some cases issuing a demand letter or a bypass

[52] GAO-14-704G.

[53] 24 C.F.R. § 291.1(a)(2).

agreement for certain properties may result in FHA marketing and selling the property more quickly than it would by reconveying the property. A quicker sale, in turn, may help avoid the negative effects of a vacant property on the surrounding neighborhood. However, if FHA accepts a property in poor condition, it may receive less in proceeds when selling the property, which negatively affects FHA's mortgage insurance fund.

FHA Does Not Have a Plan to Evaluate Its Preconveyance Inspection Pilot

FHA began a pilot program in 2017 to inspect properties that meet certain criteria before conveyance, but has not developed a plan to assess the results of the pilot program. FHA selected three large servicers to participate in this preconveyance inspection pilot. These servicers may request preconveyance inspections for properties with characteristics that increase their chances of being reconveyed, according to FHA officials.

For example, eligible properties include those that experienced recurring vandalism, received overallowable repairs of greater than $5,000, or have potential structural defects, foundation issues, or damp or wet basements.[54] Based on the inspection results, the properties are approved to convey, approved to convey subject to repair with no additional inspection, or denied conveyance through the pilot (see Table 3).

---

[54] Other eligible properties include those with code violations—including occupancy violations—for which the mortgagee requests approval to convey as-is; insurable claims with completed repairs in excess of $5,000; unrepaired borrower neglect affecting mechanical, electrical, or plumbing, or having excessive mold; uninsurable and unfinished renovations the servicer has requested to convey as-is; and completed roof repairs in excess of $2,500 that have unrepaired interior ceiling or wall damage. Properties with borrowers 35 or more months delinquent on the mortgage or that were vacant more than 12 months also are eligible, as are properties in a presidentially declared disaster zone with completed repairs exceeding $5,000 or in Puerto Rico or Washington State.
Reoccurring vandalism is defined as at least two completed vandalism repairs (paid with insurance proceeds) on a property the servicer has requested to convey as-is.

After conveyance, FHA inspectors conduct a thorough inspection to confirm that the property meets conveyance condition standards.

Properties that do not meet the standards may be reconveyed.

Table 3. Results of Federal Housing Administration (FHA) preconveyance inspection pilot, as of November 5, 2018

Inspection result	Number of properties	Percentage of inspected properties
Approved to convey	190	27.3
Approved to convey subject to repairs	260	37.3
Denied conveyance	247	35.4
Total inspections	697	100.0

Source: FHA. | GAO-19-517.

As of November 2018, FHA had not developed plans for evaluating the effectiveness of the pilot in achieving the goals of reducing the number of properties reconveyed due to property condition and minimizing the time it takes to convey properties. FHA officials told us that they will develop a plan to assess pilot outcomes when sufficient data are available.

However, without an evaluation plan, FHA may not collect the right information during the pilot to rigorously assess results. GAO's guide for designing evaluations states that key components of an evaluation design include the evaluation questions or objectives; information sources and measures; data collection methods; an analysis plan, including evaluative criteria or comparisons; and an assessment of study limitations.[55]

Certain characteristics of FHA's pilot underscore the importance of incorporating these components into evaluation design. For example, because the pilot is intended to expedite the conveyance process through preconveyance inspections, it will be important to isolate the impact of the inspections, potentially by making comparisons to a control group. A properly selected control group can rule out competing explanations for observed outcomes. Additionally, because the pilot may affect

[55] GAO, *Designing Evaluations: 2012 Revision*, GAO-12-208G (Washington, D.C.: Jan. 31, 2012).

participating servicers in ways that extend beyond the speed of the conveyance process or the probability of reconveyance, it will be important for FHA to thoroughly consider the information sources and measures it uses, including participant feedback. For example, representatives of the three participating servicers told us they had concerns about FHA holding properties in the pilot to higher conveyance condition standards than nonpilot properties and the time it takes to complete the preconveyance inspection process. According to the representatives, this process, which includes 7 calendar days for the inspection and 5 business days for the HOCs to review the inspection report, has resulted in longer holding times and increased vandalism risks.

Without a well-designed evaluation, FHA risks making decisions about preconveyance inspections based on incorrect or incomplete information on the pilot's benefits and drawbacks.

CONCLUSION

While FHA increased the use of other property disposition methods in recent years, servicers still convey thousands of foreclosed properties to FHA annually. If the process of transferring ownership from the servicer to FHA is not efficient, these properties may sit vacant for prolonged periods, deteriorate, and contribute to neighborhood decline. As a result, it is critical for FHA to have effective and efficient policies and procedures for the conveyance process. While FHA has made recent updates to its handbook, mortgagee letters, and information systems, additional improvements would better align its processes and procedures with federal internal control standards and GAO guidance on designing evaluations:

- By addressing limitations in the content (including its detail) and communication of its policies and procedures on conveyance condition, FHA could help reduce uncertainty and inconsistency in the conveyance process that may contribute to inefficiencies, such as reconveyance of properties to servicers.

- Second, by providing direction to HOC officials on factors to consider when deciding whether to use alternatives to reconveyance for properties that do not meet conveyance condition standards, FHA could increase the likelihood that alternatives will be used consistently and in line with FHA's goals for the REO program.
- Third, by developing a plan for how it will evaluate the outcomes of the pilot to inspect certain properties prior to conveyance, FHA could help ensure the pilot generates the performance information needed to make effective management decisions about future policies.

By addressing these issues, FHA could make the conveyance process more efficient and therefore help reduce negative impacts on neighborhoods.

RECOMMENDATIONS

We are making the following three recommendations to FHA:

The Commissioner of FHA should enhance the content and communication of FHA's policies and procedures on conveyance condition, including by considering the program stakeholder views discussed in this chapter and other stakeholder input. (Recommendation 1)

The Commissioner of FHA should provide written direction to HOC REO directors on factors to consider when determining whether to reconvey a property with condition issues, issue a demand letter, or enter into a bypass agreement with the servicer. (Recommendation 2)

The Commissioner of FHA should develop a formal plan for evaluating the outcomes of the preconveyance inspection pilot that includes key elements of evaluation design—such as evaluation objectives and measures—and utilizes participant feedback and control groups, as appropriate. (Recommendation 3)

AGENCY COMMENTS AND OUR EVALUATION

We provided a draft of this chapter to FHA, the Department of Veterans Affairs, and the Federal Housing Finance Agency (the conservator and regulator of Fannie Mae and Freddie Mac) for their review and comment. The Department of Veterans Affairs and the Federal Housing Finance Agency did not provide comments. FHA provided written comments reproduced in appendix II. FHA neither agreed nor disagreed with our first recommendation to enhance the content and communication of its policies and procedures on conveyance condition. FHA cited the 2016 updates to its policy handbook and mortgagee letter and said it recognized the importance of external communication, training, and in- person meetings to ensure servicers have the information they need to operate in compliance with FHA programs. Our report discusses these updates, but also identifies areas for additional improvements to address limitations in the clarity and comprehensiveness of FHA's policies and procedures and methods for communicating them. FHA agreed with our second and third recommendations to provide written direction on considering alternatives to reconveyance and to develop a plan for evaluating the preconveyance inspection pilot.

We are sending copies of this chapter to the appropriate congressional committees, the Secretary of the Department of Housing and Urban Development, and other interested parties.

Daniel Garcia-Diaz
Director, Financial Markets and Community Investment

APPENDIX I: OBJECTIVES, SCOPE, AND METHODOLOGY

Our objectives were to examine (1) timelines for Federal Housing Administration (FHA) foreclosed property conveyances in June 2010–December 2017 and the extent to which servicers and FHA met time requirements and (2) changes FHA has made to the conveyance process in recent years and any ongoing process challenges.

Time Lines for Property Conveyances

To address the first objective, we obtained data from FHA's Single Family Insurance System–Claims Subsystem and from the P260 Asset Disposition and Management System (asset disposition system) on the 610,802 foreclosed properties mortgage servicers conveyed to FHA from January 1, 2010, through December 31, 2017. For purposes of our analysis, we generally excluded properties conveyed to FHA from January 2010, through June 2010 because they were managed using different data systems and contractors than FHA currently uses.[56]

After excluding these properties, we analyzed data for 544,421 properties conveyed to FHA from July 2010 through December 2017. (We use calendar years in this chapter unless otherwise noted.) We calculated the number of days it took each property to complete the conveyance process. We defined the start of the conveyance process as the date the servicer obtained possession and acquired marketable title for a property and the end of the process as the date on which FHA assigned a marketing contractor to sell the property.[57] For each annual cohort of conveyed properties, we calculated the 25th, 50th (median), and 75th percentile time frames and compared these statistics across years.

To analyze the effect that reconveyances had on the length of the conveyance process, we compared length of time for conveyance in 2012–2017 for properties that were reconveyed to those that were not. According

---

[56] FHA launched the asset disposition system in April 2010 to manage the property conveyance process. Additionally, in June 2010, FHA launched the third generation of its Management and Marketing contractor program. Under prior arrangements, FHA's contractors were responsible for both the maintenance and marketing of FHA's real estate-owned properties. Under the current structure, separate contractors perform these functions. FHA also began a new compliance management contract in June 2010.

[57] Servicers submit a date on their claim forms indicating when they obtained possession and marketable title for the property, according to FHA officials. We used this date as the start of the conveyance process.

to FHA staff, data on reconveyances were unreliable prior to 2012, so we excluded those properties from this comparative analysis.

We interviewed FHA officials about factors that may have affected conveyance time frames from 2010 through 2017, including increased use of other disposition methods and servicers delaying foreclosure actions and the resulting impact on property conditions, since the asset disposition system does not disclose the reasons for any delays. To analyze changes in the use of different property disposition methods and to examine the loss severity rates for these methods, we reviewed FHA data for fiscal years 2010–2017. To understand the relationship between properties with long default and foreclosure periods and conveyance time frames, we measured the time between the borrower defaulting on the mortgage and the servicer obtaining title to and possession of the property (effectively, the end of the foreclosure process) for properties conveyed to FHA from July 2010 through December 2017. We divided the range of default and foreclosure periods into four quartiles. For each quartile, we calculated the length of the conveyance process at the median and at the 25th and 75th percentiles. We then compared these statistics across quartiles.

To determine the extent to which mortgage servicers and FHA contractors met their respective time requirements for the conveyance process, we identified relevant time requirements in Department of Housing and Urban Development (HUD) regulations and policies. We also reviewed the performance work statements for FHA's mortgagee compliance manager (compliance contractor) and field service managers (maintenance contractors) to identify the contractors' time requirements for the conveyance process. For servicers and contractors, we selected key time requirements for which electronic data were available, including the following:

- Servicers
  - Thirty calendar days from acquiring title and possession of a property, plus the length of any approved time extension, to convey property to FHA.

- Forty-five days from conveying a property to FHA, plus the length of any approved time extension, to provide FHA with title evidence.

- Compliance contractor
  - Five business days to review each overallowable request submitted by a servicer.
  - Five business days to review the sufficiency of title documentation submitted by the servicer.
  - Five business days to determine whether a servicer can convey a property with surchargeable damage.
  - Five business days to approve or deny a servicer's conveyance or title extension request.
- Maintenance contractor
  - Two calendar days, plus an additional 24 hours, to complete and upload the HUD Property Inspection Report from the date the property was assigned.
  - Five calendar days to complete a Property Condition Report from the date the Property Inspection Report was completed.

For each property, we calculated the number of days it took servicers and contractors to complete these required steps in the conveyance process and compared that number to the maximum number of days FHA allows for each step. For each annual cohort of properties conveyed in 2010–2017, we calculated the 25th, 50th (median), and 75th percentile time frames for completing the steps. We also calculated the percentage of properties for which servicers or FHA contractors met their time requirements for each step. We reviewed FHA's procedures for monitoring the performance of compliance and maintenance contractors for conveyed properties. We also reviewed examples of contractor quality control plans and FHA quality control reports and scorecards used to assess the contractors' compliance with minimum time frames and other requirements. Additionally, we interviewed FHA officials about the contractors' compliance with their respective time requirements and what steps FHA took, if any, to address any noncompliance.

We assessed the reliability of data from the Single Family Insurance System–Claims Subsystem and the asset disposition system by reviewing FHA documentation about the data systems and data elements. We interviewed FHA staff and contractors knowledgeable about the data to discuss interpretations of data fields and trends we observed in our analysis. We also conducted electronic testing, including checks for outliers, missing data fields, and erroneous values. We excluded from each analysis properties with missing or erroneous information in the applicable data fields. We also excluded from each analysis properties for which the applicable data fields were five absolute deviations from the median (which we consider to be outliers). In addition, we excluded certain properties conveyed in calendar years 2010–2017 that had conveyance dates that were out of sequence. For example, we excluded properties for which the date a servicer obtained possession and good and marketable title occurred after the date the servicer conveyed the property to FHA. The number of properties we excluded in any analysis using these methods represents no more than 3.2 percent of properties conveyed from July 2010 through December 2017, which we consider to be insignificant when compared to the remaining properties included in the analysis. After taking these steps, we believe that the data were sufficiently reliable for purposes of characterizing the overall length of FHA property conveyances and compliance with key time requirements.

Changes to Conveyance Process and Ongoing Challenges

To determine what changes FHA made to the conveyance process in recent years, we reviewed relevant FHA regulations, policies, and procedures issued in 2010 or later, including FHA's February 2016 mortgagee letter (a written instruction to FHA-approved lenders) on conveyances. We compared the requirements and property preservation and protection allowance amounts in the mortgagee letter to those in the prior mortgagee letter. We also reviewed FHA documentation on changes to the asset disposition system, FHA's data system for conveyed properties, and on FHA's preconveyance inspection pilot program that began in 2017. We interviewed FHA officials on the reasons for the recent changes and on the extent to which they reviewed any analogous requirements and property preservation and protection allowances of other mortgage entities (including Fannie Mae, Freddie Mac, and the Department of Veterans Affairs) when making the updates. To supplement our review of FHA's recent changes to property preservation and protection allowances, we used the asset disposition system data to analyze changes in the frequency and number of servicer overallowable requests since the 2016 mortgagee letter went into effect.

To examine what, if any, challenges exist with the conveyance process, we randomly selected a nongeneralizable sample of 20 large- and medium-sized, bank and nonbank servicers of FHA-insured mortgages. We defined large-sized servicers as those with 100,000 or more active FHA-insured mortgages as of December 31, 2017, and medium-sized servicers as those with 10,000–99,999 active FHA-insured mortgages as of that date. These servicers accounted for more than one-third of active FHA-insured mortgages as of December 31, 2017. We conducted semistructured interviews with the servicers about their experience with FHA property conveyances, including the sufficiency of FHA's policies and procedures, time lines, and allowance amounts and any challenges they experienced with the process. We also discussed the extent to which the 2016 mortgagee letter assisted or hindered their conveyance efforts.

In addition, we spoke with two national industry groups representing mortgage servicers about recent changes and any challenges their members experienced with the conveyance process.

We reviewed FHA's requirements for servicers and contractors on conveyed properties. In cases in which servicers stated that FHA's policies and procedures on particular conveyance requirements was insufficient or unclear, we examined the 2016 mortgagee letter, HUD's single-family housing policy handbook, and frequently asked questions on HUD's website—to determine whether it addressed the topics and was sufficiently thorough to be applied to properties with different circumstances. We assessed whether the policies and procedures were consistent with federal internal control standards for external communication. In particular, we examined whether the policies and procedures communicated necessary quality information to achieve program objectives and whether FHA had evaluated appropriate methods to communicate them.[58] Where applicable, we also compared FHA's policies and procedures to features of Fannie Mae's guide for servicers on how to preserve and protect vacant properties. We also assessed FHA's policies and procedures on reconveyances and alternatives to reconveyance against federal internal control standards for designing control activities.

To review the preconveyance inspection pilot that FHA began in 2017 and any challenges with the pilot, we interviewed the three participating servicers about FHA's implementation of the pilot and the extent to which preconveyance inspections reduced the likelihood of reconveyance or addressed other challenges. We spoke with FHA National Servicing Center officials about their monitoring of pilot outcomes and their plans for assessing results. We assessed FHA's planning and evaluation efforts against key components of evaluation design from GAO's guide for designing evaluations.[59]

Furthermore, we interviewed a number of individuals and entities about challenges they experienced in implementing their property conveyance responsibilities, the sufficiency of FHA's policies and procedures, and methods for assessing contractor performance. These included FHA headquarters and National Servicing Center officials with responsibilities for aspects of the conveyance process; FHA's compliance contractor; and Real Estate-Owned Division officials, the largest maintenance contractor, and staff responsible for overseeing the maintenance contractors at each of FHA's four homeownership centers.

Finally, we visited eight recently conveyed or reconveyed properties in the Baltimore, Maryland, and Atlanta, Georgia, areas to observe property conditions, learn about the maintenance contractors' property inspection processes, and understand challenges in documenting and addressing

---

[58] GAO, *Standards for Internal Control in the Federal Government*, GAO-14-704G (Washington, D.C.: Sept.10, 2014).

[59] GAO, *Designing Evaluations: 2012 Revision*, GAO-12-208G (Washington D.C.: Jan. 31, 2012).

condition issues. We chose these locations to provide some geographic dispersion and coverage of different FHA homeownership centers. The properties were selected by Philadelphia and Atlanta homeownership center staff based on our request to visit a mix of recently conveyed and reconveyed properties in metropolitan areas and time periods that we chose. As a result, the conditions we observed are illustrative rather than representative of all conveyed properties.

We conducted this performance audit from September 2017 to June 2019 in accordance with generally accepted government auditing standards. Those standards require that we plan and perform the audit to obtain sufficient, appropriate evidence to provide a reasonable basis for our findings and conclusions based on our audit objectives. We believe that the evidence obtained provides a reasonable basis for our findings and conclusions based on our audit objectives.

APPENDIX II: COMMENTS FROM THE DEPARTMENT OF HOUSING AND URBAN DEVELOPMENT

U.S. DEPARTMENT OF HOUSING AND URBAN DEVELOPMENT
WASHINGTON, DC 20410-8000

OFFICE OF HOUSING

JUN 0 5 2019

Daniel Garcia-Diaz
Director, Financial Markets and Community Investment
Government Accountability Office
441 G Street NW
Washington, DC 20548

Dear Mr. Garcia-Diaz:

Thank you for the opportunity to respond to the Draft Report GAO-19-517 entitled Federal Housing Administration (FHA) – Improved Procedures and Assessment Could Increase Efficiency of Foreclosed Property Conveyance. This letter communicates the Department of Housing and Urban Development (HUD), FHA's response to the draft report.

FHA reviewed the Government Accountability Office's (GAO) draft report and submits the following responses to the three recommendations on page 40:

Recommendation 1:
The Commissioner of FHA should enhance the content and communication of FHA's policies and procedures on conveyance condition considering the program stakeholder views discussed in this report and other stakeholder input.

FHA's Response:
HUD has made significant changes to improve the delivery of clear policy guidance into the market through the publication of HUD Handbook 4000.1 (Handbook) which is the primary source for policy on Single Family program requirements. HUD also updated Mortgagee Letter (ML) 2016-02 on property preservation requirements and expense reimbursements. Both the Handbook and ML 2016-02 are publicly available on HUD's website. The National Servicing Center (NSC) also creates open lines of communication through meetings with FHA servicers to discuss conveyance procedures. The NSC has made clear that as policy changes are considered, FHA will continue to enforce current regulations to ensure compliance and to protect the Mutual Mortgage Insurance (MMI) Fund.

FHA recognizes that policy changes and staff changes both require consistent outreach in terms of external communications, training and in-person meetings in order to ensure that servicers have the information and understanding they need to operate in compliance with our programs. It has been, and will continue to be, a central goal of FHA to meet these needs.

Recommendation 2:
The Commissioner of FHA should provide written direction to the Homeownership Center (HOC) Real Estate Owned (REO) directors on factors to consider when determining whether to reconvey a property with conveyance condition issues, issue a demand letter, or enter into a bypass agreement with the servicer.

FHA's Response:
HUD agrees that written guidance will help Homeownership Centers' REO Directors in applying consistent factors related to reconveyances, which will be determined based on a clearly defined set of criteria. This same guidance will be shared with HUD's Mortgagee Compliance Monitor (MCM) to help: (1) the MCM validate the HOC's decision for re-conveyance; and (2) the MCM to finalize the process of notifying the mortgagee of the reconveyance; and (3) the mortgagee with remedying its non-compliance with HUD's conveyance standards by issuing a Demand Letter or entering into a Bypass Agreement.

It is important to note; however, that over the past five years, HUD has been leveraging less costly upstream disposition strategies (e.g., Third Party Sales, Note Sales, etc.) with higher recovery rates which have resulted in fewer foreclosed properties getting re-conveyed. From FY2019 through June 3, 2019, the Department has only re-conveyed 613 properties out of 34,330 foreclosures processed through Third Party or REO sales' transactions.

Recommendation 3:
The Commissioner of FHA should develop a formal plan for evaluating the outcomes of the pre-conveyance inspection pilot that includes the key elements of evaluation design—such as evaluation objectives and measures—and utilizes participant feedback and control groups, as appropriate.

FHA's Response:
HUD agrees with the recommendation to formalize a plan to evaluate the existing data and inspection outcomes of its pre-conveyance inspection pilot.

We appreciate GAO's review and discussions regarding recommended improvements of FHA's property conveyance procedures.

Sincerely,

John Garvin
General Deputy Assistant Secretary for Housing

CONTENTS OF EARLIER VOLUMES

Key Government Reports. Volume 31: National Defense - May 2019

INDEX

A

B

C

D

E

F

G

H

I

L

M

N

O

P

R

S

T

U

V

W